This book is due at the **ROBERT B. HOUSE UNDERGRADUATE LIBRARY** on the last date stamped below unless recalled sooner. If not on hold, it may be renewed by bringing it to the library or renewed online at the library webpage.

DATE DUE	DATE RET'D	DATE DUE	DATE RET'D

Politics *in* The Bible

Politics *in* The Bible

Paul R. Abramson

Transaction Publishers
New Brunswick (U.S.A.) and London (U.K.)

Library of Congress Catalog Number: 2011034114
ISBN: 978-1-4128-4310-2
Printed in the United States of America

Library of Congress Cataloging-in-Publication Data

Abramson, Paul R.
    Politics in the Bible / Paul R. Abramson.
       p. cm.
    Includes bibliographical references and index.
    ISBN 978-1-4128-4310-2 (cloth)
       1. Politics in the Bible.   I. Title.
BS680.P45A27 2012

220.8'32—dc23

2011034114

To:
John H. Aldrich
Ronald Inglehart
David W. Rohde
For over a century of friendship and collaborative research.

Contents

List of Tables

Tables

Acknowledgments

Three scholars read the entire manuscript, and I am grateful for their criticism: my colleagues William B. Allen and Corwin D. Smidt at Michigan State University, and the leader of my weekly Bible study group Stephen Rayburn. Robert Alter of the University of California at Berkeley briefly looked at an early version of this book, and his insightful suggestions helped shape my approach.

Ira Sharkansky at The Hebrew University of Jerusalem read large portions of the manuscript. Several other scholars read portions of the manuscript, including my colleague Michael Colaresi. My colleague Ani Sarkissian helped with my discussions of Islam. In addition, Bonnie Honig at Northwestern University made numerous suggestions for my chapter on *Ruth*, and Scott Gates of the Peace Research Institute in Oslo (PRIO) made helpful suggestions for my chapter on *Isaiah*. Moshe Koppel of Bar Ilan University reminded me about the contentious history of Hebron. Abraham Diskin of The Hebrew University of Jerusalem provided specific information about the naming of the Jewish state as well as a recent study on Seder participation in Israel conducted by the Central Bureau of Statistics.

I also want to thank Steven J. Brams at New York University and Kenneth A. Shepsle of Harvard University for their encouragement.

My son, Lee J. Abramson, also provided comments. And, as with all my previous books, I thank my wife Janet for her assistance in copyediting.

At Transaction Publishers, I want to thank Jennifer Nippons for her enthusiastic support for my project, and to Irving Louis Horowitz for his generous praise. Larry Mintz did an outstanding job of copyediting the manuscript, and Andrew McIntosh did an excellent job shepherding my book through its production.

Paul R. Abramson

Introduction

The Bible is fundamental to Western culture, and political philosophers from Hobbes, Locke, Montesquieu, and Rousseau, to modern political theorists such as George H. Sabine (1961), Leo Strauss (1959), and Sheldon S. Wolin (2004) draw upon biblical examples. American political leaders, such as Thomas Paine, Abraham Lincoln, and William Jennings Bryan, drew heavily upon the Bible. George Shulman (2008) demonstrates the impact of the Hebrew prophets, especially Jeremiah, upon Henry David Thoreau, Martin Luther King Jr., James Baldwin, and Toni Morrison. Most contemporary politicians display less familiarity with the Scriptures, but many proudly proclaim themselves to be born-again Christians.

Many current studies of the Bible focus on textual analysis (see, for example, Richard Elliott Friedman, 1989, 2003). Friedman argues that the *Hebrew Bible* comes from four main sources, an **E** source because God is referred to as El or Elohim, a **J** source that refers to God by his proper name, Yahweh, and a **D** source responsible for *Deuteronomy*. The largest source of the *Pentateuch*, he argues, is an Aaronid priest, the **P** source. These sources were combined by a Redactor, sometimes writing material that can best be labeled **R**.[1]

But many political scientists, as well as other scholars, have studied the Bible to gain insights about political conflict and political leadership. For example, Steven J. Brams (2003, 2011) applies game theory to study the *Hebrew Bible*, Aaron Wildavsky analyzes the political leadership of Joseph (Wildavsky, 1993) and Moses (Wildavsky, 1984), and Michael Walzer (1985) studies the Exodus from Egypt as a revolution, brilliantly demonstrating its relevance to other revolutions, especially the English Civil War (1642–51). Bonnie Honig analyzes *Ruth* as an example of political assimilation (1997, 2001). There are many studies of the kings of Judah and Israel, and David has been studied more extensively than any other biblical monarch. Paul Borgman (2008), Israel Finkelstein and Neil Asher Silberman (2006), Steven L. McKenzie (2000), Robert Pinsky (2005), and Ira Sharkansky (1996) study David, although their books do not approach the comic brilliance of Joseph Heller's novel, *God Knows* (1984). The Israelite monarchy reached its heights under King Solomon, and Frederic Thieberger (1947) studies the organization and leadership style of his monarchy. There have also been analyses of the political conflicts described in the *Book of Esther* (see, for example, Yoram Hazony, 1995).

A great deal has been learned recently on the canonization of the *New Testament*.[2] But through the time of its canonization, Christians never held political power, so they are largely restricted to the views of Jesus, his apostles, and his disciples about how to respond to hostile political authority. I will focus mainly upon Jesus's major confrontation with political authority, his trial and execution (Haim Hermann Cohn, 1971; Gerard S. Sloyan, 2006), and on Paul's writings.[3] Because there is a growing interest in the "end times," I will discuss some of the the first two epistles of John and *Revelation*.

Readers will observe that I refer to the "Old Testament" as the *Hebrew Bible*, which includes thirty-nine books. For Jews, the technical name for these writings is the "Tanakh," an acronym for the Torah, meaning the Law (The Five Books of Moses), Nevi'im (The Prophets), and Kethuvim (Writings). Protestants accept these same thirty-nine books but organize them as The Pentateuch (which has the same contents as the Torah), The Historical Books, The Poetical and Wisdom Books, and the Prophetic Books. For the first seven books, both Bibles order the books in the same way, but beginning with *Ruth*, the order diverges. When I want to emphasize the Protestant ordering, I use the term the *Christian Scriptures*. Jews do not accept the books after *2 Chronicles* in the *Hebrew Bible* or after *Malachi* in the *Christian Scriptures*. They therefore reject the books between *Matthew* and *Revelation*. Most Jews refer to them as the *New Testament*. Jews and Protestants do not view the *Apocrypha* as part of the Bible, while it is included in the Catholic Bible.

Format and Goals of the Book

For each topic, I identify the text I will be discussing, summarizing it in a section labeled, "Basic Text." Each summary presents a concise discussion of the stories and enough quotations to provide a sense of the text. After each summary, I discuss its "Political Implications" (or occasionally merely "Political Implication"). These sections discuss the implications of the text for questions about authority, leadership, and political conflict.

The main goal is to help readers to think critically about how the Bible illuminates our understanding of justice, leadership, and politics.

I have two basic theses. First, for a political scientist, there are great advantages to studying the Bible. As Wildavsky argues (1989), scholars usually spend a great deal of time collecting data, and little time analyzing them. Students of the Bible have short texts to analyze, and they have a history of two thousand years of Jewish and Christian scholarly discussion. Second, as Wildavsky argues, the Bible discusses universal problems. As Wildavsky made these arguments two decades ago, my theses are borrowed. However, the scope of the biblical texts I discuss is original. Whereas Wildavsky wrote analyses of Joseph and Moses, I analyze a large number of stories drawn from eighteen of the thirty-nine books of the *Hebrew Bible* and fifteen of the twenty-seven books of the *New Testament.*

I will not discuss the historical accuracy of these stories, or even whether some of the early characters existed. For many people the accuracy of the Bible is a matter of faith. For example, according to my analysis of the 2008 American National Election Study survey, respondents were asked to choose one among three statements that "comes closest to describing your feelings about the Bible." Among the 2,263 respondents who made such a choice, 38 percent said "The Bible is the actual word of God and is to be taken literally, word for word"; 45 percent said, "The Bible is the word of God but not everything in it should be taken literally, word for word"; while only 17 percent said, "The Bible is a book written by men and is not the word of God."

For others, the accuracy of the Bible might be based on archeological evidence, which is often contradictory.[4] However, most scholars agree that there is no archeological evidence of an exodus from Egypt.[5] But even many Jews who doubt whether an exodus occurred conduct a Passover Seder commemorating the liberation of their ancestors from slavery. When the youngest person capable of asking the "Four Questions," asks, "Why is this night different from all other nights?," (*Gates of Freedom Haggadah,*1999: 17), he or she is told, "We were slaves of Pharaoh in Egypt, and the Lord our God brought us forth from there with a strong hand and an outstretched arm."

(*Passover Haggadah*, 1993: 8–9). The lack of archeological evidence does not prevent many secular Jews from participating in a Passover Seder.

In Israel, for example, the vast majority of Jews say that they always participate in a Seder.[6] In September 2010, the Central Bureau of Statistics published the results of a survey of 7,500 Jews conducted in 2009. Eight percent classified themselves as *Haredi* (ultraorthodox), 12 percent as *Dati* (religious), 13 percent as *Masorti-Dati* (traditional-religious), 26 percent as *Masorti* (traditional, not so religious), and 42 percent as secular or nonreligious. Even among secular Jews, 82 percent say that they always participate in the Seder; among the "not so religious," 93 percent always participate; while among the traditional-religious, 98 percent say they always participate. For the two most religious groups, nearly 100 percent say they always participate in the Seder.[7]

As anyone interested in Israeli politics knows, an understanding of the *Hebrew Bible* is essential because, as Ira Sharkansky shows (1991, 1996), there are many parallels between ancient and modern Israel. He makes a convincing case. But the men who composed the *Hebrew Bible* and the *New Testament* were writing under specific historical conditions, which do not have precise parallels. As Otto von Bismarck said in 1867, "Politics is the art of the possible."[8] The writers of the *Hebrew Bible* could not imagine a time when a Jewish state would possess far better weaponry than its enemies (Sharkansky, 1991: 4; 1996: 144–45), any more than the men who wrote the *New Testament* could imagine a time when Christianity would become the official religion of the Roman Empire.

Of course, much of the Bible never had any political relevance. Although the *Psalms* provide the most beautiful passages of the *Hebrew Bible*, I quote from only one of them (Ps. 89) in this book.[9] Although there is a great deal of disagreement about what the *Song of Solomon* is about, it would be hard to argue that it has political content. Sharkansky (1996: 252–56) discusses *Job*, yet I find it difficult to understand why it has political meaning.[10] The miracles of the prophets, of Jesus, and of his apostles and disciples also have no political implications. And the Beatitudes in *Matthew* have little political meaning, except for the statement, "Blessed are the peacemakers, for they will be called children of God" (Matt. 5:9), which might encourage political leaders to vie for the Nobel Peace Prize.[11] There are other passages that no longer have political relevance such as those used to support and oppose slavery in the United States. And there are other books, such as *Revelation*, which might or might not have political relevance today, depending upon how one interprets their apocalyptic vision.

But there is a great deal of material that was politically relevant at the time it was written, much that is politically relevant for thousands of years after the Bible was written, and some texts that are politically relevant today.

My second thesis is that regardless of its political significance, the Bible is a book that should be read even by those who do not believe it has any transcendental significance. The Bible can be read as the revealed word of God, a basic source of Western morality, a compilation of interesting stories, poetry, and history, and as a work of great literature.[12] Although my main goal is to select stories that have political implications, I also try to focus on works that have great literary merit. There are many passages in the *Pentateuch* that are great literature, and *1 Samuel* and *2 Samuel* are among the most beautiful works in the Western canon, as are the prophesies of Isaiah. The Gospels contain some of the most beautiful passages ever written. Unfortunately, the most beautiful English translation, the *King James Version* (*KJV*) or Authorized Version of 1611, has too many translation errors of the *Hebrew Bible* to rely upon, but I have often quoted from it because the beauty of its language often compensates for its inaccuracies. Indeed, any student of English or American literature needs to read this edition, for it has had a profound literary impact, as Robert Alter (2010a) shows.[13]

Translations Cited

For the most part, the biblical translations come from four sources, although I also quote from the *KJV* as well:

For the *Pentateuch* I quote from the following:

Robert Alter, *The Five Books of Moses: A Translation and Commentary*, translated and with commentary by Robert Alter. New York: Norton, 2004.

For *1 Samuel, 2 Samuel*, and *1 Kings* (1–2), I quote from:

Robert Alter, *The David Story: A Translation and Commentary of 1 and 2 Samuel*. New York: Norton, 1999.

There is one citation from *Psalms*, which comes from:

Robert Alter, *The Book of Psalms: A Translation and Commentary by Robert Alter*. New York: Norton 2007.

For the remainder of the Bible, I quote from:

The New Oxford Annotated Bible: New Revised Standard Version With the Apocrypha, Fully Revised Fourth Edition. New York: Oxford University Press, 2010.

Notes

1. As Freidman (1989: 52) notes, the first three persons to argue that the Bible was the combination of several sources were a German minister, Henning Bernhard Witter in 1711, Jean Astruc, a French physician in 1753, and Johann Gottfried Eichhorn in 1780. But only Eichhorn's work had any impact. As he notes (25–27), Julius Wellhausen (1844–1918) made a major contribution by synthesizing earlier research and developing a new model for examining the Bible.

2. For an outstanding summary of these developments, as well as a magisterial history of Christianity, see Diarmaid MacCulloch (2010).

3. For an interesting and controversial perspective on Paul, see John G. Gager (2000).

4. For excellent but dated volumes presenting archeological evidence on warfare during biblical times, see Yigael Yadin (1963a, b). For a more recent study, see Chaim Herzog and Mordechai Gichon (1997).

5. For two recent examples of the origins of ancient Israelites, see William G. Dever (2003) and Finkelstein and Silberman (2002).

6. For a classic study of the way religious traditions have been incorporated into Israeli civil society, see Charles S. Liebman and Eliezar Don-Yehiya (1983).

7. I am grateful to Abraham Diskin for providing me with these results.

8. Quoted in *The Yale Book of Quotations*, p. 86.

9. Psalm 137, which expresses the Jewish exiles in Babylon's passionate desire to return to Zion, makes a political statement.

10. Sharkansky disagrees. As he points out (personal communication, August 9, 2010), "*Job* deals with good, bad, and justice and by implication the weakness and evil of God." In his *The Augustian Imperative*, the eminent political theorist William E. Connolly (2002) has many insights about *Job*, but without presenting a sustained thesis that the overall book has major political implications.

11. At the signing of a peace accord between Israel and Jordan on October 26, 1994, President Bill Clinton gave a speech praising Yitzhak Rabin, the Israeli Prime Minister, and King Hussein of Jordan. Referring to the Beatitudes, he said, "Blessed are the peacemakers for they shall inherit the earth." I was at the Hebrew University at the time, and remember how much fun Israelis had suggesting that Clinton needed a new speechwriter.

12. As Huston Smith (2009: 271) writes, "It has been estimated that one-third of our Western civilization bears the mark of its Jewish ancestry. We feel its force in the names we give to our children." We see it in some of the greatest works of Western art and literature. Smith states, "The United States carries the indelible stamp of its Jewish heritage in its collective life: The phrase 'by their Creator' in the Declaration of Independence; the words 'Proclaim Liberty throughout the land' on the Liberty Bell. The real impact

of the ancient Jews, however, lies in the extent to which Western civilization took over their angle of vision on the deepest questions life poses." As for Christianity, he reminds us (p. 317) that it is the most widespread religion in the world and has the most adherents. "The figure is probably inflated, but the registries list almost one out of three persons today as Christian, bringing the number into the neighborhood of one and a half billion." For projections on the future growth of Christianity, see Philip Jenkins (2007).

13. For a discussion of how this edition was developed, see Adam Nicolson (2003).

1

Reading the Bible Politically

Ira Sharkansky (1996: 35–74) and Aaron Wildavsky (1984: 3–29) both discuss reading the Bible politically.[1] The title of Sharkansky's chapter is the same as mine, but his approach differs. He focuses mainly on the difficulty of reading the Bible politically. As he writes (p. 35),

> The Hebrew Bible provides a treasure of political material, but it does not yield easily to analysis in modern terms. It comes to us in thirty-nine books. Some were combined or organized differently in previous versions. Most seem to be compilations gathered from several oral and written sources. Portions of the rest may have been written as early as the period of David and Solomon, several hundred years after the Israelites were said to have settled the land. The material was added to, and re-edited during the next several 1,000 years or so.

Sharkansky deals with the political problems in compiling the Bible, the geopolitical context of biblical times, and the question of whether the Bible presents political reality. He concludes (p. 43) "historical Israel is not the Israel of the Hebrew Bible. Historical Israel produced biblical Israel." He also discusses appeals and problems with the Bible's literary devices, and a brief discussion of biblical commentary and scholarship.

In his study of Moses (1984: 15), Wildavsky argues, "By far the most powerful fieldwork methods in the social sciences are those of the structural anthropologists."[2] "Undeterred by gaps or apparent contradictions in chronology, able to accommodate dreams and fables, considering variants in the same story as clues to meaning, structural anthropologists take seriously the task of discovering the inner coherence of a way of life." This approach, Wildavsky (pp. 15–19) argues, is similar to that of the rabbinic scholars. Wildavsky concludes (pp. 18–19): "The best advice for fieldworkers on the Bible is . . . keep your feet on the ground, your eyes on the

1

heavens, and do not accept any proposition that explains one without the other—the institution without the ideas, or the God of Israel without His people." Moreover, Wildavsky has no use for source-based criticism. He writes (p. 19): "Even if there were agreement on what parts of the Bible belong to which source . . . this would not usually aid us in the interpretation of themes in the text. Until I learn of a better way of negotiating between the Bible and social science in regard to questions of leadership, I shall continue to rely on the structural method."

My approach differs from Sharkansky and Wildavsky's, even though I agree with many of their arguments. In demonstrating how to read the Bible politically, I will focus on a single incident.

The Text: Moses Strikes the Rock and is Denied Entry into Canaan

To illustrate how one can read the Bible in different ways, I will discuss an example that has attracted a great deal of commentary. Most casual readers of the Bible know that Moses was not allowed to enter the Promised Land, and careful readers of the *Hebrew Bible* will remember the seemingly trivial transgression that led God to deny him entry. I will recount the entire story, and then show how a political analysis differs from most other readings. As I will refer to this story again, using Robert Alter's translation, I will here use the *KJV*.[3]

The story is related in *Numbers* 20:1–13:

> Then came the children of Israel, *even* the whole congregation, into the desert of Zin in the first month: and the people abode in Kadesh; and Miriam died there, and was buried there.
>
> And there was no water for the congregation: and they gathered themselves together against Moses and against Aaron.
>
> And the people chode with Moses, and spake, saying, Would God that we had died when our brethren died before the LORD!
>
> And why have ye brought up the congregation of the LORD into this wilderness, that we and our cattle should die there?
>
> And wherefore have ye made us to come up out of Egypt, to bring us in unto this evil place? it *is* no place of seed, or of figs, or of vines, or of pomegranates; neither *is* there any water to drink.
>
> And Moses and Aaron went from the presence of the assembly unto the door of the tabernacle of the congregation, and they fell upon their faces: and the glory of the LORD appeared unto them.
>
> And the LORD spake unto Moses, saying,
>
> Take the rod, and gather thou the assembly together, thou, and Aaron thy brother, and speak ye unto the rock before their eyes;

and it shall give forth his water, and thou shalt bring forth to them water out of the rock: so thou shalt give the congregation and their beasts drink.

And Moses took the rod from before the LORD, as he commanded him.

And Moses and Aaron gathered the congregation together before the rock, and he said unto them, Here now, ye rebels; must we fetch you water out of this rock?

And Moses lifted up his hand, and with his rod he smote the rock twice: and the water came out abundantly, and the congregation drank, and their beasts *also*.

And the LORD spake unto Moses and Aaron, Because ye believed me not, to sanctify me in the eyes of the children of Israel, therefore ye shall not bring this congregation into the land which I have given them.

This *is* the water of Meribah; because the children of Israel strove with the LORD, and he was sanctified in them.

Joshua is designated as the leader to lead Israel into Canaan (Num. 27:3). Toward the end of his life, Moses makes one last plea to enter the Promised Land, but God does not relent, telling Moses "speak no more unto me of this matter" (Deut. 3:26). He lets Moses see the Promised Land, but he dies after viewing it. "No man knoweth of his sepulcher unto this day" (Deut. 34:6). "And there arose not a prophet since in Israel like unto Moses, whom the LORD knew face to face . . ." (Deut. 34:10).

Religious Interpretations: Scholars who read this text from a religious viewpoint will probably ask why Moses's disobedience deserves such harsh punishment. As the *Jewish Study Bible* (p. 323) notes, "Puzzled by the apparent harshness of God's verdict, biblical scholars . . . have tried to reconcile Moses and Aaron's punishment with their sin." The Talmudic scholar Nachmanides (1194–c1270) maintains that their error was for Moses to say, "*Are we to bring forth water?*" This expression, he argues, "might have given the people the impression that it was Moses and Aaron who by some device brought forth water from the rock." Moses should have said, "Is the Lord to bring you forth water."[4] There are numerous other religious interpretations that explain why Moses's behavior was sinful.[5]

Textual Analysis: According to Richard Elliott Friedman (2003: 276–76), the first sentence of verses 1–13, are by the Redactor, who compiled and edited various versions to form the *Pentateuch.* The remaining twelve verses are by **P**. As I mentioned at the outset, textual analysis has become a major concern of biblical scholarship, but I ignore it in this book.

Ancient Interpretations: In *The Bible as It Was,* James L. Kugel (1997) argues that ancient interpretations of the Bible are extremely valuable and that it is useful to examine stories and to group them by themes. In his more recent book, *How to Read the Bible* (2007), he provides a longer history of biblical scholarship, and also discusses the story of the waters of Meribah (pp. 239–40). Ancient interpreters argue that there was a large traveling rock that followed the Children of Israel. But the waters in this rock gave out after the death of Miriam (reported in the first verse). Ancient interpreters called this rock, "The well of Miriam."[6] "It was Miriam's virtuous nature," Kugel writes, "interpreters reasoned, that had caused God to give the Israelites the traveling rock in the first place—a rock that went far toward explaining how the Israelites managed to survive all those years in the barren wastes."

Now, Kugel argues, few would accept the traveling rock theory. Instead they note that there is a story about Moses striking a rock at Rephidim in a section of *Exodus* attributed to **J** or **E**. The same story is found in *Numbers* in a passage attributed to **P**. The same story appearing twice, Kugel explains (p. 240), is a "narrative doublet." He argues (p. 240) that these stories "are slightly different versions" of the same story. The final editor of the *Pentateuch* included both. The waters of Meribah still appear in two separate locations, Rephidim and Kadish, inspiring the traveling well theory.

However, Kugel fails to mention that there is a major difference between these two stories. In *Exodus* (17:11), Moses is told to strike the rock; in *Numbers* (20:8) he is told to speak to the rock. In the *Exodus* story, he obeys God; in *Numbers*, he disobeys. Kugel avoids discussing why Moses is punished, which seems more important than explaining the source of the water.

Political Explanations: A political scientist would approach the same story differently. I will examine Wildavsky's discussion in *The Nursing Father* (1984). Wildavsky argues (p. 182), "Interpretations of why Moses does not get to the Promised Land are less important than the fact that he does not go."

Wildavsky explains why Moses is not allowed to enter Canaan in terms of political leadership. He advances five arguments.

First (p. 187), it is important to establish that all leaders have limits. If Moses were to cross the Jordan, it would imply that "he could lead the people in perpetuity." "Moses, like his people, needs boundaries."

Second (p. 187), God does not want a Moses cult to develop. As no one knows where he is buried, this will be more difficult.

Third, by saying that there has been no prophet "like unto Moses," *Deuteronomy* is also saying no such prophet should arise. "A new Moses," Wildavsky writes (p. 187) "might also make new laws." Granted, Wildavsky recognizes that the sanction of neither adding to nor subtracting from the laws of Moses cannot be taken literally. "Without change," he writes (p. 187), "no continuity is possible. Incessant change makes continuity impossible."

Fourth, Wildavsky points out that in the final phase of his leadership, Moses introduces new laws to limit future leaders. Wildavsky (p. 188) writes, "Moses inaugurates a system of checks by institutionalizing forms of leadership and by delegating authority to numerous others, who are themselves further subdivided in function and limited in power" (p. 188). "In Deuteronomy, by then a teacher as well as a leader, Moses continually exhorts the people to remember the great events of Israel's history, rather than his personal role."

Fifth, Wildavsky (p. 188) argues, "The final events in Moses' life suggest that he who teaches continues to learn. Meribah . . . represents Moses' own supreme moment of forgetfulness. Backsliding even more than the people, Moses forgot that he was to inspire them to learn and to aim at a higher goal than slavery. . . . The generation that left Egypt is doomed to wander in the desert. Moses must affirm his bond by sharing their fate."

Wildavsky concludes (pp. 188–89) "Moses eventually understands that the chief virtue in leaders is to make themselves unnecessary. To be a 'nursing father'—knowing that the child may die, will probably rebel, and must be allowed to make history on its own—is the essence of Mosaic leadership. Teaching that leads to learning that creates new teachers is a circular process of renewal, not a linear model of leadership."

Wildavsky's analysis of this story focuses on authority and on leadership. When his book was republished in 2005, the title was dropped and the subtitle became the title, *Moses as a Political Leader*. This comes closer to describing its contents than its original enigmatic title. Justice, authority, and leadership are core questions for political scientists. Reading the Bible politically requires readers to be alert to stories that shed insight on these themes. Some biblical leaders were great men, such as Moses, Joshua, and David. Some were ineffective leaders, such as Rehoboam and Zedekiah. Some, especially the

Hebrew prophets and Jesus, had great visions of justice. Some such as Ahab, Haman, and Judas were evil, and, according to Dante, Judas was consigned to the fourth round of the ninth circle of the *Inferno*. What makes the Bible especially interesting for political analysts is that all of the leaders in the *Hebrew Bible* were flawed. In this fundamental way they are similar to real political leaders.

The political implications I discuss are not the only ones that can be derived from these biblical texts. For example, as I note throughout my discussion, there are many texts in the *Hebrew Bible* that Steven J. Brams (2003, 2011) analyzes using game theory. In discussing slavery, I even discuss a Marxist view of Paul's writings by Eugene D. Genovese (1974). Readers may find interpretations that I failed to offer, but I hope they will not find many misinterpretations.

Notes

1. In addition, the *New Testament* scholar, Richard Bauckham (1989) has also published a book, *The Bible in Politics: How to Read the Bible Politically*. For the most part, he analyses short texts, and there is very little overlap between the texts I discuss and those he discusses. His first chapter, "Issues in Interpretation," is particularly relevant.
2. Two years before, Wildavsky coauthored a book with the renowned anthropologist, Mary Douglas. Douglas herself (1999) also authored an important book on *Leviticus*.
3. I am also using the *KJV* because Wildavsky uses it, and I discuss his analysis.
4. Cited from *The Soncino Chumash*, 903.
5. For the summary of five traditional Jewish scholars, see *The Stone Chumash*, 845, an Orthodox interpretation of the *Torah*. (The *Chumash* contains the weekly readings from the Pentateuch, along with complementary readings from the Prophets.) In a recent conservative *Chumash, Etz Hayim*, Jacob Milgrom writes, "Perhaps the most persuasive explanation is that offered by Maimonides in the twelfth century and Hirsch in the nineteenth century. Moses was punished for losing his temper and patience with the people, and calling them 'rebels', striking the rock [and then striking it a second time] in exasperation with his people" (p. 885). See also Milgrom's comment on the *JPS* edition of *Numbers*, 166.
6. For a discussion of this legend, see Louis Ginzbeg 1998a: 50–54; 1998b: 14–15.

2

Genesis

Abram Goes Forth

Basic Text: Genesis begins with God creating the heaven and the earth, the serpent tempting Eve, and God punishing the serpent, Eve, and Adam, including Adam and Eve's expulsion from the Garden of Eden. It continues with Cain murdering Abel, and Cain's punishment. It relates Cain's genealogy, but more importantly the genealogy of Seth, Adam and Eve's third son and an ancestor of Noah. It tells of the Great Flood in which Noah and his family are saved, of Noah's drunkenness after the flood, Ham viewing his father's nakedness, and Noah's curse of Canaan, one of Ham's sons (Gen. 9:25–26), which was later used to justify enslaving Negroes. But Genesis moves again to genealogy and tells of the attempt to "build us a city and a tower with its top in the heavens" (Gen. 11:4), and the creation of many languages to divide the people.

Genesis moves once again to genealogy and reaches Terah. Terah has three sons, Abram, Nahor, and Haran, all from the Land of the Chaldees. Haran dies in his father's lifetime in the land of his father's birth. But the family moves to Ur. God tells Abram to "Go forth from your land and your birthplace and your father's house to the land I will show you. And I will make you a great nation and I will bless you and I will make your name great, and you shall be a blessing" (Gen. 12:1–2). Moreover, "all the clans of the earth through you shall be blessed" (Gen. 12:3). Abram departs with his wife Sarai and Haran's son, his nephew Lot.

Political Implications: Some of the stories before Abram can be modeled politically. Steven J. Brams, for example, models God's creation of the world (11–12), Eve's temptation by the serpent (21–24), Eve's offering the forbidden fruit to Adam (24–28), God's punishment of Adam and Eve (28–34), and Cain murdering Abel (55–59). Although these antediluvian tales can be modeled, it seems more reasonable to begin looking for political messages at the beginnings of the founding of what became the Jewish people, as well as for the founding of Christianity (Matt. 1:1).[1] The story establishes Abram's descendants as a chosen people, and provides Abram's descendents with a claim to this unnamed land.

We are not told why Abram is selected, but there are many *midrashim* (tales about the Bible) arguing it was because he hated idolatry.[2] As we will see, both Jews and Arabs view themselves as Abram's descendants. Moreover, beginning with Abram seems logical since, as Thomas L. Pangle (2003: 127) correctly argues, "Noah and his family were called to be the surviving remnant of the whole human race; Abram and his family are called to separate themselves, to distinguish themselves, from the rest of the race. Accordingly, Abram/ Abraham and Sarai/Sarah are the first real personalities in the Bible." "From this point forward" Pangle (p. 127) writes, "Genesis bristles with characters defined and to some extent ranked by unique qualities, both admirable and questionable—qualities that disclose themselves for the most part through the drama, and only to readers who do some serious thinking for themselves." Avivah Gottlieb Zornberg (2010: 72) argues, "The story of Abraham is both beginning and end. Here begins the drama of the central family-nation of the Torah; here ends the prehistory, the rough drafts of God's intent. One such essay in creation had ended in exile (Adam driven from the Garden), the second in Destruction (the Flood)."

Abram Rescues Lot

Basic Text: Lot resides in Sodom and is captured in a battle of four kings versus five kings. Abram leads three hundred and eighteen of his men and rescues Lot. Abram refuses to take any reward from the king of Sodom, saying "I will take not a single thread or sandal strap of all that is yours, lest you say 'I have made Abram rich'" (Gen. 14:23).

Political Implication: Abram establishes himself as a military leader who rejects gifts from questionable allies.

Melchizedek Blesses Abram

Basic Text: After the battle, Melchizedek ("righteous king"), the King of Salem [Jerusalem], who is also priest to "El Elyon" (Gen. 14:18–20) blesses Abram.

Political Implication: This brief story is politically important because it establishes Jerusalem as a holy city, although it will be about a thousand years before Abram's descendants capture it.

God Establishes a Covenant with Abraham

Basic Text: Abram is ninety-nine years old and his wife Sarai ninety. Sarai remains childless. Abram's only son Ishmael, was born to Hagar, Sarai's slave. God now establishes a covenant with Abram, changing his name to Abraham and Sarai's name to Sarah. Abraham and all the males in his household are circumcised, and in future his male descendants are to be circumcised when they are eight days old.

Political Implication: Circumcision provides a crucial difference between Abraham's male descendents (both Jews and Muslims), and most men who do not claim this descent. It becomes an important marker to identify Jews during the Holocaust (see Timothy Snyder, 2010: 183, 204).

Abraham Bargains for Sodom

Basic Text: Abraham hosts three angels who are disguised as men. One of them predicts that within a year Sarah will give birth to a son. Sarah, past menopause, "laughed inwardly" (Gen 18:12). The Lord asks Abraham why Sarah laughed, asking "Is anything beyond the LORD?" (Gen. 18:13) and Sarah, fearful because the visitor has heard her silent laughter, denies laughing. But God tells her that she did laugh. God reveals to Abraham that he plans to visit Sodom and Gomorrah because their outcry is very great. If what He has heard is true, he will destroy them. Abraham bargains with God, appealing to His sense of justice, asking whether He will destroy the just along with the wicked. "Perhaps there may be fifty innocent within the city. Will You really wipe out the place and not spare it for the sake of the fifty innocent within it?" (Gen. 18:24). God agrees and eventually Abraham gets God to agree to spare the city for ten innocent people. Two angels visit Sodom, and all the men of Sodom threaten to rape them. They take shelter in Lot's house. Sodom is destroyed, but Lot and two of his daughters escape. A year later Sarah bears a son, who is named Isaac ("he laughs").

Political Implication: Abraham understands the importance of justice. He must know that there may be a few just people in Sodom, and argues they should be spared. *Jonah* presents a much different view of justice. When Jonah warns the people that Nineveh will be overthrown, the people repent and God spares the city. Although Jonah is disappointed, God tells him, "And should I not be concerned about Nineveh, that great city, in which there are more than a hundred and twenty thousand persons who do not know their right hand from their left, and also many animals?" (Jon. 4:11).

Abraham Buries Sarah

Basic Text: Sarah dies, and Abraham does not want to bargain when purchasing her gravesite. She dies in Kiriath-Arba, which the Bible says is now Hebron. (There is a Jewish settlement named Kiriath-Arba near the West Bank city of Hebron.) Although he has been promised this land, he says, "I am a sojourning settler with you. Grant me a burial-holding with you, and let me bury my dead now before me" (Gen. 23:4). He specifically wants to purchase the cave of Machpelah that belongs to Ephron, a wealthy Hittite. Ephron offers to give Abraham the cave, but in effect asks an exorbitant price. "Land for four hundred silver shekels between me and you, what does it come to? Go bury your dead" (Gen. 23:15).[3] Abraham pays the full price. The cave of Machpelah is the traditional burial site of all three patriarchs and three of the four matriarchs.[4]

Political Implications: Abraham is establishing a claim to the land by purchasing it, rather than accepting it as a gift, but he still is a sojourner. Hebron remains a site of great conflict. In 1929, during the British Mandate (1923–48), Arab riots in Hebron killed sixty-nine Jews. Between the War of Independence (1948–49) and the Six-Day War (1967) no Jews lived in Hebron. But the cave of Machpelah now contains both a mosque and a synagogue. In 1994, Baruch Goldstein, a Jewish settler, entered the mosque and killed twenty-nine Muslims before he was killed.

Abraham's Chief Servant Finds Rebekah

Basic Text: Ishmael, Abraham's firstborn son, is expelled from Abraham's household after Isaac is weaned. His mother finds him an Egyptian wife. But Isaac is to receive the inheritance and Abraham must be careful in choosing his wife. He tells his chief servant, "You shall not take a wife for my son from the daughters of the Canaanite in whose midst I dwell. But to the land of my birthplace you shall go, and you shall take a wife for my son, for Isaac" (Gen. 24:3–4). The servant, laden with gifts carried by ten camels (an anachronism, as camels had not yet been domesticated), finds Rebekah, the granddaughter of Nahor, Abraham's brother (and Isaac's second cousin). Rebekah's brother, Laban, approves of Rebekah marrying Abraham's son, and Rebekah agrees to marry her second cousin. Even though her mother and brother suggest that she wait ten days before leaving, she returns with Abraham's servant the next day.

Political Implication: The story demonstrates that Abraham is not established in Canaan, holds the inhabitants in contempt, and orders his servant to make a lengthy journey to his homeland to find an appropriate wife for Isaac.

God Speaks to Rebekah

Basic Text: Rebekah has difficulty conceiving, and Isaac prays on her behalf. When she becomes pregnant, she has a difficulty pregnancy. When she laments her pregnancy, God tells her two nations are in her womb and that, "People over people shall prevail, the elder, the younger's slave" (Gen. 25:23).

Political Implication: Esau is born first with Jacob, the second born, holding his heel.[5] Rebekah knows that Jacob is the favored son, while Isaac does not. Jacob's supremacy is politically significant because his descendants (the children of Israel, the name God later gives him), will have a claim to the Promised Land.[6]

Jacob Drives a Hard Bargain

Basic Text: After Esau and Jacob grow up, Esau becomes a hunter, whereas Jacob becomes a "simple man, a dweller in tents" (Gen. 25:27). One day Esau comes back from the hunting and is famished. Jacob is preparing lentil stew and Esau wants some. But Jacob will feed him only if Esau sells him his birthright. Esau replies, "Look, I am at the point of death, so why do I need a birthright?" (Gen. 25:32). Esau agrees to sell his birthright.

Political Implications: The story establishes Jacob's superiority. Esau "spurned" his birthright (Gen. 25:34). (In the *KJV* Esau "despised" his birthright.) Brams (2003: 59–66) analyzes this story using a game theoretic approach, but I disagree with his arguments. One outcome in Brams' game is that Esau sells his birthright, but that Jacob refuses to feed him and that Esau dies. But despite saying, "I am at the point of death" it seems very unlikely that Esau would have starved without the lentil stew.

Isaac's Many Weaknesses

Basic Text: Genesis spends relatively little space discussing Isaac, although there are many *midrashim* about him. Among his faults, he favors Esau for a trivial reason, since he likes the game that Esau hunts. Like his father he attempts to pass off his wife as his sister (Abraham makes two attempts). But God intervenes to protect Sarah whereas

Isaac betrays his subterfuge by "playing" ("sporting" in the *KJV*) with Rebekah (Gen. 26:8). Despite his suspicion, he allows himself to be deceived by Jacob, although this may also be seen as a virtue.

Political Implication: Despite his faults, Isaac has been chosen as the designated successor of Abraham's line, and God honors his promise. And Isaac remains faithful to God throughout all his difficulties. In his translation of *The Five Books of Moses*, Everett Fox writes (p. 111), "Yitzhak [Isaac] functions in Genesis as a classic second generation— that is, as a transmitter and stabilizing force, rather than as an active participant in building the people. . . . His main task in life is taking roots in the land of Canaan [see below], an admittedly important task in the larger context of God's promises in Genesis." As Fox writes (p. 111), "The true dynamic figure of the second generation here is Rivka [Rebekah]. It is she to whom God reveals his plan, and she who puts into motion the mechanism for seeing that it is properly carried out." Rebekah's role in the narrative is brilliantly discussed by Tikva Frymer-Kensky (2002: 5–23).

Isaac Digs Wells

Basic Text: Despite his weaknesses, Isaac has some strengths. When Rebekah bemoans her barrenness, Isaac prays for her to have children, a sharp contrast to Jacob's rebuke to Rachel (Gen. 30:2). And even though he suspects the son he is about to bless may not be his first born, Esau, he proceeds to bless Jacob, perhaps realizing that Jacob is more worthy to carry Abraham's blessing. Isaac's main political contribution is establishing a claim to the Promised Land. His father had dug many wells, which the "Philistines" (another anachronism) have filled in. He reopens them. He also finds a new well fed by fresh water.

Political Implications: By re-opening his father's wells, Isaac makes an important political contribution by establishing a claim to the Promised Land. Although he is nearly blind when he blesses Jacob, he is blessed with the longest life of any of the three patriarchs, dying at the age of one hundred eighty.

Jacob Deceives Isaac

Basic Text: Isaac is losing his eyesight and tells Esau to find fresh game, and prepare it so that he can give his first born and favorite son his blessing. Rebekah overhears this conversation and devises a scheme to trick Isaac into giving his blessing to her favorite son, the second born Jacob. Jacob objects that his father will detect the ruse, because Esau is a hairy man, whereas he is not. Rebekah clothes Jacob in Esau's garments and covers Jacob's hands and neck with goatskins. She prepares a stew from goat's meat. Isaac is suspicious and asks to feel Jacob. Isaac says, "The voice is the voice of Jacob and the hands are Esau's hands" (Gen. 27:22). Isaac proceeds to bless Jacob, a blessing he cannot retract. When Isaac learns he has been deceived, he is "seized with a very great trembling" (Gen. 27:33).[7] Esau has already sold his birthright to Jacob for lentil stew and now cannot have his father's blessing.

Political Implication: The story establishes that the line of descent will go through Jacob (later to be named Israel). Through his manipulation and duplicity, Jacob has both the birthright and his father's blessing and is ready to begin to establish what will become the children of Israel.

Isaac Sends Jacob to Find a Wife

Basic Text: Esau is furious and "said in his heart"(Gen. 27:41) that he will kill Jacob after their father dies. Wanting to protect Jacob, Rebekah must persuade Isaac to send him away. In doing so, she blames Esau for marrying two Hittite women, telling Isaac, "I loathe my life because of the Hittite women! If Jacob takes a wife from Hittite women like these, from the native girls, what good to me is life?" (Gen. 27:46). Isaac follows her advice and commands Jacob, "You shall not take a wife from the daughters of Canaan. Rise, go to Paddan-Aram to the house of Bethuel, your mother's father, and take you from there a wife from the daughters of Laban, your mother's brother" (Gen. 28:2).

Political Implication: The story once again establishes that despite being a wealthy man, Isaac recognizes the corrupting effects of living among Canaanites. Abraham's birthright must be continued through marriage within Abraham's family, and the political position of his descendants in the Promised Land remains tenuous.

Leah Deceives Jacob

Basic Text: Jacob travels to Paddan-Aram, making a conditional contract with God along the way. He finds his way to Haran, and meets Laban's youngest daughter, Rachel, his first cousin. Jacob kisses Rachel. He agrees to work for Laban for seven years, "for Rachel your younger daughter" (Gen. 29:18). But on his wedding night, Leah, Laban's oldest daughter, whom Jacob finds unattractive, is substituted for Rachel.[8] Laban tells Jacob that if he waits another week, he can marry Rachel as well, but he must serve for another seven years. Laban gives Leah a handmaiden, Zilpah, and he gives Rachel a handmaiden, Bilhah. They become important as well because they each bear Jacob two sons.

Political Implications: The story accounts for Jacob having twelve sons, who become the ancestors of the tribes of Israel. Moreover, except for the two handmaidens, Zilpah and Bilhah, the line is carried by women from Abraham's family.

Jacob Becomes Israel

Basic Text: By the time he returns to the Promised Land, Jacob has eleven sons (six by Leah, two by Bilhah, two by Zilpah, and one by Rachel), as well as Dinah, a daughter by Leah. When he returns, he is about to be confronted by Esau, with a band of four hundred men. The night before he must confront his brother, he wrestles with what appears to be a man. The man asks him his name, and he answers "Jacob." The man replies, "Not Jacob shall your name hence be said, but Israel, for you have striven with God and men, and won out" (Gen. 32:29).

Political Implication: Now Jacob becomes Israel, and thus the ancestor of the Children of Israel, and the name of the current Jewish state.

Shechem Rapes Dinah

Basic Text: Jacob and his family settle near Shechem, near the current West Bank city of Nablus. Dinah is raped by Shechem, the son of Hamor the Hittite, and the prince of the land.[9] But after raping her, Shechem loves Dinah, and asks his father to arrange a marriage with her. Jacob holds his peace until his sons come home from the fields. Hamor makes Jacob a generous offer for Dinah's bride price, pointing out the many advantages that would come from cooperation between Jacob's family and the people of Shechem. The sons of Jacob answer "deceitfully" (Gen. 34:13), saying they cannot agree unless the men of Shechem are circumcised. Hamor agrees, and persuades the Shechemite men to agree also. Three days later, when the recently circumcised Shechemites are in pain, Simeon and Levi, two of Dinah's full brothers, lead an attack on Shechem, kill Shechem and Hamor, kill the other adult males, sack the town, and carry off the women and children.

Jacob is furious, but only because of the trouble Simeon and Levi have caused for him. "You have stirred up trouble for me, making me stink among the land's inhabitants, among Canaanite and Perizzite, when I am a handful of men. If they gather against me and strike me, I shall be destroyed, I and my household" (Gen. 34:30). But Simeon and Levi reply, "Like a whore should our sister be treated?" (Gen 34:31).[10]

Political Implications: The story shows that Jacob's sons have no moral superiority. The punishment for the rape of a virgin goes far beyond the sanctions later specified in the *Pentateuch.* Moreover, Jacob does not rebuke his sons for the immorality of their actions. They use a ritual God establishes with Abraham as a ruse for mass murder. As many scholars note, from this point onward, Jacob reacts to events, and his sons become the prime movers.

Jacob Prefers Joseph

Basic Text: Rachel dies giving birth to Benjamin, and shortly after Reuben, Jacob's oldest son, has sex with Bilhah, Rachel's handmaiden. Jacob learns of this, but takes no action. Jacob shows remarkable favoritism toward Rachel's firstborn son, but his eleventh son, Joseph, by giving him "an ornamented tunic" (Gen. 37:3) (In the *KJV,* "a coat of *many* colours.") Joseph becomes increasingly estranged from his older brothers. And Jacob is foolish enough to send Joseph on a lone mission to find his older brothers who have taken his sheep to pasture, and Joseph sets out wearing his special tunic.

Political Implications: It is important to establish a story that makes Joseph's presence in Egypt possible, and thereby to establish the basis for the Exodus story. From the standpoint of family politics, Jacob fails as a father by displaying such great favoritism to Joseph. Granted, his firstborn son, Reuben, has forfeited his rights by having sex with Bilhah and his second and third oldest sons, Simeon and Levi, have committed the atrocity at Shechem.

Joseph is Sold into Slavery

Basic Text: Joseph is the most extensively discussed character in *Genesis.* His father's favoritism causes great resentment among his ten older half-brothers. Joseph further alienates them by telling them about two dreams suggesting that he will rule over them, and one of which suggests he will even rule over Jacob.

Jacob sends his ten oldest sons to tend his sheep, and they lead them to graze near Shechem. Jacob sends Joseph to see how they are faring, and Joseph sets out wearing his special tunic. Through the aid of a mysterious stranger, Joseph finds his older brothers. Seeing the "dream-master" (Gen. 37:19) approaching, they decide to throw him down a waterless pit. Reuben objects to murdering Joseph, but the other brothers strip Joseph of his tunic and throw him down the pit.

As the brothers are eating lunch, a caravan approaches. Judah says, "What gain is there if we kill our brother and cover up his blood? Come, let us sell him to the Ishmaelites and our hand will not be against him" (Gen. 37:26). The brothers sell him into slavery. The brothers slaughter a kid, cover Joseph's tunic with its blood, and trick Jacob into believing that beasts have killed him.

Political Implications: Although Joseph will become a great political leader, he is a remarkably naïve teenager. How else can we explain his enthusiasm for telling his family his dreams of future supremacy or wearing a special tunic on a lone mission to find his brothers? Up to now, Joseph has shown no talent for leadership, and a great talent for alienating others.

The story may also lay the groundwork for conferring special merit upon Judah. Judah may recognize that after throwing Joseph into a pit it would be dangerous to return him to Jacob but convinces his brothers to spare his life. As Judah will be the ancestor of David and of future kings, it is important to establish his merits. On the other hand, one can argue that Judah should have done more to try to help his brother. Elie Wiesel writes (1976: 154), "For it had been Yehuda's [Judah's] idea: better to live in bondage than to die. A compromise the Midrash judges harshly. It is forbidden to praise Yehuda. When human life and dignity are at stake, one has no right to settle for half measures; Yehuda should have fought to the end to save his brother, not only from death but also from shame."

Judah, Tamar, and Perez

Basic Text: Before the Joseph story resumes, there is an interlude in which Judah plays a key role (Gen: 38). Judah moves away from his family, and marries the daughter of a Canaanite man named Shua. She bears Judah three sons, Er, Onan, and Shelah. When Er is grown, Judah finds a wife for him, Tamar. But God finds Er to be evil and kills him. Judah then orders his second-born son to do his duty for his dead older brother and to have a child with Tamar. But a son will be counted as Er's son, and have precedence over Onan. Rather than refuse to have sex with Tamar, Onan does have intercourse, but when he did he "would waste his seed on the ground, so to give no seed to his brother"(Gen. 38:9). God finds Onan's behavior evil, and He puts him to death. Judah fears that his youngest son, Shelah, will die if he has sex with Tamar. He tells Tamar to return to her household and wait until Shelah is grown.

A long times passes and Judah's wife dies, but he does not fulfill his promise to Tamar. When Tamar learns that Judah is going to a shearing festival, she wears a veil and Judah believes she is a whore. Judah wants to procure her services, not knowing the woman he desires is Tamar. But Tamar demands payment in advance, and Judah has nothing to pay her. He offers to send her a kid, but she demands a pledge, and he agrees, leaving her with his seal-and-cord and his walking staff. But when he sends his friend with the kid, he asks where the cult-harlot is, and is told none has been there.

Three months later Judah learns that Tamar is pregnant, and is pregnant from being a whore. Judah orders her to be burned. Tamar presents Judah's seal-and-cord and walking staff, saying that the owner of them is the father. Judah acknowledges they are his and says, "She is more in the right than I, for have I not failed to give her to Shelah, my son?" (Gen. 38:26). Tamar gives birth to twin sons. There is a detailed description of the childbirth. A baby sticks out its hand and the midwife ties a scarlet thread around it. But the baby withdraws its hand, and the other baby is born. The baby that fully emerges is named Perez (breach; bursting through), although he is considered to be the second-born. The second baby, who is considered the firstborn, is named Zerah (shining).[11]

Political Implications: As Judah is the ancestor of David, the Davidic monarchy, and the Messiah, it is important to demonstrate his virtues. He has already saved Joseph from being murdered, and now he acknowledges the paternity of Tamar's unborn child (or, as it happens, children). As *The Torah: A Women's Commentary* (2008: 2109) notes, "This is the first reported occasion where anyone has called Judah to account for his actions; he rises to the occasion by taking responsibility for his earlier words and actions—albeit indirectly. It marks a definite step in his maturation." Moreover, the birth of Perez is also important because he has many descendants, including King David. And Tamar is among the five women mentioned, and one of the four named, in Matthew's genealogy of Jesus (Matt. 1:3). The story also demonstrates that Jacob's descendants can no longer find women from Abraham's family, and now marry local women.

Joseph and Potiphar's Wife

Basic Text: Joseph is transported to Egypt and is sold to Potiphar, one of the Pharaoh's courtiers. God favors him, and he now begins to show his administrative ability and becomes the head of the household. But Joseph has inherited his mother's good looks, and Potiphar's wife orders him to "Lie with me" (Gen. 39:7). Joseph spurns her advances. But one day he enters the house when only Potiphar's wife is present. When she once again demands that Joseph have sex with her, Joseph flees, and she seizes his garment. Potiphar's wife screams, accusing Joseph of attempted rape, and uses his garment as evidence. Once again, Joseph's garments play a role in his undoing. Joseph is imprisoned.

Political Implication: Before serving in Potiphar's household, Joseph demonstrates little judgment. Now he shows enough administrative ability to run a large household but scarcely the ability to run a country. Unfortunately, he enters Potiphar's house when only his wife is present.

From Prisoner to Minister for Pharaoh

Basic Text: Even in prison, God continues to favor Joseph, and the warden places him in charge of the other prisoners. The Pharaoh's chief cupbearer and his chief baker are sent to the prison, and the warden assigns Joseph to serve them. One night they both have dreams, and are morose because there is no one to interpret them. Joseph tells them, "Are not solutions from God? Pray, recount them to me" (Gen. 40:8). Joseph correctly interprets both dreams. In three days, the cupbearer will be recalled to office; in three days, the baker will be impaled. Joseph asks the cupbearer to mention him to Pharaoh since he is unjustly imprisoned. Joseph's interpretation proves correct. The cupbearer does not mention him to the Pharaoh, and forgets him.

Political Implications: Joseph, with God's help, demonstrates his administrative ability. Now he does not tell others about his own dreams but interprets the dreams of others. Joseph becomes increasingly skilled, but running a prison is a far cry from running a country. The story establishes the basis for Joseph meeting the Pharaoh.

Joseph Becomes Pharaoh's Chief Minister

Basic Text: Two years later, Pharaoh has his two dreams. First, he dreams of seven fair and fat cows coming out of the Nile, but they are devoured by seven scrawny cows that eat the fat cows. Pharaoh awakens, but when he falls asleep he has a second dream. There are seven good ears of corn on a single stalk, but they are devoured by seven meager ears. None of Pharaoh's advisors can (or will) provide a satisfactory explanation. The cupbearer now remembers the "Hebrew lad" (Gen. 41:12) who had correctly interpreted his dream and that of the chief baker. Joseph is prepared for an audience with Pharaoh. Pharaoh repeats the dreams in greater detail.

Joseph explains that the two dreams are really the same. There will be seven years of plenty followed by seven years of famine. Moreover, Joseph not only interprets the dream(s), but also recommends action for dealing with the impending crisis. Pharaoh should appoint a wise man and set him over the land of Egypt. Food should be collected during the years of plenty, guarded, and a reserve maintained to enable Egypt to survive the seven years of famine. Pharaoh not only accepts Joseph's interpretation, but also appoints Joseph to rule over Egypt. He changes Joseph's name to Zaphenath-Paneah, and gives him an Egyptian wife, Asenath, daughter of Potiphera, priest of On, although according to one story she later converts to Joseph's religion (*Joseph and Aseneth* and *The Marriage and Conversion of Aseneth*).[12] She and Joseph have two sons, Manasseh and Ephraim.

Political Implications: Not only did Joseph interpret Pharaoh's dream(s), but by making an unsolicited suggestion about how to meet the impending crisis, he all but suggests that he should be appointed to run Egypt. To a large extent he has become Egyptian. Thomas Mann uses his imagination to expand on this theme in his classic novel *Joseph and His Brothers* (see especially, "Joseph the Provider").[13] Aaron Wildavsky (1993, 119–37) compares the Egyptianization of Joseph with the Hebraicization of Daniel and Esther.

Joseph Transforms Egypt

Basic Text: Joseph serves the Pharaoh well, but how well does he serve the Egyptian people? During the seven good years, Joseph acquires surplus food and stores it under guard. "And Joseph piled up grain like the sand of the sea, very much, until he ceased counting, for it was beyond count" (Gen. 41:49). Although he provides food for the Egyptians during the years of famine, they pay dearly for it. He acquires the people's money, their livestock, their land, and relocates people throughout the country. By the end of the famine, the people are still grateful. "You have kept us alive! May we find favor in the eyes of our lord, in being Pharaoh's slaves" (Gen. 47:25).

Political Implications: According to the biblical account, Joseph transforms Egyptian society, reducing the people to serfdom or slavery. Granted, the people's lives have been spared by his abilities, but they could have been spared at much lower cost. Wildavsky (1993: 142) compares the Egyptian social relocation to actions by Joseph Stalin, arguing that there was no moral justification for Joseph's policies.

Joseph Tests His Brothers

Basic Text: The famine affects the known world, and Jacob hears provisions are available in Egypt. Jacob sends his ten oldest sons to purchase grain, but keeps Benjamin, his youngest son, whom he believes to be Rachel's only surviving child, at home. The brothers appear before Joseph. Although Joseph has not seen his brothers for twenty years, he recognizes them, but his brothers do not suspect that the official dressed in Egyptian garb and speaking to them through an interpreter, is Joseph. Joseph accuses them of being spies. They tell him that they are ten brothers, from a family of twelve brothers, one of whom has died and the youngest of whom (Joseph's full brother, Benjamin) remains with his father. Joseph insists they are spies. But he agrees to sell the brothers grain (although he secretly returns their money), but holds Simeon hostage. He says he will not see them again, unless they return with their younger brother.

They go home and relate their story to Jacob, who is furious that they have mentioned Benjamin's existence. But the family is running out of food. Finally, Judah persuades his father that they have no choice but to return to Egypt with Benjamin. Now Joseph treats his brothers well and releases Simeon. But Joseph has the head of his household place his silver goblet in Benjamin's baggage. After the brothers depart, Joseph sends his servant after them to demand they return and face a charge of theft. Joseph says that the man who stole his goblet, Benjamin, must be his slave, but the other brothers can return to their father.

At this point, Judah makes the longest speech in *Genesis* (44:18–34). Judah offers to serve as Joseph's slave in place of Benjamin. At this point, Joseph breaks down, and speaks in Hebrew, "I am Joseph. Is my father still alive?" (Gen. 45:3). Joseph tells his brothers that the famine will last five more years and tells them they should come to Egypt and live in the land of Goshen. Jacob now learns that his favorite son is not only alive, but is the leading official under the Pharaoh. He says, "Enough! Joseph my son is still alive. Let me go and see him before

I die" (Gen. 45:28). On the way to Egypt, God assures Jacob that he is right to go to Egypt and that he will become a great nation there.

Political Implications: The story makes two important political points. It establishes one more reason for Judah's primacy. As a leader he must assume the position of his followers and be willing to share their fate, or even trade his place for theirs (Wildavsky, 1993: 104). The story also provides yet another basis for establishing that the Israelites were once in Egypt.

Jacob's Blessings

Basic Text: Although Jacob has been tricked into marrying Leah, and deceived by his ten oldest sons into believing that wild animals have killed Joseph, as he nears his death, he displays prophetic abilities. When blessing Joseph's two sons, he crosses his hands to give Joseph's youngest son his primary blessing since he knows that, although Joseph's firstborn son will be a great people, Joseph's younger son "shall be greater than he, and his seed shall be a fullness of nations" (Gen. 48:19). When he "blesses" his twelve sons, he once again displays prophetic abilities. He condemns Reuben for violating Bilhah, and condemns Simeon and Levi for their atrocities at Shechem. (Yet Moses is a descendant of Levi, and the Levites will become the priests.)

Judah, Jacob's fourth son, is the first to actually be blessed. "The scepter shall not pass from Judah, nor the mace from between his legs, that tribute to him may come and to him the submission of peoples" (Gen. 49:10). He blesses his remaining eight sons and asks to be buried in the cave of Machpelah. Jacob is embalmed and his body is carried to Hebron in an impressive funeral procession.[14]

Political Implications: The main goal is to establish Judah's supremacy since he is to be the ancestor of David. Judah is central to the ancestry of Jesus (Matt. 1: 6–23 and Luke 3:23–38) and Jews believe that the Messiah will be a descendent of David.

Joseph Dies

Basic Text: When Jacob dies, Joseph's older brothers fear that he will seek to revenge their wrong of selling him into slavery. But Joseph assures them he will not harm them. "Fear not, for am I instead of God? While you meant evil toward me, God meant it for good" (Gen. 50:19–20). And Joseph lives until he is one hundred ten years old, and asks that his bones be carried back to the Promised Land when the "sons of Israel" (Gen. 50: 25) return to Canaan. "And they embalmed him and he was put in a coffin in Egypt" (Gen. 50:26).When the Israelites depart from Egypt, Moses takes Joseph's bones (Exod. 13:19), and they are eventually buried at Shechem (Josh. 24:32).

Political Implications: Joseph now displays an understanding of justice in not seeking revenge against his older brothers. Moreover, despite becoming very Egyptianized, Joseph does not want to be buried in Egypt. To be buried in Canaan, he, like his father, must be embalmed, contrary to Hebraic custom.

Notes

1. Islam views Abraham as a prophet and he is mentioned frequently in *The Koran* (see either of the two editions cited in the Bibliography).
2. For a compilation of these legends, see Louis Ginzberg (2005: 209–20; 2008: 135–43).
3. As J. H. Hertz writes in *The Pentateuch and Haftorahs* (p. 81), "The sum demanded, four hundred shekels of silver, is a very substantial sum. In the contemporary Code of Hammurabi . . . the wages of a workingman for a year are set at six or eight shekels."
4. Anyone familiar with Genesis will recognize that I have not discussed the Binding of Isaac (the *Akedah* in Hebrew), which occurs after the destruction of Sodom and Gomorrah, but before Sarah's death. God was "testing" Abraham's willingness to "Take, pray, your son, your only one, whom you love, Isaac, and go forth to the land of Moriah and offer him up as a burnt offering on one of the mountains which I shall say to you" (Gen. 22:2). In *Fear and Trembling*, Kierkegaard famously challenges Abraham's willingness to sacrifice Isaac. (For a discussion, see Thomas L. Pangel [2003: 172–81].) In my view, this story, while it is well worth discussing for other reasons, has no political implications. For game theoretic discussions, see Brams (2003, 37–45; 2011, 31–50).
5. In Hebrew, Jacob's name is *"Ya'aqob"*; the Hebrew for "heel" is *"aqeb."*
6. As the tribes from the Kingdom of Israel had disappeared (see chapter 13), it may seem odd that in 1948 Jewish leaders chose Israel as the name of their state. Abraham Diskin (personal communication, July 27, 2010), informs me that there was considerable controversy about what the Jewish state should be named. Throughout the British Mandate, official documents refer to it as "Eretz Israel" (the Land of Israel). This was not considered acceptable to Jewish leaders who argued it implied that Jews would rule over only part of the land. The terms, Judah or Zion (which refers to Jerusalem) were rejected for similar reasons. The final vote on the name to be used in the Declaration of Independence was made by the Mo'etzet Ha'Am (People's Council) on May 14, 1948, and the Declaration actually uses two names, Medinat Yisrael (State of Israel) and simply Yisrael. The Declaration of Independence was proclaimed later that day. Despite opposition by the U.S. State Department, Harry S. Truman recognized Israel eleven minutes later. His reading of the Bible influenced his decision. For a discussion of Truman's role in U.S. support for Israel, see Allis Radosh and Ronald Radosh (2009).

7. As Leon R. Kass observes in the PBS series, *Genesis: A Living Commentary* (Bill Moyers editor 1996: 260), "When he discovers that he has been deceived, Isaac doesn't get angry, he trembles—perhaps an experience of awe that somehow, unbeknownst to him himself, something working through him has given the blessing to the right son, even though that son is not Esau."

8. As Robert Alter points out (pp. 155–56), the Midrash Bereishit Rabba links Jacob's deception of Isaac with Leah's deception of Jacob. "And all that night he cried out to her 'Rachel!' and she answered him. In the morning, 'and, . . . look, she was Leah.' He said to her, 'Why did you deceive me, daughter of a deceiver? Didn't I cry out Rachel in the night, and you answered me!' She said: 'There is never a bad barber who doesn't have disciples. Isn't this how your father cried out Esau, and you answered him?'"

9. In *The Torah: A Woman's Commentary* (2008: 191–92), the commentator argues that the word *innah* does not have the same meaning as "he took hold of her" used for rape in *Deuteronomy* and in the Tamar/Amnon story (see Chapter 11), and should not be considered rape in the modern sense of the word.

10. For a substantial retelling of this story, see Thomas Mann, "The Stories of Jacob," in *Joseph and His Brothers*. Throughout the biblical account, Dinah is silent. For a fictionalized account of the story from Dinah's point of view, see Anita Diamant (1997). Like the *Torah: A Woman's Commentary*, Diamant does not view Shechem's action as rape.

11. For a discussion of Tamar's actions, see Frymer-Kensky (2002: 264–77) and Jonathan Kirsch (1997: 100–54).

12. The first translation is in James H. Charlesworth ed. (1985); the second and shorter version is in Lawrence E. Wills ed. (2002).

13. See also, Leon R. Kass (2003: 550–72).

14. As Everett Fox (p. 234) reminds us in *The Five Books of Moses*, the *Iliad* ends with Hector's burial. (Homer ends his epic, "And so the Trojans buried Hector breaker of horses."[Book 24: 944]) "The contrast," Fox writes, "is instructive: the Homeric epic celebrates the deeds and mourns the lost youth of the hero (Hector). Genesis reflects Yosef's [Joseph's] standing at the court and the desire to bury Yaakov [Jacob] in the land of Canaan, in the family plot."

3

Exodus

The Israelites are Enslaved

Basic Text: Exodus begins by naming the sons of Israel who came to Egypt with Jacob, a total of seventy persons (see also Gen. 46:8–27). They "were fruitful and swarmed and multiplied, and grew very vast and the land was filled with them" (Exod. 1:7). A new king rules Egypt "who knew not Joseph" (Exod. 1:8). The king fears the growing size of "the people of the sons of Israel" (Exod. 1:9). Even if Israel cannot defeat the Egyptians, "should war occur, they will actually join our enemies and fight against us and go up from the land" (Exod. 1:10). Pharaoh sets taskmasters over the Israelites, but their numbers continue to grow. The king orders the Hebrew midwives, Shiphrah and Puah, to put all the boys to death, but to let the girls live. But the midwives disobey, and explain that they cannot comply because the Hebrew women give birth too quickly. God rewards the midwives.

Pharaoh now commands that every Hebrew boy be flung into the Nile, but that girls be allowed to live. A Levite man takes a Levite woman and she gives birth to a son, whom they hide for three months. She puts him into an ark, which she puts in the Nile, while his older sister watches over him. Pharaoh's daughter finds him, realizes he is a Hebrew, but adopts him. She gives the boy an Egyptian name, Moses, "For from the water I drew him out"(Exod. 2:10). Moses is brought up as an Egyptian. When he grows up, he sees an Egyptian man striking a Hebrew man. He "turned this way and that and saw that there was no man about, and he struck down the Egyptian and buried him in the sand" (Exod. 2:12). However, the next day Moses realizes that he has been seen, and he flees Egypt and goes to the land of Midian.

Political Implications: The Israelites have grown into a people, and Pharaoh is the first to use this term to describe them. Pharaoh views the Israelites strategically. Egypt is often at war, and the Israelites may join Egypt's enemies. When forced labor does not prevent the Israelites from multiplying, he institutes partial genocide, by trying to kill newborn Hebrew boys, a restricted genocide compared with the Nazis in the twentieth century, who made no distinctions between men and women, and between male and female children. The midwives who defied Pharaoh are rewarded, and their names are recorded, whereas the Bible does not report the name of the Pharaoh. Joseph Telushkin (1997: 92–93) considers their refusal to comply with Pharaoh's command "the first recorded act of civil disobedience." The birth, adoption, and exile of a future Hebrew leader is described, although Sigmund Freud (1939) famously argues that Moses is an Egyptian.

Moses at the Burning Bush

Basic Text: Moses sits down by a well and meets the seven daughters of the priest of Midian. The daughters come to the well to water their father's flock, but shepherds come and drive them off. Moses rises to protect them. The father (Reuel, later named Jethro) invites Moses for dinner. Moses agrees to dwell with the man, who gives Moses one of his daughters, Zipporah. She gives birth to a son, whom Moses names Gershom. A long time passes, and the king of Egypt dies.

God hears the Israelites' cries of affliction and decides to have Moses lead them to their deliverance. Moses sees a burning bush near Mount Horeb, but the bush is not consumed. Moses turns to see this sight. God now speaks: "Moses, Moses! . . . Come no closer here. Take off your sandals from your feet, for the place you are standing on is holy ground" (Exod. 3:4–5). God tells Moses that he is the God of Abraham, the God of Isaac, and the God of Jacob. Moses is to act for God by rescuing his people, and bringing them to "a land flowing with milk and honey, to the place of the Canaanite and the Hittite and the Amorite and the Perizzite and the Hivite and the Jebusite" (Exod. 3:8). Moses is not to ask that the Israelites be freed, only that he should be allowed to lead them from Egypt to "worship God on this mountain" (Exod. 3:12). Moses argues that the Israelites will not listen to him unless he can tell them God's name. God answers him, *"Ehyeh-'Asher'-Ehyeh,* I-Will-Be-Who-I-Will-Be. And He said, Thus, shall you say to the Israelites, *'Ehyeh* has sent me to you'" (Exod. 3:14).

Even though God promises to strike Egypt with signs and wonders, and although he shows Moses some tricks, and promises major signs, Moses protests that "I am heavy-mouthed and heavy-tongued" (Exod. 4:10). (In the *KJV,* "but I *am* slow of speech, and am of a slow tongue.") But God replies that his older brother Aaron the Levite is eloquent and is on his way to meet him. Moses takes his wife and two sons and heads toward Egypt, although it appears he sends them back before reaching his destination.

Political Implications: Moses proves to be a great political leader. But he is a very reluctant leader, although if he had known of the problems that the Israelites would cause him he would have been even more reluctant. As Aaron Wildavsky (1984, 34–35) points out, Moses must learn a great deal about leadership during the next four decades.

Moses Becomes "a God unto Pharaoh"

Basic Text: Moses and Aaron speak to Pharaoh and demand that he allow Israel to worship God in the wilderness. But Pharaoh says he does not know the Lord, and instead retaliates against the Israelites by demanding that they make the same quota of bricks without being supplied with straw. The Israelites complain to Moses, and Moses complains to God. But God tells Moses, "See, I have set you as a god to Pharaoh, and Aaron your brother will be your prophet" (Exod. 7:1). But God is determined to demonstrate his powers against Pharaoh, even though many innocent Egyptians will suffer as well. God turns the Nile into blood. Pharaoh recognizes that this is a powerful sign but "Pharaoh's heart toughened" (Exod. 7:22) and he refuses to let the Israelites worship in the desert. After a plague of frogs, his heart hardens. When God afflicts the Egyptians with a plague of lice, even his advisors recognize that "God's finger it is!" (Exod. 8:15). God then sends a swarm of flies, but Pharaoh once again hardens his heart.

God next turns to a plague of cattle disease, but, once again Pharaoh's heart hardens. Finally, God uses a cloud of dust to cause skin disease among Egyptians, which affects Pharaoh's soothsayers. But now, "the LORD toughened Pharaoh's heart, and he does not heed them [his soothsayers]" (Exod. 9:12). God next afflicts Egypt with hail. He is about to relent, but his heart hardens. Moses threatens that the next plague will be locusts to destroy what is left of Egypt's crops. But after the plague of locusts, God toughens Pharaoh's heart (Exod. 10:20). Even three days of darkness do not convince Pharaoh, for once again God toughens his heart (Exod. 10:27). Pharaoh tells Moses to leave his presence "for on the day you see my face, you shall die" (Exod. 10:28). And Moses says, "Rightly have you spoken—I will not see your face again" (Exod. 10:29).

Moses then warns the Israelites to sacrifice a lamb and mark their houses with its blood. And that night the Lord strikes down the firstborn of Egypt, "from the firstborn of Pharaoh sitting on his throne to the firstborn of the captive who was in the dungeon, and every firstborn of the beasts" (Exod. 12:29). But the Lord passes over the houses of the Israelites. Now the outcry in Egypt is so great that the Israelites are expelled in great haste, not even having time to leaven their bread. But Pharaoh and his advisors have another change of heart. God again "toughened the heart of Pharaoh king of Egypt" (Exod. 14:8), and Pharaoh pursues the Israelites with six hundred chariots. Backed up against the Sea of Reeds, the Israelites chastise Moses, "Was it for lack of graves in Egypt that you took us to die in the wilderness?" (Exod. 14:11). But Moses holds his rod over the sea, the sea parts, and the Israelites cross on dry land.

When Pharaoh's chariots follow them, the sea closes and the horses and charioteers drown. The people are thankful and sing the Song of the Sea, one of the oldest passages in the Bible. "And Miriam, the prophetess, Aaron's sister, took the timbrel in her hand, and all the women went out after her with timbrels and dances. And Miriam sung out to them:

'Sing to the LORD for He has surged, O surged,

Horse and its rider He hurled into the sea!'" (Exod. 15:20–21).

Political Implications: The unnamed Pharaoh is also a political leader, and even if he has only recently become the Pharaoh, he should have greater leadership experience than Moses, who has spent most of his adult life tending sheep. But Pharaoh, who is worshipped as a god, is contending with a real god, as both his advisors and he eventually realize. Moreover, several times Pharaoh is about to make an expeditious decision, since holding the Israelites in captivity is far too costly for him and his people.

But is Pharaoh a free agent? God is determined to show his power, and Pharaoh is willing to relent four times, but God toughens his heart. The text raises the question of whether Pharaoh had free will. Of course, the Pharaohs, especially the Pharaoh who introduced the murder of male Hebrew babies, were evil. But were all the firstborn of Egypt evil, even their animals (compare with Jon. 4:11)?

Jethro Advises Moses

Basic Text: Jethro, the priest of Midian and Moses' father-in-law, has heard of the great events in Egypt. He brings Zipporah and Moses' two sons, Gershom and Eliezer. The following day, Jethro observes Moses judging the people. He sees that Moses is overworked and offers advice. "The thing that you are doing is not good. You will surely wear yourself out—both you and this people that is with you" (Exod. 18:17–18). He advises Moses to teach others the statutes and to divide the responsibility of judging the people among God-fearing men who can be put over the chiefs of thousands, hundreds, fifties, and tens. Moses, he advises, should only judge the difficult cases. Moses follows Jethro's advice, and his father-in-law departs.

Political Implications: Moses learns about organizational principles. Moreover, he accepts Jethro's advice even though Jethro does not convert to become a worshipper of Moses' God. Moses understands that he should take good counsel from any source.

God's Covenant with the Children of Israel

Basic Text: Just before Moses ascends Mount Sinai to receive God's commandments, God tells him he wants to establish a covenant with the Israelites. He instructs Moses to tell them, "You yourselves saw what I did to Egypt, and I bore you on the wings of eagles and I brought you to Me. And now, if you truly heed My voice and keep My covenant, you will become for Me a treasure among all the peoples, for Mine is all the earth. And as for you, you will become for Me a kingdom of priests and a holy nation. These are the words that you shall speak to the Israelites" (Exod. 19:4–6). "And all the people answered together and said, 'Everything that the LORD has spoken we shall do" (Exod. 19:8).

Political Implications: This covenant is made through Moses with the entire people of Israel, and, as Michael Walzer (1985: 75) notes, according to *midrashic* tales, it is with women as well because God realized He had erred by warning Adam not to eat the fruit from the tree of knowledge, but did not directly warn Eve. By creating a covenant with the Israelites, God creates a new form of civil society. According to Rousseau, Moses' greatest achievement was transforming "wretched fugitives" into a "free people" by giving them laws (Rousseau, *The Government of Poland*, 6).

Moses and the Golden Calf

Basic Text: God gives the Decalogue to Moses on Mount Sinai, and through Moses to the Israelites. The prohibition against murder goes back to Noah, "He who sheds human blood by humans his blood shall be shed" (Gen. 9:6), but the Hebrew in *Exodus* 20:13 clearly prohibits "murder" (mistranslated in the *KJV* as "Thou shalt not kill"). The first two commandments, according to the Jewish enumeration, prohibit idolatry. "I am the LORD your God Who brought you out of the land of Egypt, out of the house of slaves. You shall have no other gods beside Me" (Exod. 20:1–2); and "You shall make no carved likeness and no image of what is in the heavens above or is on the earth below or what is in the waters beneath the earth" (Exod. 20:3–4).

In addition to the ten basic laws, God gives Moses laws about the treatment of slaves, strongly suggesting that Hebrew slaves have special rights (Exod. 21:1–6). But all slaves have rights against cruel mistreatment that results in bodily injury (Exod. 21:26). God establishes the concept of limited retribution (Exod. 21:22–37), distinctions between robbery and theft (Exod. 22:1–3), and the establishment of three festivals (Exod. 23:14–19). And when he took these commandments to the people, they repeated, "All that the LORD has spoken we will do and we will heed" (Exod. 24:8).

Moses returns to the mountain and God gives him extensive instructions for building an Ark and tabernacle (Exod. 25:10–31:11). He stays on the mountain so long that the people demand that Aaron make them gods. Aaron asks them to provide the gold, but they have a great deal of gold since they despoiled Egypt. Aaron melts this gold and makes a golden calf, proclaims a festival, and the people celebrate. God tells Moses to hurry down from the mountain. Aaron acknowledges that he asked the people for gold and that he flung it into the fire, "and out came this calf" (Exod. 32:24). God is furious and threatens to destroy the Israelites. But Moses intercedes and saves them. But not all. Moses cries, "Whoever is for the LORD, to me!" (Exod. 32:26). The Levites gather and kill about three thousand men.

Political Implications: Walzer (1985: 55–61) analyzes the political implications of this episode. The main lesson is the importance of purges. It was necessary to destroy the hidden idolaters but not the entire people. He notes that Saint Augustine favored persecuting heretical Christians, that John Calvin (1509–64) saw *Exodus* 32 as a precedent, and that Lincoln Steffens (1926: 108) saw this purge as a justification for the Red terror in Russia. Everett Fox (p. 442) argues that the story "focuses not only on the great crime of idolatry, but also on the nature of Moshe [Moses] as a leader."[1]

Notes

1. Steven J. Brams provides a game theoretic discussion of this rebellion in Brams (2003: 94–98) and extends the analysis in Brams and D. Marc Kilgour (2009: 236–37).

4

Leviticus

The Priesthood is Established

Basic Text: Although God through Moses establishes a covenant with all of the Israelites, *Leviticus* spells out rules for the priests. Analysts of biblical sources conclude that the priestly writers had a major role in writing this book (see especially, Richard Elliott Friedman, 2003). The book provides a great deal of detail about rituals, dietary laws, and establishes the basis for ritual purity.

One of the most interesting chapters is 18, part of the Holiness Code, which is read in many synagogues on Yom Kippur (the Day of Atonement). It warns the people not to behave like the people of Egypt or the people of Canaan. "No man of you shall come near any of his own flesh to lay bare nakedness" (Lev. 18:6). (In the *KJV*, "None of you shall approach to any that is near of kin to him, to uncover *their* nakedness.") The portion prohibits intercourse during a woman's period, as well as male homosexuality. There is no mention of female homosexuality, but women are prohibited from copulating with beasts. Chapter 20 makes male homosexuality a capital offence (Lev. 20:13), and for both sexes bestiality is a capital offence (Lev. 20:15–16).

Political Implications: Most argue that the main purpose of this code was to separate the Israelites from the inhabitants of the Promised Land. But it also shows that Abraham and Jacob violated these incest prohibitions. Abraham tells Abimelech that he did not lie when he said that Sarah was his sister, because she had the same father (prohibited by Lev. 18:9). And Jacob has sex with two sisters, Leah and Rachel, in their same lifetime (prohibited by Lev. 18:18). Granted, these rules had not been promulgated, but some argue that the Patriarchs should have known them anyway.

There are harsh rules condemning male homosexuality, and Paul later condemns female homosexuality (Rom. 1:26). Controversies about homosexuality, especially about same-sex marriage, remain important in the United States, and throughout the world people with what Ronald Inglehart calls materialist values are more negative toward homosexuality than those he calls postmaterialists.[1]

God Warns the Israelites

Basic Text: In the penultimate chapter of *Leviticus* (26), God reminds the Israelites that they will be rewarded if they follow His laws, and severely punished if they do not, and He again reminds them of the prohibition against idolatry. If the people obey, God will provide rain in its season, the land will yield abundantly, wild beasts will leave the Promised Land, and foreign enemies will not invade. "And you will pursue your enemies and they will fall before you by the sword. And five of you will pursue a hundred, and a hundred of you will pursue ten thousand, and your enemies will fall before you by the sword"(Lev. 26:7–8).

If the people do not obey God's laws, His vengeance shall be seven-fold. Enemies will invade the land, and even if the people grow crops, others will eat them. "And I will break the pride of your strength and make your heavens like iron and your earth like bronze" (Lev. 26:19). "Ten women shall bake your bread in one oven and dole out your bread by weight, and you shall eat and not be sated" (Lev. 26:26). People will even resort to cannibalism and devour their children's flesh.

Political Implications: God makes a covenant with the Israelites, but he will protect them only if they obey his laws. He will punish them severely if they do not. During the Roman siege of Jerusalem in 70 CE, some residents practiced cannibalism. The prohibition against idolatry (Lev. 19:3 and earlier in Exod. 20:1–4) is also extremely strong in Islam. And during the Civil War in England (1642–51), the Puritans accused Anglicans, who they saw as too close to Roman Catholics, of being idolaters.

Note

1.   See Ronald Inglehart and Paul R. Abramson (1999), Inglehart, Miguel Basañez, and Alejandro Moreno (eds.) (1998, Table V307), and Inglehart et al., (eds.) (2004, Table F118).

5

Numbers

God Orders a Census

Basic Text: Although God refers to a census in *Exodus* 30:11–16, He again tells Moses to "Count the heads of all the community of the Israelites by their clans, by their fathers' houses, according to the number of names, every male by their heads. From twenty years old and up, everyone who goes out in the army in Israel, you shall reckon them by battalions, you and Aaron" (Num. 1:2–3). The total, not including the Levites, comes to 603,550 men. (For a detailed account at the beginning and end of *Numbers*, see Jacob Milgrom's commentary, Chapter 26.) (Although old men could fight effectively, there were relatively few old men during this period.) But there were males younger than twenty, and probably about as many women as men. So many scholars say that, if these figures are taken literally, there were about 2,000,000 Israelites.

Political Implications: The goal of the census was to determine the Israelite military strength. The Roman emperor Augustus (63 BCE–14 CE; Emperor 23 BCE–14 CE) orders the most famous biblical census (see Chapter 18). The most famous English census resulted in the *Domesday Book,* completed in 1086 under William the Conqueror (c1028–87; reigned 1066–87), to assess what he could tax in the country he conquered twenty years earlier. As Kenneth Prewitt (2003), the director of the 2000 U.S. Census, points out the United States Census of 1790 was the first census used to determine how people should be represented (*U.S. Constitution,* Article 1, Section 3).[1]

God Orders Moses to Establish a Council of Seventy Elders

Basic Text: God tells Moses that he now has six hundred thousand foot soldiers. It seems like time to invade Canaan. But first God orders Moses to establish a council of elders. And Moses "gathered seventy men of the elders of the people and stood them round about the Tent"

(Num. 11:24). God's spirit rested on the elders. Two of these elders, Eldad and Medad, begin prophesying, but Moses does not object.

Political Implications: Although God has earlier established a covenant with all the Israelites, He continues to be more restrictive. First, He has established a priesthood, and now a Council of Elders. But, according to Aaron Wildavsky (1984: 161–62), establishing the council demonstrates Moses' willingness to delegate authority. This higher council, Wildavsky acknowledges, is scarcely democratic. Unlike the directly elected U.S. Senate (since 1913), the Council of Elders is selected from above, although, unlike the British House of Lords until 1958, membership was not basically hereditary.

The Sin of the Scouts

Basic Text: Moses is now about to invade Canaan, but God tells him to dispatch scouts, "every one of them a chieftain" (Num. 13:2). (In the *KJV*, "every one a ruler among them.") All twelve are named, but in the case of Hosea, the son of Nun, from the tribe of Ephraim, Moses has changed his name to Joshua. Moses asks them to assess the land's fertility and its defenses. The scouts are gone for forty days and come back with proof of Canaan's fertility. But all but Caleb, from the tribe of Judah, and Joshua, advise against invading. The people are too strong to overcome. But Caleb argues, "We will surely go up and take hold of it" (Num. 13:30). But all the other scouts except Joshua now put forth "an ill report" about the Land (Num. 13: 32). "The land through which we passed to scout is a land that consumes those who dwell in it" (Num. 13:32).

The community bewails this bad report. "Would that we have died in the land of Egypt, or in this wilderness would that we had died" (Num. 14:2).They plan to return to Egypt. Now Caleb and Joshua argue that the land is very good, and if God helps them, they can conquer it. Moses and Aaron also plead with the people, but the people pelt them with stones. God threatens to destroy the people and to make Moses a new nation. But Moses pleads with God, appealing to God's ego, saying that if He destroys the Israelites, the Egyptians will claim it is because He was not able to deliver upon his promise. He also appeals to God's sense of compassion.

God relents, but He inflicts a severe punishment. The people will eventually enter the Promised Land, but "in this wilderness your corpses will fall and all of your reckoned ones from twenty years old and up, for you have complained against Me. . . . And your little ones, of whom you said they would become booty, I shall bring them and they will know the land that you have cast aside"(Num. 14:29, 14:31). God kills the ten scouts who gave the ill report. The older generation will spend a total of forty years in the wilderness, one for each day the chieftains scouted the Land.

Political Implications: The story demonstrates that the Israelites liberated from Egypt are not ready to be a free people. A new generation must be raised to conquer Canaan; in other words, there must be a new political generation (Paul R. Abramson, 1989, 2001, 2011; Abramson and Ronald Inglehart, 1995). This concept can be found in Greek philosophy as well. Plato argued that philosophers could establish the ideal polity more quickly if they expelled all citizens above the age of ten from the republic (*Republic* 541a). Presumably, unlike William Golding in his novel, *Lord of the Flies* (1954), Plato would provide adult supervision.

Moses and Korah's Rebellion

Basic Text: Korah, a Levite, leads a rebellion of two hundred fifty prominent men against Moses and Aaron. They challenge Moses and Aaron proclaiming, "You have too much! For all the community, they are all holy, and in their midst is the LORD, and why should you raise yourselves up over the LORD's assembly?" (Num. 16:3). Moses challenges Korah and his followers. He asks that they prepare fire-pans. Korah and his followers prepare their fire-pans, and Moses and Aaron prepare theirs. Moses asks God to judge between him and the rebels. Everyone dies. Moses says, "But if a new thing the LORD should create, and the ground gapes open its mouth and swallows them and all of theirs and they go down alive to Sheol, you will know that these men have despised the LORD" (Num. 16:30).

And as soon as Moses speaks these words, the ground opens up, swallowing "every human being that was Korah's, and all their possessions. And they went down, they and all that was theirs, alive to Sheol" (Num. 16:32). Fire destroys all two hundred fifty of the men who challenge Moses.

Political Implications: What were Korah's goals? Ira Sharkansky argues that it is not clear whether Korah wanted more popular input or whether he wanted to establish a new oligarchy (1996: 84). On the other hand, Michael Walzer (1985: 111) concludes, "Korah is the first left opportunist in the history of radical politics." But even before the rebellion it was clear that challenging Moses was dangerous.

Moses at the Waters of Meribah

Basic Text: At the Wilderness of Zin, the entire community complains to Moses and Aaron to demand water. God tells Moses to assemble the people and to speak to the rock and that it will yield water. But Moses is furious with the people. Instead of speaking to the rock, he strikes it twice with his staff. Water flows. But God tells Moses and Aaron, "Inasmuch as you did not trust Me to sanctify Me before the eyes of the Israelites, even so you shall not bring this assembly to the land that I have given to them" (Num. 20:12). This infraction at the waters of Meribah is the reason God refuses to let Moses enter Canaan. (For the full story, as related in the *KJV*, see Chapter 1.)

Political Implications: We can ask whether the Lord, like Gilbert and Sullivan's Mikado, has the sublime object of making "the punishment fit the crime." But as Aaron Wildavsky points out, Moses has defied explicit instructions (1984: 175). Milgrom also sees God's actions "as a fitting and fair punishment" (commentary on Chapter 20). Being a political leader is difficult, especially if one is being supervised by God. Moreover, as Wildavsky has pointed out (see my discussion in chapter 1), it is important for Moses' leadership to end.

Balak, Balaam, and the Idolatry at Baal-Peor

Basic Text: Balak, the King of Moab, is frightened by the Israelites and hires Balaam, a non-Hebrew prophet, to curse them. Since he cannot issue false prophesies, he winds up blessing them. On a trip to curse Israel, the she ass Balaam is riding refuses to walk forward, and in anger, he whips her. But the she ass speaks to her master, "What have I done to you, that you should have struck me these three times?" (Num. 22:28). Apparently, Balaam fails to recognize that it is unusual for animals to speak, for he answers the she ass. But the ass sees the Lord's messenger barring her path and prevents Balaam from continuing his journey.

Although cursing Israel does not succeed, sex does. At Shittam, "the people began to go whoring with the daughters of Moab" (Num. 25:1). Worse yet, they worship Moabite gods. Phinehas, a grandson of Aaron, spears the son of an Israelite leader and a Moabite woman who are openly having sex. God has caused a plague that killed 24,000 Israelites. But Phinehas's actions assuages Him and the plague ends. He grants Phinehas His covenant of peace.

Political Implications: Moses is severely punished for striking a rock, whereas Phinehas is rewarded for murder. But the danger of intermarriage is a persistent theme in the *Hebrew Bible*, even though, as we shall see, at least one of King David's ancestors was probably a Canaanite (Tamar) and one was a Moabite (Ruth). But idolatry is a far greater sin. The story warns the Israelites against the danger of assimilation but, especially, against the sin of idolatry.

God Orders a Second Census

Basis Text: The Israelites are now close to invading Canaan, and God orders another census of men twenty years old and over. The overall totals have changed very little, a decline from 603,550 to 601,730 (not including the Levites). Only the tribe of Simeon has declined markedly, falling from 59,300 to 22,200, probably because it was being absorbed by Judah. The tribe of Manasseh has grown from 32,200 to 52,700 (Milgrom, Comments on Chapter 26). But although the numbers are similar, the men are not. Among the men tallied in the first census (two years after the Exodus), only Caleb and Joshua remain alive for the second census. For the adults who wanted to return to Egypt after the report of the scouts were "doomed to die in the wilderness" (Num. 26:65).

Political Implication: Generational change is now complete, and Israel has a large contingent of men to conquer Canaan. If this story is accepted literally, it means all men except Caleb and Joshua who were counted in the first census are dead thirty-eight years later. Most would be dead, but one would expect there to be some survivors. God could easily assure there were none.

Joshua is Appointed the Next Leader

Basic Text: As Moses cannot enter the Promised Land, a successor must be chosen. God instructs Moses to select Joshua, the son of Nun. Moses and Eleazar the priest instruct Joshua in using the Urim, a device for forecasting. And Moses "laid his hands upon him and charged him as the LORD had spoken through Moses" (Num. 27:23).

Political Implication: In Max Weber's terminology, the laying of hands upon Joshua is an attempt to "routinize charisma." This is a major point of the elaborate ceremonies used to transfer political authority. Max Weber provides the most important theoretical discussion (see Max Weber [1946, 1947]).

Towns of Asylum

Basic Text: God differentiates between voluntary and involuntary killing. Even a murderer deserves to be judged and God tells the Israelites to establish "towns of asylum" where they can take sanctuary until they are tried. Moreover, some may have killed accidentally, and the victim's relatives may seek vengeance. The Israelites should establish six "towns of asylum" where they can take refuge and where they can remain until the high priest dies (Num. 35:10–34).

Political Implications: Montesquieu comments favorably on providing sanctuary for people who kill involuntarily. He writes, "The laws of Moses were very wise. Those who murdered involuntarily were innocent, but they had to be removed from the sight of the relatives of the deceased; therefore, Moses established an asylum for them" (*The Spirit of the Laws*, Part 5, Book 25, Chapter 3). Today, it is illegal for people to take personal revenge against someone who has killed their relatives, although such practices continue among criminals and in some non-Western societies. Therefore, cities of asylum are no longer necessary.[2] But there are still witness protection programs that perform a similar function.

Notes

1. Although the original provisions of the Constitution strongly suggest that the allocation of U.S. House seats to the states will be based upon population, population-based representation was not guaranteed since each state could have been allocated a single representative. Federalist 54, 55, and 58 (all by James Madison) argue that one of the purposes of the decennial census would be to allocate representatives. This principle was further institutionalized when Thomas Jefferson's formula for allocating House seats was applied to the 1790 Census results (see Prewitt, 2003: 3).

2. For a discussion of Montesquieu's views on the Bible in his *The Spirit of the Laws*, see Thomas L. Pangle (2010: 38–44).

6

Deuteronomy

Moses Restates the Law

Basic Text: In *Deuteronomy* Moses restates the law, as well as adding new regulations. Scholars agree that the style of this book is profoundly different from the four earlier books of the Pentateuch (see Richard Elliott Friedman, 1989, 2003, as well as Moshe Weinfeld's [1991] *Anchor Bible* translation and commentary of *Deuteronomy* 1–11, passim[1]). The most important message of the book is: "Justice, justice shall you pursue, so that you may live and take hold of the land the LORD your God is about to give you" (Deut. 16:20).[2]

The most important new regulations are the laws regulating future Israelite kings. The Israelites must have no foreign kings, their kings must not have many horses, nor many wives (Deut. 17:15–17). The king shall write his own copy of the book of laws to keep with the Levitical priests (Deut. 17:18), and "fear the LORD his God" (Deut. 17:19) and keep his statutes.[3]

Political Implications: As there was no Israeli monarchy at the time of Moses, many argue that these regulations were added much later. One of the leading political scientists of the last half of the twentieth century, Gabriel A. Almond, argues (1996: 53), "Love for the Bible cannot convert the advice given to Moses by his father-in-law as to how he might more efficiently adjudicate the conflicts among the children of Israel, or the Deuteronomic doctrine of kingship, into serious political science." Almond is correct, but he is picking two examples, whereas the Bible provides scores of examples of leaders dealing with political problems.

The Boundaries of the Promised Land

Basic Text: After a poetic warning of the benefits of following God's laws and the dangers of flouting them, Moses climbs to the top of Mount Nebo to see the Promised Land that he will not be allowed to enter. He is allowed to see the entire Land. "And the LORD let him see all the land, from Gilead as far as Dan, and all Naphtali, and the land of Ephraim and Manasseh, and all of the land of Judah as far as the Hinder Sea, and the Negeb, and the plain of the Valley of Jericho, town of the palm trees, as far as Zoar" (Deut. 34:1–3). "This is the land I swore to Abraham, to Isaac, and to Jacob" (Deut. 34:4).

Moses dies at the age of one hundred and twenty, and until the time of his death, "his eye had not grown bleary and his sap had not fled" (Deut. 34:7). (According to the *KJV*, "his eye was not dim, nor his natural force abated.") To this day, no one knows where he is buried. "No prophet again rose in Israel like Moses, whom the LORD knew face to face, with all the signs and the portents which the LORD sent him to do in the land of Egypt to Pharaoh and to all his servants and to all his land, and with all the strong hand and with all the great fear that Moses did before the eyes of all Israel" (Deut. 34:10–12).

Political Implications: About to embark upon the conquest of the Promised Land, the leaders must know its boundaries. Granted, the boundaries described to Moses are far less precise than those that could be established using a Global Positioning System, but they provide a clearer idea than any provided up to this point, with the exception of *Numbers* 34: 1–12. Moreover, as much as Moses is praised, there is no site to worship his remains or the place of his burial. And there is only a passing reference to Moses in the Passover *seder* that most Jews in Israel observe on the first evening of Passover, and which many Jews outside Israel observe on both the first and the second evening.[4]

Notes

1. The *Anchor Bible* translation and commentary of the remaining chapters of *Deuteronomy* have not yet been published. Weinfeld passed away in April 2009 at the age of eighty-four.
2. Robert Alter (p. 962) argues that scholars have interpreted this repetition; it simply emphasizes that "justice, and justice alone, shall you pursue."
3. For a discussion of the way that *Deuteronomy* attempts to limit kingship, see Joshua A. Berman (2008: 56–80).
4. See my summary of Aaron Wildavsky's argument in Chapter 1.

7

Joshua

Rahab, the Spies; The Walls of Jericho; and the Sun at Gibeon

Basic Text: Joshua is best known for three famous stories. First, we have the account of Joshua sending two spies into the walled city of Jericho, where they are hidden by the prostitute Rahab. The people of Jericho have heard of the victories of the Israelites, and Rahab tells the spies that "all the inhabitants of the land melt in fear before you" (Josh. 2:9). She will help the spies leave Jericho undetected if Joshua will spare her life and that of her family. They agree, in a bargain analyzed by Brams (2003: 107–113). Joshua leads the people across the Jordan, orders a mass circumcision, and then directs priests carrying trumpets made of rams' horns to march around the city.

The second famous story relates the collapse of Jericho's walls. On the seventh day they march around the city seven times, and on the seventh time the city "wall fell down flat; so the people charged straight ahead into the city and captured it" (Josh. 6:20). Only Rahab and her family are spared, and "[H]er family has lived in Israel ever since" (Josh. 6:25).

The third story relates the most famous miracle of the *Hebrew Bible.* It occurs when Joshua defeats the Amorites at Gibeon (Josh. 10). Hailstones destroy the Amorites, but Joshua wants more time to annihilate them. Joshua asks God, "Sun, stand still at Gibeon, and Moon, in the valley of Aijalon" (Josh. 10:12). The Lord complies. This event, we are told, is described in the *Book of Jashar*, which no longer exists. But *Joshua* 10:14 records, "There has been no day like it before or since, when the LORD heeded a human voice; for the LORD fought for Israel."

Political Implication: Among these three stories, the rescue of Rahab has the greatest political significance. Rahab and her family are spared after Jericho is destroyed, and her family "has lived in Israel ever since" (Josh. 6:25). Although she disappears from the *Hebrew Bible,* she reappears in Matthew's genealogy as the great-great-grandmother of King David, among the four women named (and among the total of five women mentioned) (Matt. 1: 5). As for the Sun and Moon standing still, see the discussion by Robert C. Boling and C. Ernest Wright in the *Anchor Bible* edition of *Joshua* (1982: 282–85).[1]

Joshua Conquers and Divides the Land

Basic Text: Most of *Joshua* describes his extensive military conquests, and the allocation of the territory to the tribes, with Judah receiving the largest portion.[2] In addition, Joshua resists any attempt to form a hereditary kingship. For example, at God's instructions, when he defeats the Canaanites, he burns their chariots and hamstrings their horses (Josh. 11:9). Joshua renews the covenant at Mount Ebal (Josh. 8) and sets up a seat of government, but not a capital, at Shiloh (Josh. 18).

Joshua gives a series of farewell addresses, but the most eloquent is delivered shortly before his death before all the tribes of Israel. He recounts the past history of the people from Terah, Abraham's father, through the conquest of Canaan. God has given the people "a land on which you had not labored, and towns that you had not built, and you live in them; you eat the fruit of vineyards and oliveyards that you did not plant" (Josh. 24:13).

Joshua warns the people to "revere the LORD, and serve him in sincerity and in faithfulness; put away the gods that your ancestors served beyond the River and in Egypt, and serve the LORD" (Josh. 24:14). The people answer that "Far be it that we should forsake the LORD to serve other gods" (Josh. 24:16). But Joshua reminds them that they must serve no other gods. "No, we will serve the LORD!" (Josh. 24:21) the people reply. Joshua reminds the people that they are witnesses to their own oath. Joshua dies at the age of one hundred and ten, and is buried near Shechem, along with the bones of Joseph.

Political Implications: Daniel J. Elazar (1989) considers the *Book of Joshua* to be a political classic. He analyzes the book as a political document, arguing that its goal was not to provide a chronology of the conquest or the division of the land, but rather to explain the rules by which Israel could live in a federal covenant.

Elazar was an expert on federalism, but in my view the rules discussed in *Joshua* do not clearly differentiate between the central government and that of the tribes. But it is probably true that in all federal governments the boundaries between the central government and the local units are always in a state of flux (see Karl J. Friedrich,

1950: 189–221; William H. Riker, 1964). Also, it is important to emphasize that Joshua never accomplished the goal God set for him—to rid the land of its polytheistic indigenous peoples. In fact, he even makes agreements with some of them.[3] Moreover, it could be argued that the Israelite tribes under Joshua or under the judges were never centralized enough to be classified as a federal system. Thus, while a great hero (Chaim Herzog, 1989: 1–12), Joshua's failures had major political implications for the Israelites during the period of the judges.

Notes

1. During the Scopes "monkey trial" held in Tennessee in July 1925, a high school teacher, John T. Scopes, was tried for teaching Darwin's theory of evolution. When famed criminal defense lawyer Clarence Darrow called William Jennings Bryan to testify as an expert witness on the Bible, he asked Bryan about this miracle. Bryan conceded that God had stopped the earth from rotating, rather than actually stopping the sun. But, as Edward J. Larson (1997: 189) writes, Bryan "had no idea what would happen to the earth if it stopped moving."
2. For an analysis of Joshua's campaigns, see Chaim Herzog and Mordechai Gichon (1997: 44–62).
3. The most famous pact comes about with the Gibeonites fooling Joshua into believing that they too are recent immigrants. Joshua makes a pact with them. He does not abrogate the pact when he learns of the deception, (Josh. 9:3–26), but he does make them "hewers of wood and drawers of water" (Josh. 9:21). Brams (2003, 113–18) formally models this story.

8

Judges

Gideon Rejects the Rulership

Basic Text: After Joshua's death, Israel is led by a series of tribal leaders, some of whom perform legendary exploits. There is a woman prophet, Deborah, whose general Barak, defeats Sisera and his nine hundred chariots. Sisera is dispatched by Jael, the wife of a Kenite, who serves him milk, and drives a tent peg into his temple. The Song of Deborah, one of the oldest portions of the Bible, praises Jael, "Most blessed of women be Jael, the wife of Heber the Kenite" (Judg. 5:24). There is Jephthah, who as the result of a rash oath, is forced to sacrifice his only child, a virgin daughter (for a discussion, see Steven J. Brams, 2003: 45–51). Samson is tricked by a Philistine woman, Delilah, into revealing the secret of his strength, loses it when his hair is shaven, and is blinded (see Brams, 2003: 153–60; 2011, 50–67). But he is placed between two pillars at the temple of the Philistine god Dagon; he asks God, "Let me die with the Philistines" (Judg. 16:30). He uses his restored strength to push aside the pillars of the temple, and it collapses killing Samson, along with about three thousand Philistines.

The most worthy of the judges is Gideon, for he rejects the kingship. The Israelites ask, "Rule over us, you and your son and your grandson also" (Judg. 8:22). Gideon emphatically refuses. "I will not rule over you, and my son will not rule over you; the LORD will rule over you" (Judg. 8:23). Gideon has seventy sons. After his death, the men of Shechem chose Abimelech, Gideon's son by a concubine. Abimelech murders all but one of his half-brothers, but three years later is killed at Thebez when a woman drops a millstone on his head. He asks his sword bearer to kill him, so that people will not be able to say "a woman killed him" (Judg. 9:54).

Political Implications: According to the traditional chronology, the period of the judges lasts about four hundred years, and it is a time of constant backsliding by the people. When foreign tribes dominate them, they call upon God, who provides them with a charismatic leader. But they invariably revert to idolatry when that leader dies. The people of Israel are increasingly unable to defend themselves, especially when the Philistines, who have iron weapons and a high level of civilization, become their primary challengers. Although the Philistines disappear, they give an alternative name to the land— Palestine. The distinction between calling the land Israel and calling it Palestine remains politically relevant.

The Men at Gibeath Rape a Concubine

Basic Text: The last three chapters (19–21) relate the story of a Levite man and the gang rape of his concubine. The story begins when his concubine escapes from him and returns to her father. Eventually, he persuades her to return. On their way home, they receive shelter in the Benjaminite town of Gibeah. The perverse men of the city begin banging on the door and demand that the master of the house bring out the man "so that we may have intercourse with him" (Judg. 19:22). (In the *KJV*, "that we may know him.") The host pleads with the men not to violate his guest and offers instead his virgin daughter and the concubine. But the men will not listen.[1]

Eventually, the Levite throws his concubine outside the house. The men "wantonly raped her, and abused her all through the night until the morning" (Judg. 19:25). Although they let her go at daybreak, she is dead.

The Levite cuts his dead concubine into twelve pieces and sends her body parts throughout the territories of all of the Israelites. He asks, "Has such a thing ever happened since the day that the Israelites came up from the land of Egypt until this day? Consider it, take counsel, and speak out" (Judg. 19:30).

The Israelites rally to punish the Benjaminites, but they refuse to yield up the perpetrators. Many Benjaminites are killed, and the other tribes decide not to give their daughters for the men of Benjamin to marry. But they realize this punishment is so severe that it will kill off the tribe of Benjamin. So they make peace with the Benjaminites and attack the inhabitants of Jabesh-gilead to provide women for the Benjaminites. *Judges* concludes, "In those days there was no king in Israel; all the people did what was right in their own eyes" (Judg. 21:25). (According to the *KJV*, "In those days, *there was* no king in Israel: every man did *that which was* right in his own eyes.")

Political Implications: This story reveals a picture of near anarchy. The people are lawless. Granted, despite the last verse in *Judges* (21:25), society had not reached a Hobbesian "time of war, where every man is enemy to every man" (*Leviathan* Part 1, Chap. XIII, v. 9), but Israel was a tribal society (see Francis Fukuyama, 2011: 64–79), and only the gravest threat or offense can get the tribes to act in unison. Although the people have not explicitly repudiated their covenant with God, God is so weary of their backsliding that he is no longer willing to protect them against the Philistines, who have become their most dangerous foe. The people themselves begin to recognize that they need more centralized leadership.

Note

1. This story parallels the story of the two angels who visit Sodom and who take refuge in Lot's house (Gen. 19:3–10). Lot offers to give the mob his two virgin daughters if they will spare his guests. For a brief account, see Chapter 2.

9

Ruth

Ruth Follows Naomi

Basic Text: *Ruth* is the second of the five *Megillot* (scrolls) of the *Hebrew* Bible, and is part of the Writings. It is the thirty-eighth book of the *Hebrew Bible*, coming after *The Song of Songs* and before *Lamentations*. In the *Christian Scriptures*, *Ruth* is one of the Historical Books and is the eighth book of the Bible, coming after *Judges* and before *1 Samuel*. It is read as part of Jewish liturgy during *Shavuot*, the Feast of Weeks, which comes at the time of the barley harvest. From a chronological perspective, the Christian placement makes sense, since the story occurs "in the days when the judges ruled" (Ruth 1:1).

The entire book consists of four chapters and of eighty-five verses. There is a famine in the land and Elimelech, a man from Bethlehem in Judah goes to live in Moab along with his wife, Naomi, and his two sons, Mahlon (meaning "sickness") and Chilion (meaning "vanishing"). Elimelech dies, but Naomi and her sons remain, and, in violation of the injunction in *Deuteronomy* 23:3, they marry Moabite women, Orpah and Ruth. (Only in *Ruth* 4:10 do we learn it is Mahlon who marries Ruth.) Both sons die, and Naomi learns that the famine has ended. She decides to return to Bethlehem, and her two daughters-in-law follow her. Naomi asks Orpah and Ruth to return, and Orpah complies.

Ruth is not persuaded. Naomi tells her, "See, your sister-in-law has gone back to her people and to her gods" (Ruth 1:15). But Ruth insists on continuing with Naomi. "Do not press me to leave you or to turn back from following you! Where you go, I will go; where you lodge, I will lodge; your people shall be my people, and your God my God. Where you die, I will die—there I will be buried. May the LORD do thus and so to me, and more as well, if even death parts me from you!" (Ruth 1:16–17). In the *KJV*, Ruth says, "Intreat me not to leave thee, *or* to return from following after thee: for whither thou goest, I will go; and where thou lodgest, I will lodge: thy people *shall be* my people, and thy God my God: Where thou diest, will I die, and there

49

I will be buried: the LORD do so to me, and more also, *if ought* but death part thee and me."

Political Implications: Why does Ruth insist on following Naomi to Bethlehem? In her beautiful retelling of the story, Cynthia Ozick (1994) points out that Orpah's decision was far more conventional, but by returning she is all but erased from history. There is, Ozick reminds us, no Book of Orpah. Ozick (1994: 227) argues that Ruth decides to follow Naomi because she has become a monotheist. "She is drawn to Israel because Israel is the inheritor of the One Universal Creator." Julia Kristeva (1991) argues that Ruth wants to continue to Bethlehem because of her love of Naomi. We can only speculate about why Ruth follows Naomi. The text does not criticize Mahlon and Chilion for marrying Moabite women. Some speculate that the storyteller is protesting directives to dissolve mixed marriages as mandated in *Nehemiah* (13) and *Ezra* (10).

Ruth Marries Boaz

Basic Text: Naomi and Ruth arrive in Bethlehem during the barley harvest. Naomi's husband had a rich kinsman, Boaz. Naomi tells Ruth to glean in Boaz's fields. Boaz comes to his fields and sees Ruth gleaning. He asks his reapers who she is. Boaz tells Ruth not to glean in any other field, and that he has ordered his young men not to bother her. She asks, "Why have I found favor in your sight, that you should take notice of me, when I am a foreigner?" (Ruth 2:10). Boaz tells her he has heard of her kindness to her mother-in-law.

Naomi gives Ruth detailed instructions, explaining that Boaz is her near kinsman. She should enter his tent at night and uncover his feet, a term often used as a euphemism for male genitals. Boaz discovers Ruth at his feet in the middle of the night and asks, "Who are you?" (Ruth 3:9). She explains, "I am Ruth, your servant; spread your cloak over your servant, for you are next-of-kin" (Ruth 3:9). Boaz explains that he is a near kinsman, and that he will do what he can do to help her, but that there is a nearer kinsman.

But when Boaz, the elders of the city, and the nearer kinsman meet at the city gate to dispose of a parcel of land owned by Naomi, the near kinsman is told he cannot have the land unless he marries Ruth. Not wanting to marry Ruth, he rejects his claim. Boaz marries Ruth, and she bears him a son. Naomi takes the child and nurses it (as Edward F. Campbell, 1975: 164–65 explains, this cannot mean wet-nurse). The women of the town name the boy, Obed, who became the father of Jesse, the father of David. *Ruth* concludes, "Now these are the descendants of Perez [the son of Judah]: Perez became the father of Hezron, Hezron of Ram, Ram of Amminadab, Amminadab of Nahshon, Nahshon of Salmon, Salmon of Boaz, Boaz of Obed, Obed of Jesse, and Jesse of David" (Ruth 4:18–22).

Political Implications: The main political purpose of the story is to spell out the genealogy of David, and therefore of the Messiah. This ancestry corresponds, with minor spelling differences, to the genealogy presented by Matthew 1:3–6, except that *Ruth* does not mention Rahab as being the mother of Boaz. Ruth is one of the four named women, and one of the five women, mentioned in Matthew's genealogy.

It is hard to account for the *Hebrew Bible* including a book documenting King David's Moabite ancestry. However, Tikva Frymer-Kensky (2002: 254) speculates that "David himself may have told this story of his ancestry in order to show his 'legitimate' claim to Moab." Bonnie Honig (1997, 2001) emphasizes the importance of Ruth's immigrant status to the story, and the way she is portrayed as a foreigner. Her marginal position is "stabilized by a marriage and birth that provide the founding energy for a new monarchic regime" (Honig, 2001: 44).

10

1 Samuel and 1 Chronicles 10, 12 (The Reign of Saul)

The People Demand a King

Basic Text: Samuel becomes the last judge. When Samuel grows old, he attempts to establish his sons as judges. "But his sons did not go in his ways and they were bent on gain and took bribes and twisted justice" (1 Sam. 8:3). The elders tell Samuel, "Look, you yourself have grown old and your sons have not gone in your ways" (1 Sam. 8: 4). So they demand, "so now, set over us a king to rule us, like all the nations" (1 Sam. 8:5). Moreover, the military position of Israel is weakened after the battle at Aphek, in which Israel is defeated by the Philistines and loses the Ark of God, although by inflicting plagues God forces them to return it (1 Sam. 5–6).[1]

Samuel warns the people that a king will take their sons to serve in his army, and their daughters to serve in his household. "Your flocks he will tithe, and as for you, you will become his slaves" (1 Sam. 8:17). But God tells Samuel to heed the people's voice. Although Samuel makes a strong argument, political conditions demand more centralized leadership. Saul, a Benjaminite, is a tall man with an imposing appearance, but he is God's choice, not Samuel's. When Samuel first sees Saul, God tells him that he is the man He has chosen (1 Sam. 9:18).

Political Implications: Samuel provides one of the strongest arguments ever made against kingship. During Solomon's reign, Samuel's warnings prove correct, and during the divided kingdoms, many of the leaders are tyrannical. Of the nineteen kings of the Kingdom of Israel, three are not assessed in *Kings*. Of the sixteen who are, only Jehu is given credit for having "wiped out Baal from Israel" (2 Kings 10:28), but he did little else to suppress idolatry (see Table 13.2). The Kings of Judah fare much better. From the end of the United Monarchy until the Babylonian Conquest, there are nineteen kings and one queen, the usurper Athalia. All nineteen kings are assessed. Many of them are evil, and most of those who "do what is right in the sight of the LORD" fail to tear down the high places where idolaters worship. Only two, Hezekiah and Josiah, are seen as righteous monarchs (see Table 13.4).

In his famous essay favoring American independence, *Common Sense*, Thomas Paine (1776) quotes Samuel's arguments at length. In his translation of *1 Samuel* and *2 Samuel* (*Give Us a King!*, pp. 33–34), Everett Fox argues that "Shemu'el's [Samuel's] warning forms an ominous backdrop out of which monarchy is to emerge. Many cultures' traditions tend to stress from the outset a new king's military exploits and charisma, choosing to build kingship on a firm popular foundation; but in the Bible, a note of misgiving needs to be sounded before anything else happens. In this sense, Shemu'el is both the last of the old-time practitioners of theocracy, the rule of God, and the first (excepting Moshe [Moses]) of the prophetic critics of human kingship."

Samuel Anoints Saul

Basic Text: Saul, the son of Kish, is reluctant to be king. "Am I not a Benjaminite, from the smallest of the tribes of Israel, and my clan is the least of the tribe of Benjamin?" (1 Sam. 9:21). But as soon as Samuel anoints him, Saul has the chance to prove his military and political skills.

Nahash the Ammonite demands a pact with the Israelites. "This is how I shall make a pact with you—with the gouging out of the right eye of every one of you, and I shall make it a disgrace for all Israel" (1 Sam. 11:2). The elders ask for eleven days to consider this offer. Saul hacks a yoke of oxen into pieces and sends it by messengers to all of Israel proclaiming, "Whoever does not come out after Saul and after Samuel, thus will be done to his oxen!"(1 Sam. 11:7). Saul is victorious. The people once again proclaim Saul's kingship.

But in a later victory over the Philistines, Saul does not wait for Samuel's blessing and sacrifices on his own. Samuel warns him that not waiting for him has cost Saul a permanent kingship over Israel (1 Sam. 13:13). All the same, Saul's attack is successful.

Political Implication: Saul achieves a military victory over the Philistines, but by failing to wait for religious authorities to bless his attack, he undermines the legitimacy of his kingship. Fox (p. 34) argues that Saul "is physically imposing and a great warrior and even, to the surprise of his people, can at times be seized by the spirit of

God 'like-a-prophet.' But Saul disobeys God, and Fox (p. 35) writes, "In this disobedience, apparently, lies the reason for the forfeiture of his kingship, similar to the fate of many of the later kings of Israel (although their disobedience almost always involved the practice of idolatry, of which Sha'ul [Saul] seems not to be guilty.") (For a discussion of these later kings, see Chapter 13.)

Saul Threatens Jonathan

Basic Text: Saul has another battle with the Philistines. He warns his men not to eat before the battle, but Jonathan, his most important son, does not learn of the order and tastes some honey. Even though Jonathan plays a major role in winning the battle, Saul proclaims that he must die. Saul's troops intervene, and Jonathan is saved (1 Sam. 14:45).

Political Implication: Saul shows bad judgment as a military commander by having his troops fight while hungry, and even worse judgment as a king in condemning his first-born son and the main soldier responsible for his victory.

Saul and the Amalekites

Basic Text: God tells Samuel to direct Saul to annihilate the Amalekites. They must be wiped out because they attacked the Children of Israel when they were fleeing Egypt. God tells Saul, "Now, go and strike down Amalek, and put under the ban everything that he has, you shall not spare him, and you shall put to death man and woman, infant and suckling, ox and sheep, camel and donkey"(1 Sam. 15:3). Saul achieves total victory, but he does not follow God's orders. Saul and his troops spare Agag, the king of the Amalekites, and they do not kill the best of the Amalekite livestock. God now tells Samuel, "I repent that I made Saul king, for he has turned back from Me" (1 Sam. 15:10). Saul acknowledges he has not killed the animals but has saved them to sacrifice. Samuel answers (1 Sam. 15:22–23):

> Does the LORD take delight in burnt offerings and sacrifices
>   as in listening to the voice of the LORD?
> For listening is better than sacrifice,
>   hearkening, than the fat of rams.
> For the diviner's offense is rebellion,
>   the transgression of idols—defiance.
> Since you have cast off the word of the LORD,
>   He has cast you aside as king.

Samuel kills Agag, saying (1 Sam. 15:33):

> As your sword has bereaved women,
> more bereaved than all women your mother!

(In the *KJV*, "As thy sword hath made women childless, so shall thy mother be childless among women.") Samuel "cut him apart" (1 Sam. 15:34). Although Saul prays for Samuel's forgiveness, Samuel leaves "and Samuel saw Saul no more till his dying day" (1 Sam. 15:35).

Political Implications: Samuel has withdrawn his support, and Saul must muddle through the rest of his reign without divine guidance. Moreover, once Samuel anoints David, Saul is attacked by evil spirits and becomes paranoiac. Some scholars see Saul as more of a chieftain than a monarch (for a summary of differing views, see the entry on Saul by Diana V. Edelman in the *Anchor Bible Dictionary*, vol. 5, 989–99). Moreover, neither *1 Samuel* nor *1 Chronicles* report Saul providing justice for the people he ruled.

Samuel Anoints David

Basic Text: David claims, via Joseph Heller (1984: 5), "I don't like to boast—I know I boast a bit when I say I don't have to boast—but I honestly think I've got the best story in the Bible." Ira Sharkansky (1996, 101) does not go quite as far when he states:

> For those concerned with the politics that appears in the Hebrew Bible, David is an obvious subject for inquiry. He is the Bible's most sharply defined political figure. More than other characters, the Bible details his youth, his development, and decline as a person and political actor. He is a complex figure, who experiences conflicting pressures, wrestles with temptation and failure, and expresses norms of political and religious significance. His story is crucial to the development of the Israelite monarchy. The Davidic dynasty ruled for over four hundred years until it was ended by the Babylonian conquest and has served until now as a symbol of glory and hope in Judaism and Christianity.

David's anointment is relatively straightforward, even though it must be conducted in secrecy lest Saul retaliate (1 Sam. 16:2). God tells Samuel to quit grieving over Saul, and to go the house of Jesse the Bethlehemite. Samuel is ready to anoint Jesse's oldest son but God tells him, "Look not to his appearance and to his lofty stature, for I have cast him aside. For not as a man sees does God see. For man sees with the eyes and the LORD sees with the heart" (1 Sam. 16:7).[2] But after seeing Jesse's seven older sons, Samuel asks if there is yet another son. When David, the youngest son, appears, God tells Samuel to anoint him. As soon as he is anointed, "the spirit of the LORD . . . turned away from Saul, and an evil spirit from the LORD . . . struck terror in him" (1 Sam. 16:14).

Political Implication: David has now been anointed. The anointing of David is a major political turning point for four hundred years of history.

David Serves Saul

Basic Text: An evil spirit from God afflicts Saul, but one of his young men reports, "Look, I have seen a son of Jesse the Bethlehemite, skilled in playing, a valiant fellow, a warrior, prudent in speech, a good-looking man, and the LORD is with him" (1 Sam. 16:18). Saul sends a messenger to summon David, "And so, when the spirit of God was upon Saul, David would take up the lyre and play, and Saul would find relief, and it would be well with him, and the evil spirit would turn away from him" (1 Sam. 16:23).

When the Philistines gather before Saul and his men at Sicoh, they bring forward a champion, Goliath of Gath, who was six cubits and a span (about nine feet) tall, and "the shaft of his spear [was] like a weaver's beam" (1 Sam. 17: 7). A man of Israel tells David that the king has promised wealth, and even his daughter's hand in marriage, to a man who will slay him (1 Sam. 17:19).

David volunteers, but Saul warns him, "You cannot go against this Philistine to do battle with him, for you are a lad and he is a man of war from his youth" (1 Sam. 17:33). David is not dissuaded, but he decides not to wear Saul's armor. Rather, he wears his shepherd's clothes and carries stones and a slingshot. Goliath scornfully asks, "Am I a dog that you should come to me with sticks?" (1 Sam. 17:43). David replies, "You come to me with sword and spear and javelin, and I come to you with the name of the LORD of Hosts, God of the battle lines of Israel that you have insulted" (1 Sam. 17:45). David hurls a stone from his slingshot, knocking him to the ground, and uses Goliath's own sword to behead him.

Seeing their champion dead, the Philistines flee, pursued by the avenging men of Israel and Judah. Saul sends David on new military missions, but David wins more accolades than Saul. Saul's youngest daughter, Michal, loves David, and, according to Robert Alter (1999: 115), she is the only woman in the *Hebrew Bible* who is explicitly reported to love a man. As David is poor, he has no money for a bride price, but Saul sets a price that he hopes will ensnare him, a hundred Philistine foreskins. David either does not suspect a ruse or is highly confident of his ability to dispatch Philistines. He provides Saul with two hundred foreskins. Saul weds Michal to David, linking David to the royal family.

Political Implications: David provides Saul with a useful military ally, but he is dangerous. Saul wants to preserve his lineage, but there is no tradition of hereditary rule. David is not only more successful militarily than Saul himself, but also more successful than Saul's son Jonathan, who in any event loves David. And Saul's youngest daughter is more loyal to her husband than to her father, warning him of an attempted assassination.

In my opinion, the biblical account provides no reason to fault David's service.[3] He is a loyal son-in-law and a faithful subject. But he has been placed close to the throne in a monarchy that has no long-term claim to legitimacy. Saul's legitimacy is based on defeating the enemies of Israel and Judah, and the legitimacy provided by his anointment has been stripped away by Samuel for not obeying God's orders to destroy the Amalekites. Although David has been anointed in a secretive ceremony witnessed by his father's household, his right to the kingship may be stronger than Saul's.

Saul Declines

Basic Text: The monarchy depends largely upon religious authority, and when Samuel withdraws his support, Saul's secular authority is imperiled. Saul declines quickly. David gains greater acclaim than Saul, and the women sing (1 Sam. 18:7):

> Saul has struck down his thousands
> and David his tens of thousands![4]

Later Saul becomes furious with Jonathan. He curses him, saying "O, son of a perverse and wayward woman! Don't I know you have chosen the son of Jesse to your own shame and to the shame of your mother's nakedness? For as long as the son of Jesse lives on the earth, you and your kingship will not be unshaken!" (1 Sam. 20:30–31). He throws a spear at Jonathan, and "Jonathan knew it was resolved by his father to put David to death" (1 Sam. 20:33). David flees the court and is aided by the head priest of Nob. Saul orders his men to kill the priest of Nob, but they refuse. Doeg the Edomite kills eighty-five priests of Nob, as well as the men, women, children, and animals of the town (1 Sam. 22:15–19).

Political Implications: Saul's anger at Jonathan is partly political. He wants to establish a dynasty, and Jonathan has demonstrated military skill. He is clearly a possible successor, and David is an obvious rival. Still, throwing a spear at Jonathan suggests that Saul had lost control of his reason. Even his own servants refuse to obey his order to kill the priests of Nob (1 Sam. 22:17).

David Rebels

Basic Text: David is provided with incontrovertible evidence, mainly by Jonathan and Michal, that Saul seeks his life. He takes refuge, along with four hundred men, "And every man in straits and every man in debt and every man who was embittered gathered round him, and he became their captain" (1 Sam. 22:2). At one point, David catches Saul relieving himself and could have killed him; instead, he cuts off the skirt of his cloak (1 Sam. 24:5). But David is remorseful even for this action. Samuel dies, but this does not lead to reconciliation between Saul and David. Shortly thereafter, David and his nephew Abishai find Saul asleep, and Abishai wants to kill Saul. But David does not let him, saying, "The LORD forbid that I should reach out my hand against the LORD'S anointed" (1 Sam. 26:11).

While in refuge, David marries Abigail, whose husband, Nabal, conveniently dies of natural causes when he learns that she has aided David (1 Sam. 25), another story that Brams (2003: 149–53) analyzes. This marriage, Steven L. McKenzie (2000, 99), argues is politically crucial because it makes David the leader of Calebites, which later facilitates his kingship of Judah.

All the same, David decides that his forces are not strong enough to maintain a rebellion against Saul. David and six hundred men join with the Philistines. But as a major battle approaches between Saul and the Philistines, many Philistine leaders do not trust David. So David leaves the Philistine territory and goes to Ziklag while the Philistine army marches to defeat Saul.

Political Implications: Although David attempts to be a loyal subject, he is forced to rebel. He spares Saul twice, and Joel Rosenberg (1987: 129) writes, "Whether or not David has designs on the throne (and it is important to remember that throughout Saul's lifetime, neither David nor the narrator says so explicitly), his refusal to harm Saul is an investment in the stability of the future regime—any future regime." David is a great leader and warrior, but he is also lucky.[5] Nabal's fortuitous death allows him to marry Abigail. And if the Philistines trusted him to fight Saul, he might have been their ally at the Battle of Mount Gilboa. As it is, we will never know on whose side David would have fought, since he was encamped away from the battle at Ziklag.

Saul's Death

Basic Text: At the end of his reign, Saul confronts the Philistines on Mount Gilboa. God will not advise Saul, either through dreams, the Urim, or prophets. Even though he has banned witchcraft, Saul asks his advisors, "Seek me out a ghostwife, that I may go to her and inquire through her" (1 Sam. 28:7). They direct him to the woman of En-dor.

Although Saul is disguised, the woman is afraid because Saul has promised to eliminate "ghosts" and "familiar spirits" in his kingdom. But Saul assures her that she will not be harmed. Saul asks her to summon up Samuel. Samuel asks, "Why have you troubled me to summon me up?" (1 Sam. 28:15). (In the *KJV*, "Why hast thou disquieted me, to bring me up?") Samuel tells Saul he will die in battle the next day. When Saul sees that the battle of Mount Gilboa is lost, he falls on his own sword (1 Sam. 31:4).Three of his sons are killed, including Jonathan. Saul's head is cut off, and his body is impaled on the wall of Beth-shan.

Political Implications: Although there will be a civil war between the followers of David and the followers of Saul, the House of David will prevail. This is politically important because David's House will provide the longest lasting of the dynasties, as well as the ancestors of the Messiah.

Notes

1. For an analysis of the confrontation between Samuel and the elders, see Allan Silver (2000).
2. Bear in mind that God, not Samuel, chose Saul (1 Sam. 9:18).
3. For an interesting but polemical book that views Saul more favorably than David, see Adam Green (2007).
4. This sentence is also found in 1 Samuel 21:12 and in 1 Samuel 29:5. As Robert Alter (1981) brilliantly demonstrates, biblical narrative depends heavily upon repetition.
5. The importance of luck in politics should not be underestimated. As Niccolò Machiavelli wrote nearly five centuries ago, "Fortune is arbiter of half our actions, but . . . she leaves the other half, or close to it, for us to govern" (*The Prince*, Chapter 25. Translation by Harvey C. Mansfield).

11

2 Samuel, 1 Kings 1–2, and 1 Chronicles 11, 13–28 (The Reign of David)

David's Eulogy

Basic Text: After Saul's defeat, a man with torn clothes prostrates himself before David. He explains he is an Amalekite who chanced upon the battle. He reports that both Saul and Jonathan have died. He says he found Saul badly wounded, and Saul, seeing that he was mortally wounded, said, "Pray, stand over me and finish me off" (2 Sam. 1:9). The Amalekite presents David with Saul's diadem and his armband.

Although it seems likely the Amalekite is lying about killing Saul (a more plausible account is presented in 1 Sam. 31:4), he is punished as if his account were truthful. David orders one of his lads to kill the Amalekite. "Your blood is on your own head, for your mouth bore witness against you, saying, 'I was the one who finished off the LORD'S anointed'" (2 Sam. 1:16).

David then delivers his famous eulogy to Saul and Jonathan, which, the *Bible* tells us, is also recorded in the *Book of Jashar* (2 Sam. 1:19–27):

> The splendor, O Israel, on your heights lies slain,
> How have the warriors fallen!
> Tell it not in Gath,
> proclaim not in Ashkelon's streets.
> Lest the Philistine daughters rejoice,
> lest the daughters of the uncircumcised gloat....
> Saul and Jonathan, beloved and dear,
> in their life and their death they were not parted.
> They were swifter than eagles,
> and stronger than lions....
> How have the warriors fallen

in the midst of battle.
Jonathan, upon your heights slain!
I grieve for you, my brother, Jonathan.
    Very dear you were to me.
More wondrous your love to me
    than the love of women.
How have the warriors fallen,
    and the gear of battle is lost.

In the more familiar poetry of the *KJV*, these lines are:

The beauty of Israel is slain upon thy high places: how are the mighty fallen!

Tell *it* not in Gath, publish *it* not in the streets of Askelon; lest the daughters of the Philistines rejoice, lest the daughters of the uncircumcised triumph....

Saul and Jonathan *were* lovely and pleasant in their lives, and in their death they were not divided: they were swifter than eagles, they were stronger than lions....

How are the mighty fallen in the midst of battle! O Jonathan, *thou wast* slain in thine high places.

I am distressed for thee, my brother Jonathan: very pleasant hast thou been unto me: thy love to me was wonderful, passing the love of women.

How are the mighty fallen, and the weapons of war perished!

Political Implications: David demonstrates his political acumen in two ways. He has the Amalekite killed for slaying "God's anointed," not for killing Israel's king. The kingship may be in dispute, but since Samuel has anointed David, David is the only man who can rightly claim to be God's anointed. Moreover, although David's love for Jonathan is genuine, his praise for Saul is duplicitous. Although he is Saul's son-in-law, Saul has been seeking his death. Even so, he wants the support of Israelites who remain loyal to Saul. His eulogy, unstinting in its praise of Saul, may help gain their support.

The House of David Versus the House of Saul

Basic Text: God tells David to establish his kingship in Hebron. But Abner the son of Ner, the commander of Saul's army, takes one of Saul's sons, Ish-bosheth ("man of shame") and supports him as a rival. The fighting went on "a long time" (2 Sam. 3:1), but "David grew stronger and stronger and the house of Saul weaker and weaker" (2 Sam. 3:1). Abner is murdered by Joab the son of Zeruiah, David's general, as part of a personal vendetta. Shortly thereafter, Ish-bosheth is murdered. Lacking both a military leader and a royal pretender, the Israelites make a pact with David, and David becomes the monarch of a united kingdom.

Political Implication: Although the length of the civil war is uncertain, David has the upper hand from the outset. He has better generals, more political skill, as well as God's favor. Moreover, as Steven L. McKenzie (2000: 126) argues, David's entire strategy may have been based on key strategic moves made during his rebellion against Saul. "The David who has emerged in our biographical portrait was a shrewd politician. . . . Astute political maneuvering involving mercenary agreements with the Philistines, usurpation of the Calebite chieftaincy, key marriages, and gifts (not to say bribes) to local leaders made David the natural choice to be king over Judah. Indeed, the local leaders had no other real option, because the guerilla tactics of David's outlaw band gave him control of the Negev and of Judah."

David Captures Jerusalem

Basic Text: Jerusalem is the ideal capital. It occupies high ground and is easily defended. Moreover, it is not in any of the tribal allotments, and is therefore on neutral ground. But Jerusalem has never been taken from the Jebusites, and they are confident they can defend it. They tell David, "You shall not enter here unless you can remove the blind and the lame" (2 Sam. 5:6). But David apparently learns of a conduit that will give him access to the city. Using this route, he takes Jerusalem and makes it his capital. This further enhances his prestige and solidifies his kingship.

David moves his wives and concubines from Hebron to Jerusalem. When the Ark is moved to Jerusalem, David celebrates by dancing, exposing himself. Michal is furious with David, but in retaliation David chastises her. "And Michal daughter of Saul had no child till her dying day" (2 Sam. 6:23). David begins a series of conquests. He subdues the Philistines, strikes down the Moabites, defeats the king of Zobah, and even defeats the Arameans of Damascus. According to 2 *Samuel* 8, his kingdom becomes a regional superpower. As David says in *God Knows*, "I was proud as a peacock, for I had taken a kingdom the size of Vermont and created an empire as large as the state of Maine!" (Heller, 256). According to 2 *Samuel* 8:15–18,[1] "And David was king over all Israel, and it was David's practice to mete out true justice to all his people. And Joab son of Zeruiah was over the army, Jehoshaphat son of Ahilud was recorder. And Zadok son of Ahitub and Abiathar son of Ahimelech were priests, and Seraiah was scribe. And

63

Benaiah son of Jehoidah was over the Cherethites and the Pelethites,[2] and David's sons served as priests."

Political Implication: Despite his estrangement from Michal, David has solidified his kingship. David is at the peak of his power. Moreover, he is noted for administering justice to all his people and has set up a rudimentary royal administration.[3]

David and the Wife of Uriah

Basic Text: During the spring when the heavy winter rains end, Joab and the army go to besiege Rabbah, the capital of the Ammonites, but "David was sitting in Jerusalem" (2 Sam. 11:1). (In the *KJV*, "But David tarried still at Jerusalem.") One evening while walking on the palace roof, he sees a beautiful woman bathing. He asks his servants who she is, and a servant reports "Why, this is Bathsheba daughter of Eliam wife of Uriah the Hittite" (2 Sam. 11:3).

David sends for her, and has intercourse with her, for she is ritually clean having "just cleansed herself of her impurity" (2 Sam. 11:4).[4] She becomes pregnant, and informs David, "I am pregnant" (2 Sam. 11:5). (In the *KJV*, "I *am* with child.")

As Bathsheba has just had her period, Uriah cannot be the father, and the most obvious cover-up is to have Uriah have sex with his wife. David orders Uriah back from the front, but after two nights in Jerusalem fails to get him to visit her. David sends Uriah back to the front with a sealed letter to Joab, "Put Uriah in the face of the fiercest battling and draw back, so that he will be struck down and die" (2 Sam. 11:15).

Joab recognizes these measures are too transparent, Robert Alter argues in his translation and commentary on *The David Story* (1999: 254). Instead he sends several men to a dangerous location and several die, including Uriah. He tells the messenger that if David questions his tactics, the messenger should add, "your servant Uriah the Hittite also died" (2 Sam. 11:24). But the messenger recognizes that this is the information David wants to hear and reports the news of Uriah's death before David can question him. David philosophizes about battle: "Let this thing not seem evil in your eyes, for the sword devours sometimes one way and sometimes another'" (2 Sam. 11:25). Uriah's wife mourns for him, and when the mourning period is over, she moves to David's house and became his wife. She bears David a son, but "the thing that David had done was evil in the eyes of the LORD" (2 Sam. 11:27).

Political Implications: David has committed adultery and murder. From a political standpoint, committing adultery with the wife of one of the leading warriors of his army (1 Chron. 11:41) is extremely ill advised, since the army is a main bulwark of David's power. In most despotisms of 1000 BCE, a monarch would not worry about committing adultery with an officer's wife, or with disposing of him even more crudely than David. But Israel is God's chosen people. Its leaders should know the law, and there were too many people who must have had at least partial knowledge of David's transgressions for him to believe that a cover-up would succeed. Although the story of David and Bathsheba does not appear in *Chronicles* and although David is whitewashed in the Talmud, the author(s) of *2 Samuel* devote their full literary powers in telling it, as both Alter (*The David Story, 1999*: 257–58) and Everett Fox *(Give Us a King!,* 1999: 187–90) demonstrate. Both Alter (1999: 249) and Robert Polzin (1993: 103–30) emphasize the importance of the word "messenger" in Chapter 11, noting that the Hebrew for messengers *malakhim* is very close to the Hebrew for kings, *melakhim.* And Alter notes that "to send" messengers occurs eleven times in *2 Samuel* 11. David has already become less active as a king, and more likely to rely on intermediaries.

As Fox writes (1999, 189–90), "The David and Bat-Sheva story is an intimate look at David's many moods, and shows what he is capable of, for good and for ill, in a variety of situations. In the writer or editor's scheme of things in 2 Samuel, it is a point from which David, despite the happy ending . . . (Shelomo's [Solomon's] birth and David's capture of Rabba), can never fully recover. From this point on, the misfortunes of the country will be identical with those of the House of David."

David's behavior can still provoke controversy. In a debate in the Knesset in December 1994, a rightwing member of the Knesset argued that King David had conducted wars of occupation. Foreign Minister Shimon Peres replied, "not everything that King David did on the ground or on the rooftops is Jewish in my eyes." In replying, Avraham Verdiger of the United Torah Judaism, an ultraorthodox party, became so upset that he fainted and was taken to the Knesset infirmary. Peres wrote a letter to Israeli religious leaders saying that he never "had any intention of insulting the 'Sweet Psalmist of Israel.'" There were even attempts to bring down the government because of Peres's remarks.[5]

Nathan's Parable and His Prophesy

Basic Text: The Lord sends the prophet Nathan to David. He relates the story of two men, one of whom was rich and one of whom had one little ewe, which he fed out of his own cup. When the rich man invites a traveler to dinner, he takes the poor man's ewe and serves it, even though he owns a great deal of livestock. David is furious. "As the LORD lives, doomed is the man who has done this!" (2 Sam. 12:5). "You are the man!" Nathan replies (2 Sam. 12:7). Nathan continues speaking in God's name: "It is I Who anointed you king over Israel and it is I Who saved you from the hand of Saul. And I gave you your master's house and your master's wives in your lap, and I gave you the house of Israel and of Judah. And if that be too little, I would give you even as much again" (2 Sam. 12:7–8). Since David had Uriah the Hittite cut down by the sword of the Ammonites, "the sword shall not swerve from your house evermore" (2 Sam. 12:10). David has taken Uriah's wife in secret, but God will give David's wives to other men "before all Israel and before the sun" (2 Sam. 12:11).

The Lord will not kill David, but the son born to David and Bathsheba will die. The child dies, but David comforts Bathsheba and they have another son, and she names him Solomon. The Lord loves him and has Nathan name him Jedediah.

Political Implications: The story reveals that even monarchs are subject to higher authority. David's punishment will be severe, and there will constantly be strife, murder, and rebellion within his household. Moreover, whatever Nathan and Bathsheba say later, there is no biblical report of David promising Solomon the kingship.

Amnon Rapes Tamar

Basic Text: David has a beautiful daughter, Tamar, the full sister of Absalom "father of peace," who is a very handsome man. David's firstborn son, Amnon, loves Tamar, but can't think of anyway "to do anything to her" (2 Sam. 13:2). A cousin suggests a strategy. Amnon feigns illness and says he can only be cured if Tamar prepares food at his bedside. Amnon has the room cleared. He asks his half-sister to lie with him. She refuses, but he overpowers her. But, unlike Shechem, who loves Dinah after he violates her, Amnon now loathes Tamar. Two years later at a shearing festival, Absalom directs his servants to murder Amnon. Absalom flees to Talmai, son of Amihur, the king of Geshur, that is to say to the court of his maternal grandfather.

Political Implications: As in the case of the murder by Levi and Simeon, the punishment greatly exceeds the crime. However, there may have been no remedy for Amnon's crime. According to Deuteronomy, a man who raped a virgin was required to marry her and could not divorce her (Deut. 22:28). But if the incest rules in *Leviticus* applied, Amnon could not marry his half-sister. But part of Nathan's prophecy has come to pass with the murder of David's firstborn son. The sword has entered David's house.

Absalom's Rebellion

Basic Text: Absalom spends three years in exile. Eventually, through the behind-the-scenes work of Joab, Absalom returns to Jerusalem, but David does not see him for another two years. Absalom begins a campaign to subvert David's kingship. He sets up an alternative site for rendering judgments. Preparing for a full-scale rebellion, he has his agents declare, "When you hear the sound of the ram's horn, you shall say 'Absalom has become king in Hebron'" (2 Sam. 15:10).

David learns that the conspiracy is strong, that Absalom's support is growing, and he flees eastward from Jerusalem with his household, leaving behind his ten concubines. Although he initially takes the Ark, he returns it to Jerusalem. To fulfill Nathan's prophecy, Absalom pitches a tent on his father's roof and has sex with his concubines. Ahitophel, one of Absalom's key advisors, urges him to attack David before he can regroup. But David has left behind a spy, Hushai the Archite, to give false counsel. He tells Absalom, "You yourself know of your father and his men that they are warriors and that they are bitter men, like a bear in the field bereaved of its young. . . . And so I counsel you—let all Israel gather round you, from Dan to Beersheba, multitudinous as the sand that is on the seashore, and you in person will go forward into battle" (2 Sam. 17:8–12). Absalom decides that Hushai has provided the better advice, and Ahitophel, his advice rejected, hangs himself.

David marshals his troops and the battlefield becomes the Forest of Ephraim in Gilead. David has many seasoned troops, led by Joab. Although Absalom is a rebel, David still loves him, and orders his troops, "Deal gently for me with the lad Absalom" (2 Sam. 18:5). But in the battle, Absalom's long hair becomes ensnarled in the branches of a large terebinth tree. Joab and his followers kill him. David grieves for his son, crying "My son Absalom! Absalom, my son, my son!" (2 Sam. 19:5). Joab tells David that he has shamed himself and his followers. He is acting as if Absalom's death were worse than his own defeat and the defeat of his own armies. King David regains his composure and returns to Jerusalem.

As he was fleeing Jerusalem, David is cursed by Shimei the son of Gera, a Benjaminite. He yells, "Get out, get out, you man of blood, you worthless fellow! The LORD has brought back upon you all the blood of the house of Saul, in whose place you became king, and the LORD has given the kingship into the hands of Absalom your son, and here you are, because of your evil, for you are a man of blood" (2 Sam. 16:7–8). After David is victorious, Shimei pleads for his life, and David decides not to kill him, and tells Shimei, "'You shall not die.' And the king swore to him" (2 Sam. 19:24).

Political Implications: Absalom's rebellion is the most serious challenge to David's kingship. Allowing Absalom to set up an alternative judicial site was a major blunder, for as Max Weber pointed out about 3,000 years later, "a state is a human community that (successfully) claims the *monopoly of the legitimate use of physical force* within a given territory" (Weber, 1946: 78; originally published in 1919).

It is one thing to decentralize judicial authority, as Moses did following Jethro's advice. It is quite another thing altogether to allow an alternative judicial system to emerge. We do not know the conditions that led to Absalom's temporary success, but David's victory demonstrates that an established monarch is likely to hold the upper hand in suppressing rebellions.

Shebah's Rebellion

Basic Text: Shortly after suppressing Absalom's rebellion, another rebellion begins led by "a worthless fellow named Sheba son of Bichri, a Benjaminite" (2 Sam. 20:1). But whereas Absalom rebelled against his father's personal rule, Sheba rebels against the tribe of Judah, and proclaims (2 Sam. 20:1):

> We have no share in David,
> no portion have we in Jesse's son—
> every man to his tent, O Israel.

David dispatches several generals to deal with the threat. Asama the son of Jether fails, and Joab kills him. Sheba appears to be able to muster support only from his immediate clansmen, and eventually takes refuge in Abel of Beth-maacah, which is besieged. Joab declares that he doesn't want to destroy the town, only to capture Sheba. And a woman from the town replies, "Look, his head is about to be flung to you from the wall" (2 Sam. 20:21). "And the woman came in her wisdom to all the people, and they cut off the head of Sheba son of Bichri and flung it to Joab" (2 Sam. 20:22).

The final chapter of 2 *Samuel* (Chapter 24) ends with a strange account of a census. An angry God orders David to "Go, count Israel and Judah" (2 Sam. 24: 1), although in *1 Chronicles* 21:1, Satan "incited David to count the people of Israel."[6] Joab objects because he thinks a census is unnecessary. Nonetheless, a census is conducted. Even though, at least according to *2 Samuel*, this appears to be an authorized census, God punishes Israel and Judah, although the punishment may have nothing whatever to do with the census. David is given three choices to end the punishment. He can choose seven years of famine, three months in which he will flee from his foes, or three days of plague. He rejects the second option. God inflicts a plague and 75,000 people die.

Political Implications: Although there is some reorganization of the army after the rebellions of Absalom and Sheba, it is not at all clear that these changes result from these rebellions. Sheba's rebellion may be a minor precursor to a successful rebellion by Israel against King Rehoboam after King Solomon's death (1 Kings 12) (see Chapter 12).

Adonijah's Rebellion

Basic Text: "And King David had grown old, advanced in years, and they covered him with bedclothes, but he was not warm. And his servants said to him, 'Let them seek out for my lord the king a young virgin, that she may wait upon the king and become his familiar, and lie in your lap, and my lord the king will be warm.' And they sought out a beautiful young woman through all the territory of Israel, and they found Abishag the Shunamite and brought her to the king. And the young woman was very beautiful, and she became a familiar to the king, and ministered to him, but the king knew her not" (1 Kings 1:1–4).

At this point, Adonijah, the son of Haggith, David's oldest surviving son, proclaims himself king. Joab supports Adonijah, as does Abiathar the priest. Adonijah rides in a chariot with fifty men before him, proclaiming, "I shall be king!" (1 Kings 1:5).

Nathan informs Bathsheba (who has not been mentioned since she named Solomon). He instructs her to inform David and says he will come in as she is recounting Adonijah's actions, as well as to remind David of his purported promise to name Solomon his successor. Bathsheba enters the inner chamber and bows to the king. She tells King David, "My lord, you yourself swore by the LORD your God to your servant, 'Solomon your son shall be king after me, and he shall sit on my throne'" (1 Kings 1:17).[7] But now, she informs him, Adonijah has proclaimed himself king. Nathan enters and confirms that Adonijah has proclaimed himself king.

David realizes that he must either accept Adonijah's usurpation or proclaim Solomon king. He makes Solomon his successor that very day. David calls together Nathan the prophet, Benaiah son of Jehoiada, commander of David's bodyguards, and several other highly regarded warriors. Solomon is mounted on a mule and led to Gihon. Zadok the priest blows a ram's horn, anoints Solomon, and the people shout, "Long live King Solomon!" (1 Kings 1:39). Adonijah's supporters flee, and Adonijah holds on to the horns of the altar for protection. King Solomon tells Adonijah and his supporters to return to their houses.

Political Implications: Up to now, Bathsheba has only stated a single sentence, informing David that she is pregnant. Now she has acquired considerable political skill. On the other hand, Adonijah proves remarkably inept. If David has made no promise to make Solomon his successor, and perhaps even if he has, Adonijah makes a major blunder in not waiting for his father to die.[8]

David's Deathbed Advice

Basic Text: David tells Solomon he is about to die. He first provides two verses of Deuteronomistic advice, out of character with the rest of the narrative. "And keep what the LORD your God enjoins, to walk in His ways, to keep His statutes, His commandments, and His dictates and His admonitions, as it is written in the Teachings of Moses, so that you may prosper in everything you do and in everything to which you may turn. So that the LORD may fulfill His word that He spoke unto me saying, 'If your sons keep the way to walk before Me in truth with their whole heart and with their whole being, no man of yours will be cut off from the throne of Israel'"(1 Kings 2:3–4).

Then, David gets down to cases:

> And, what's more, you yourself know what Joab son of Zeruiah did to me, what he did to the two commanders of the armies of Israel, Abner son of Ner and Asama son of Jether—he killed them, and shed the blood of war in peace and put the blood of war on his belt that was round his waist and on his sandals that were on his feet. And you must act in your wisdom, and do not let his gray head go down in peace to Sheol. . . . And, look, with you is Shimei son of Gera the Benjaminite from Bahurim, and he cursed me with a scathing curse on the day I went to Mahanaim. And he came down to meet me at the Jordan, and I swore to him by the LORD saying, 'I will not put

you to death by the sword.' And now, do not hold him guiltless, for you are a wise man, and you will know what you should do to him, and bring his gray head down in blood to Sheol! (1 Kings 2:5–10)

David now dies, having passed along his advice to Solomon.

Political Implications: Only a short portion of David's dying advice reminds Solomon to follow God's laws. Most of his advice is provided to assure that David's scores will be settled. David does not bother to tell Solomon to settle his own scores. Perhaps David recognizes that Solomon does not need such advice.

Comparing Saul and David

Even though I focus on politics, the reasons for Saul's failure and David's difficulties are to be found mainly in their moral weaknesses.[9] As *1 Chronicles* 10:13–14 explains, "Saul died for his unfaithfulness; he was unfaithful to the LORD in that he did not keep the command of the LORD; moreover, he had consulted a medium, seeking guidance. . . . Therefore the LORD put him to death and turned the kingdom over to David son of Jesse."

The Bible reveres David as Judah and Israel's greatest king. In *Kings,* he is constantly praised for doing "right in the sight of the LORD," although *1 Kings*: 15:5 adds . . . "except in the matter of Uriah the Hittite." He has two faults, both of which result from excessive love, albeit very different types of love.

David has seven named wives before he commits adultery with Bathsheba. Having sex with her after her period, while her husband was away at the battlefront, was extremely reckless since Uriah could not possibly be the father if she became pregnant.

Secondly, although David is "greatly incensed" (2 Sam. 13:21) after Amnon rapes Tamar, he takes no action against him. The Qumran Samuel writes that David was "furious" with Amnon, "But he would not inflict pain on his son Amnon's spirit, because he loved him, since [he was his] firstborn" (*The Dead Sea Scrolls Bible* 2 Sam. 13:21). According to the Septuagint, David, "did not grieve the spirit of his son Amnon, because he loved him, for he was his first-born" (*Septuagint* II Kings 13:21) (see Alter, 271). Several English translations, including the *New Revised Standard Version*, but not the *KJV*, appear to rely upon the Septuagint at this point. But whatever David's reasons for not punishing Amnon were, in retrospect it seems clear that David had to take decisive action against Amnon to prevent further problems. David's logical response *might* have been political. Had he banned

Amnon from the kingship, Absalom might not have murdered Amnon, gone into exile, rebelled against David, and been killed in battle. But all this is counterfactual. And if Absalom had become king, there would never have been a King Solomon.

Coda

Some of the world's greatest poetry is attributed to King David. Granted, it was traditional to ascribe the authorship of poems to past historical or mythical figures. Alter labels 67 of the 150 poems included in the *Book of Psalms* as "David psalms," but that does not mean that David wrote them. On the other hand, in his introduction to his translation of *Psalms*, he writes (2007, xv) that "one cannot categorically exclude the possibility that a couple of these psalms were actually written by David." As with all great non-English poets, such as Homer, Virgil, Dante, or the authors of the Sanskrit epic, the *Mahābhārata,* a great deal is lost when translating their poetry, although Alter (2007) makes an excellent attempt to convey the compactness of the Hebrew. In some of the last words attributed to David, we are told (2 Sam. 23:1–2):

> Thus spoke David son of Jesse,
>   thus spoke the man raised on high,
> anointed of the God of Jacob,
>   and sweet singer of Israel.
> The LORD's spirit has spoken in me,
>   his utterance on my tongue.

(In the *KJV*, "David the son of Jesse said, and the man *who was* raised up on high, the anointed of the God of Jacob, and the sweet psalmist of Israel said, The Spirit of the LORD spake by me, and his word *was* in my tongue.")

Notes

1. The paragraph is repeated in *1 Chronicles* 18:14–17.
2. Robert Alter argues that there is widespread agreement that the first group had Cretan origins, but that there is debate over the origins of the second. He maintains that these people were a special palace guard directly loyal to David (Alter, 1999: 239).
3. However, *1 Chronicles* 11:10–47 and 12 provide an extensive description of his military organization.
4. Tikva Frymer-Kensky (2002: 147) argues that this statement is based upon an anachronistic interpretation of purification practices at the time. Even so, depending upon how long Uriah has been at the front, Bathsheba's pregnancy would be proof of her adultery, although not of David's.

5. From Ella Bancroft, "Names in Mideast News," *Washington Report on Middle East Affairs*, March 1995, 38–41, http://www.washington-report.org/backissues/0395/9503038.htm, accessed August 12, 2010. I discuss the political implications of this incident in Paul R. Abramson (1997).

6. In the *Christian Scriptures*, the two books of *Chronicles* appear after the two books of *Kings*. In the *Hebrew Bible*, they are included with "The Writing," and are the last two books of the Bible.

7. As Alter notes (p. 367), Bathsheba edits Nathan's suggested speech, most importantly by adding the words "by the LORD your God." Perhaps, Alter speculates, since David never promised to make Solomon king, Nathan was reluctant to invoke God's name to support the claim that he had. However, all we know is that the text never reports David making such an oath. In his novel, Torgny Lindgren (1989: 224) writes that during Absalom's rebellion, Bathsheba has David swear that Solomon was his first choice to succeed him.

8. As Frank H. Polack (1994: 139–40) argues, Solomon's succession story demonstrates there was a precarious political equilibrium in David's kingdom.

9. Saul may have had serious psychological problems as well, but we do not have enough evidence to evaluate what appears to be his paranoiac behavior that begins as soon as David is anointed.

12

1 Kings 3–12 and 2 Chronicles 1–10 (The Reign of Solomon through the Division of the Kingdom)

Solomon Consolidates His Power

Basic Text: Adonijah challenges Solomon. He asks Bathsheba to present a "one petition" on his behalf asking Solomon to give him Abishag the Shunamite as a wife (1 Kings 2:16). Bathsheba conveys the request, with a subtle variation,[1] to which King Solomon replies, "And why do you ask Abishag the Shumanite for Adonijah? Ask the kingship for him, as he is my older brother; and Abiathar the priest and Joab son of Zeruiah are for him." (1 Kings 2:22). Solomon sends Benaiah to kill Adonijah. Solomon banishes Abiathar the priest. Joab grabs the horns of the altar for protection, but Benaiah kills him.

David has promised not to kill Shimei. Solomon tells him that he can live in Jerusalem but will die if he crosses the Wadi Kidron. Three years later he leaves Jerusalem to search for escaped slaves, and he too is killed. We are told, "And the kingdom was unshaken in Solomon's hand" (1 Kings 2:46).

Political Implications: In having Joab killed, Solomon is fulfilling David's deathbed request, but David has not condemned Adonijah, his eldest surviving son. But Solomon may see Adonijah's request for Abishag as part of a larger political conspiracy. "This behaviour on Solomon's part," according to Frederic Thieberger (1947: 127) "can be understood only if we realize that Adonijah's request for Abishag was the sign of a new move on the part of the opposition, which had rallied its forces after David's death." Adonijah's request was remarkably inept, for he had not thought through his actions if his brother opposed his "petition." Indeed, Frank Moore Cross (1973: 237) argues claiming Abishag would be tantamount to claiming the throne and doubts the veracity of the story. "We doubt that even the most fervid supporter of Solomon could have made this claim without tongue in cheek" (see also, Jonathan Kirsch, 2000: 282–84).

Solomon's Wisdom

Basic Text: Solomon makes an alliance with Egypt and marries Pharaoh's daughter. He goes to Gibeon to sacrifice, and the Lord appears to him in a dream. God says, "Ask what I should give you" (1 Kings 3:5). He asks God "Give your servant . . . an understanding mind to govern your people, able to discern between good and evil" (1 Kings 3:9). God is pleased with Solomon's request and tells him that he will grant it. Moreover, since Solomon did not ask for a long life or for riches he will have them as well. Solomon's first opportunity to display his wisdom comes when he judges between the claims of two prostitutes. The first says that she and the other woman live in the same house. She gave birth, and three days later the other woman gave birth. No one else was in the house. She says the second woman lay on her son and killed it, but that the second woman switched the babies in the middle of the night. The first woman thought her baby was dead, but in the morning she saw that the live baby was hers, and that the dead baby belonged to the other woman. But the second woman claims that the live son is hers, while the dead son belongs to the first woman.

The technology for determining their veracity will not be available for nearly 3,000 years. So Solomon asks for a sword, and says, "Divide the living boy in two; then give half to the one, and half to the other"(1 Kings 3:25). But the first woman, who is the true mother, has compassion for her baby, and asks Solomon to give the child to the second woman. The second woman says, "It shall be neither mine nor yours; divide it" (1 Kings 3:26). Solomon then renders his famous judgment, "Give the first woman the living boy; do not kill him. She is his mother" (1 Kings 3:27). "All Israel heard of the judgment that the king had rendered; and they stood in awe of the king, because they perceived that the wisdom of God was in him, to execute justice" (1 Kings 3:28).

Although there are later references in *1 Kings* and *2 Chronicles* to Solomon's great wisdom, especially his ability to answer the questions posed by the Queen of Sheba (1 Kings 10; 2 Chron. 9), none of them provide the detail of Solomon's first judgment.

Political Implications: As Plato points out, the greatest goal of politics is to provide justice.[2] By establishing that he was a wise ruler, Solomon bolsters his legitimacy. As for judging the claims of the two prostitutes, the second woman makes his decision easy by enthusiastically endorsing his initial ruling to divide the baby.

Perhaps Brams (2003: 120) is correct in arguing that the second woman's willingness to divide the baby is designed to win Solomon's favor by endorsing his judgment. If so, she was a poor game-player. It is easy to see this in retrospect, whereas the prostitute is standing in the king's presence.

Although this judicial trick can only be employed once, it provides Solomon with so much fame that we refer to "the wisdom of Solomon" and "Solomonic" wisdom nearly three thousand years later. The story also shows that even the lowly in society deserve justice.

Solomon's Administration

Basic Text: I Kings 4 provides an extensive description of Solomon's administrative apparatus, providing the names of his officials. He has a priest, two secretaries, a recorder, a commander of the army, two additional priests, a supervisor of officials, and a priest who was also his friend. An additional official was in charge of the palace and another in charge of forced labor. Solomon had twelve officials to govern Israel, each of whom was responsible for providing food. There was another official responsible for Judah. Solomon, it is claimed, ruled all the land from the Euphrates to the land of the Philistines, and all the land to the border of Egypt. All these people provided Solomon with tribute. Moreover, the people were content. "During Solomon's lifetime Judah and Israel lived in safety, from Dan even to Beer-sheba, all of them under their vines and fig trees" (1 Kings 4:25). Apart from his construction projects, Solomon composed 3,000 proverbs, and 1,005 songs. "People came from all the nations to hear the wisdom of Solomon; they came from all the kings of the earth who had heard of his wisdom" (1 Kings 4:34).

Political Implications: Saul's monarchy had little administrative structure, and relatively few officials are named in describing David's kingship. Now we have a full-blown administrative apparatus, although how these officials interact with each other is not explained. As Thieberger points out (1947: 169) the relationship of Judah to the rest of the kingdom is unclear. This may have contributed to problems after Solomon's death.

Solomon Builds the Temple and His Palaces

Basic Text: In addition to his ties by marriage with Egypt, Solomon establishes ties with King Hiram of Tyre, a man who greatly admired David. Hiram helps Solomon build a temple to house the Ark both by supplying materials and sending gifted craftsmen. Solomon conscripts labor "out of all Israel" (1 Kings 5:13). Four hundred and eighty years after the Exodus, and in the fourth year of his reign, he begins to build the temple, which took seven years to complete. He spends thirteen years building his own house. A great deal of detail is provided describing the temple and Solomon's houses. Solomon calls the people to Jerusalem and dedicates the temple, saying (1 Kings 8:12–13):

> The LORD has said that he would
>   dwell in thick darkness.
> I have built you an exalted house,
>   a place for you to dwell in forever.

And Solomon holds a seven-day festival throughout the land.

Political Implications: Solomon reigns for forty years, and he uses massive resources, including forced labor, to build the temple and his royal household. Critics note that he spent almost twice as long to build his own house as he did to build the temple. The temple provides a center for national worship and a potentially unifying symbol for the kingdom. However, this construction came at great economic and social cost. Although it seems very unlikely that his empire was as grandiose as that described in *I Kings*, he opened Israel and Judah to foreign contacts, some of which may have undermined religious beliefs.

God's Covenant with Solomon

Basic Text: God is pleased. He tells Solomon he has heard his prayer and is pleased that he has consecrated the temple. God's eyes will always be over the temple. "As for you, if you will walk before me, as David your father walked, with integrity of heart and uprightness, doing according to all that I have commanded you, and keeping my statutes and my ordinances, then I will establish the royal throne over Israel forever, as I promised your father David saying, 'There shall not fail you a successor on the throne of Israel'" (1 Kings 9:4–5). But, God continues, "If you turn aside from following me, you or your children, and do not keep my commandments and my statutes that I have set before you, but go and serve other gods and worship them, then I will cut Israel off from the land that I have given them; and the house that I have consecrated for my name I will cast out of my sight; and Israel will become a proverb and a taunt among all peoples" (1 Kings 9:6–7).

Political Implications: God reminds Solomon that his covenant with Israel is conditional. If it obeys God's laws, he will favor Israel. If not, he will withdraw his favor. The worst offense, he reminds Solomon, is to serve other gods.

Seven Hundred Wives; Three Hundred Concubines

Basic Text: "King Solomon loved many foreign women along with the daughter of Pharaoh: Moabite, Ammonite, Edomite, Sidonian, and Hittite women . . .. Among his wives were seven hundred princesses and three hundred concubines; and his wives turned away his heart. For when Solomon was old, his wives turned away his heart after other gods; and his heart was not true to the LORD his God, as was the heart of his father David. For Solomon followed Astarte the goddess of the Sidonians, and, Milcom, the abomination of the Ammonites. So Solomon did what was evil in the sight of the LORD, and did not completely follow the LORD, as his father David had done" (1 Kings 11:1–6).

God warns Solomon not to follow other gods, but Solomon persists. So God tells Solomon that he will tear away his kingdom. "Yet," God says, "I will not do it in your lifetime; I will tear it out of the hand of your son. I will not, however, tear away the entire kingdom; I will give one tribe to your son, for the sake of my servant David and for the sake of Jerusalem, which I have chosen" (1 Kings 11:12–13). God raises up enemies against Solomon, the most important of which turns out to be Jeroboam, a servant of Solomon. Eventually, Jeroboam flees to Egypt. Many of Solomon's remaining actions are recorded in the *Book of the Acts of Solomon*, which no longer exists. Solomon dies, is buried in Jerusalem, and Rehoboam, Solomon's son by Naamah, an Ammonite princess and Solomon's only named wife, succeeds him.

Political Implications: The Ancient Greeks knew that the love of one man for one woman could lead to the destruction of a mighty city. How much more trouble could be caused by the love of one man for hundreds of women? Chapter 11 of *I Kings* is consistent with the tradition of condemning intermarriage. Solomon had ample warning before being told that his kingdom would be divided. And even though the *Deuteronomistic* (17:17) injunction against a king having "many wives" lacks specificity, seven hundred is clearly many.

Rehoboam and the Division of the Kingdom

Basic Text: Rehoboam recognizes that he will have problems governing Israel, for he goes to Shechem where Israel's leaders are waiting to proclaim him king. Upon hearing of Solomon's death, Jeroboam returns from Egypt to Israel. And all the assembly of Israel, including Jeroboam, state Israel's grievances. "'Your father made our yoke heavy. Now therefore lighten the hard service of your father and his heavy yoke that he placed on us, and we will serve you" (1 Kings 12:4). Rehoboam asks for three days to consider his reply.

The older men who had counseled King Solomon advise him to accept their proposal, and "they will be your servants forever" (1 Kings 12:7). But he turns to the young men whom he grew up with. They advise him, "Thus you should say to this people who spoke to you.... My little finger is thicker than my father's loins. Now, whereas my father laid on you a heavy yoke, I will add to your yoke. My father disciplined you with whips, but I will discipline you with scorpions" (1 Kings 12:10–11). (In the *KJV*, "my father hath chastised you with whips, but I will chastise you with scorpions.") Rehoboam follows the advice of his young advisors. The people of Israel answer (1 Kings 12:16):

> What share do we have in David?
>> We have no inheritance in the son of Jesse.
> To your tents, O Israel!
>> Look now to your own house,
>>> O David.

When King Rehoboam sends Adoram, the head of forced labor, to make Israel comply, he is stoned to death. Rehoboam mounts his chariot and flees to Jerusalem. The people of Israel accept Jeroboam as their king, and only Judah accepts Rehoboam. Although he plans an attack to conquer Israel, he is persuaded by a man possessing God's word not to fight his own kindred. Israel and Judah are never reunited, although Israel dominated Judah for much of the ninth century. There also was some intermarriage between the ruling families.

Political Implications: Differences between Judah and Israel were probably too great to be overcome. On the other hand, Solomon's older advisors may have been correct. Clearly, Rehoboam's actions were stupid. Barbara Tuchman (1984: 9–11) sees his actions as a classic case of "folly," which she defines as "the pursuit of policy contrary to the self-interest of the constituency of the state involved (1984, 5)." Folly must meet three criteria: (a) it must be perceived as counterproductive in its own time, (b) another feasible course of action must have been available at the time, and (c) the policy must go beyond any one time. The first two criteria clearly apply to Rehoboam's actions. Rehoboam rules Judah for seventeen years and Jeroboam rules Israel for twenty-two. By that time any opportunity for reconciliation may have been over. The Kingdom of Israel lasted between 931 BCE and 722 BCE, and the separate Kingdom of Judah from 931 BCE to 587 BCE (see Tables 13.1 and 13.3).

One may also discuss Rehoboam's actions in more abstract social scientific language, as Gabriel A. Almond and Sidney Verba (1963) do when discussing "The Parochial-Subject Culture." This is a type of political culture "in which a substantial portion of the population has rejected the exclusive claims of diffuse tribal, village, or feudal authority and has developed allegiance toward a more complex political system with specialized governmental structure" (p. 23). The change between these patterns is difficult and often unstable.

Almond and Verba write that "the classic case is that of the succession to Solomon in the kingdom of Israel. When Solomon died, the parochial (tribal and lineage) leaders of Israel came to Rehoboam, saying, 'Thy father has made our yoke hard; but do thou now make lighter the hard service of thy father, and his heavy yoke to which he put upon us and we will serve thee (p. 23).'" As we have seen, Rehoboam rejects the counsel of his father's advisors, follows the advice of the younger men, and threatens to add to Israel's yoke. As Almond and Verba (p.24) write, "The consequences of Rehoboam's acceptance of the advice of the young modernizers, as told in the rest of *Kings*, suggest that too violent an attack on parochialism may cause both parochial and subject orientations to decline to apathy and alienation. The results are political fragmentation and national destruction."

Now that we have many well-trained social scientists to advise political leaders major mistakes seem far less likely than they were 3,000 years ago.

Coda

Three of the books of the Bible are traditionally attributed to Solomon—*Proverbs, Ecclesiastes*, and the *Song of Solomon* (also known as the *Song of Songs*). But as Thieberger argues (1947: 227), "critical investigations raise grave doubts about his authorship." As we saw, *1 Kings* reports that he wrote 3,000 proverbs, but these were supposed to be allegories about trees and animals, and these subjects are rarely mentioned in *Proverbs*. Archeologists Israel Finkelstein and Neil Asher Silberman (2006: 231) argue that their authorship is postexilic. In his commentary in the *Anchor Bible* series, Michael V. Fox (2000, 2009) points to a wide range of authorship and in another *Anchor Bible* translation and commentary, R. B. Y. Scott (1965: 15) maintains that *Proverbs* was "composed by the bringing together of various collections and independent pieces, each with its own history." In his translation of *Ecclesiastes* for the *Anchor Bible* series, Choon-Leong Seow (1997: 37) argues that even though Solomon was thought to be a patron of wisdom literature "the language of the book does not permit a Solomonic date." He argues that the book can be dated no earlier than the fifth century BCE. Israel Finkelstein and Neil Asher Silberman (2006: 234) argue that the Hellenistic influence upon *Ecclesiastes* demonstrates that it could be written no earlier than the late third century BCE. They also argue that the *Song of Solomon* is generally believed to be postexilic.

In his translation of the *Song of Songs* for the *Anchor Bible* series, Marvin H. Pope (1977: 22–33) discusses alternative dates when the book could have been written. Some scholars argue the book, although not written by Solomon, may be closely associated with his reign. But, as Pope also notes, theories about when it was written are not nearly as varied as those about what the poem means. At its simplest level, it could be a song between two lovers. Jewish interpretations might view the book as the love of the people of Israel for their God, or a Christian view may see it as celebrating the marriage between Christ and his Church. I am sure that, were he alive today, King Solomon would have the wisdom to provide a definitive interpretation for the book that bears his name.

Finally, in his translation and commentary of *Job, Proverbs*, and *Ecclesiastes*, Robert Alter (2010b), concludes that Solomon wrote neither Proverbs nor Ecclesiastes. Even though it begins, "The proverbs of Solomon, son of David, king of Israel" (Prov. 1:1), Alter argues (p. 193) that this headnote "follows the Late Biblical practice of ascribing texts to famous figures from the national past." *Qohelet* (*Ecclesiastes*) begins with "The words of Qohelet, son of David, king in Jerusalem" (Eccles. 1:1). Alter (p. 345) maintains that "This editorial superscription, together with the account in the second half of the chapter of Qohelet's amassing wisdom, is the basis for the traditional ascribing of the authorship to Solomon, though Solomon's name is never mentioned in the book. Virtually all scholarly assessments date the text nearly six centuries after Solomon."

Notes

1. As Robert Alter (1999:379) points out, Bathsheba asks for "one small petition" (1 Kings: 2:20) on Adonijah's behalf. Alter argues that she knows that her son, Solomon, will see this as a huge demand.
2. In his *City of God*, Saint Augustine (354–430 CE) makes an eloquent argument that a state must provide justice (Book IV, Chapter 4). He relates the encounter recounted by Cicero (106 BCE–43 BCE) between Alexander the Great (356 BCE–323 BCE; King of Macedon, 336 BCE–323 BCE) and a captured pirate. Alexander asked, "What is your idea, in infesting the sea?" And the pirate answered with uninhibited insolence. "The same as yours in infesting the earth! But because I do it with a tiny craft, I'm called a pirate; because you have a mighty navy, you're called an emperor." Augustine argues that the pirate gave "a witty and truthful rejoinder." "Remove justice," Augustine writes, "and what are kingdoms but gangs of criminals on a larger scale? What are criminal gangs but petty kingdoms? A gang is a group of men under the command of a leader, bound by a compact of association, in which the plunder is divided according to an agreed convention." "If," Augustine writes, "this villainy wins so many recruits from the ranks of the demoralized that it acquires territory, establishes a base, captures cities, and subdues peoples, it then openly arrogates to itself the title of kingdom, which is conferred on it in the eyes of the world, not by the renunciation of aggression but by the attainment of impunity."

13

1 Kings 13–22, 2 Kings, and 2 Chronicles (The Divided Kingdoms)

The Chronology of the Kings of Israel

Basic Text: 1 Kings, 2 Kings, and *2 Chronicles* relate the stories of the monarchies of Israel and of Judah until their end. In the Bible the discussion of these monarchies is merged, which makes sense given the constant relationships each monarchy had with the other. The monarchs of Israel are presented in Table 13.1, along with their fathers, the year in the reign of the king of Judah in which their reign began, the dates of their reigns, the length of their reigns, and their tribe.

There were nineteen kings in a mere 209 years, so that the average reign was only eleven years. Six are assassinated (Nadab [1 Kings 15:28], Elah [1 Kings 16:10], Jehoram [2 Kings 9:24], Zechariah [2 Kings 15:10], Shallum [2 Kings 15:14], and Pekah [2 Kings 15:30]), Zimri commits suicide (1 Kings 16:18) to avoid assassination, and Ahab (1 Kings 22:34–37) is killed in battle. Moreover, no king establishes an enduring dynasty, although Jehu is followed by four descendants, and the period between the beginning of his reign (841 BCE) and the end of Zechariah's (747 BCE) lasts ninety-four years. During the kingdom of Israel, leaders became increasingly weaker compared with their foreign neighbors, eventually succumbing to the Assyrian Empire in 722 BCE.

Political Implications: The monarchy never developed a means of transferring power. There was no royal family comparable to the House of David, which ruled Judah. Even though there was widespread agreement that future subjugation from Judah must be avoided, it was difficult to establish central authority over the competing tribes. Although the new capital of Shechem had some symbolic value and was not clearly part of any tribal allotment, it was overshadowed by

Table 13.1 Kings of Israel

Name	Father	Accession according to who was the king of Judah	Dates of reign (all dates are BCE)	Length of reign according to *Kings*	Tribe
Jeroboam	Nebat	In Rehoboam's first year	931–910	22	Ephraim
Nadab	Jeroboam	Second year of King Asa	910–909	2	Ephraim
Baasha	Ahihah	Third year of King Asa	909–886	24	Isaachar
Elah	Baasha	Twenty-sixth year of King Asa	886–885	2	Isaachar
Zimri	Not known	Twenty-seventh year of King Asa	885	7 days	Not known
Omri	Not known	Thirty-first year of King Asa	885–874	12	Not known
Ahab	Omri	Thirty-eighth year of King Asa	873–853	22	Not known
Ahaziah	Ahab	Seventeenth year of King Jehosophat	853–852	2	Not known
Jehoram (Joram)	Ahab	Eighteenth year of King Jehosophat	852–841	12	Not known
Jehu	Nishmi; or son of Jehosophat, son of Nishmi	King Ahaziah begins to reign	841–813	28	Not known
Jehoahaz	Jehu	Twenty-third year of King Joash	813–797	17	Not known
Jehoash (Joash)	Jehoahaz	Thirty-seventh year of King Joash	797–782	16	Not known

Jeroboam II	Jehoash (Joash)	Fifteenth year of King Amiziah	782–747	41	Not known
Zechariah	Jeroboam II	Thirty-eighth year of King Azariah	747	6 months	Not known
Shallum	Jabesh	Thirty-eighth year of King Azariah (Uzziah)	747	1 month	Not known
Menahem	Gadi	Thirty-ninth year of King Azarah (Uzziah)	747–742	10	Not known
Pekahiah	Menahem	Fiftieth year of King Azariah (Uzziah)	742–740	2	Not known
Pekah	Remaliah	Fifty-second year of King Azariah (Uzziah)	740–731	20	Not known
Hoshea	Elah	Twelfth year of King Ahaz	731–724	9	Not known

Assyrian conquest in 722

Sources: 1 Kings, 2 Kings, and 2 Chronicles. I also used the chronology tables in the Soncino editions of Kings (ix) and Chronicles (x), chronologies in the Anchor Bible editions of 1 Kings (2000: 508) and 2 Kings (1988: 341), and Gelb (2010: 234–34). In addition, I used the Anchor Bible Dictionary for information about specific monarchs.

Notes: As Steven W. Holloway notes in his Anchor Bible entry on the Books of Kings (vol. 4: 75), "A few minutes' labor with a hand calculator will convince the reader not only of serious discrepancies between tallies of the individual regnal years of the kings of Judah and Israel, but outright contradictions between different citations of the same chronological text." The contradictions in these tables are most apparent in cases where the number of years a monarch is claimed to have reigned does not match our contemporary calendar of the dates in which they served. In the actual texts, the accession of kings of Israel is calculated by the number of years that the contemporary king of Judah has served, whereas, until the Northern monarchy ended, the accession of kings of Judah are calculated by the number of years that the contemporary king of Israel served.

Jerusalem and by the magnificent temple that King Solomon had constructed.

Evaluating the Kings of Israel

Basic Text: The regime has very little moral authority. Even before the division of the kingdom, idolatry is much more prevalent in the north than in the south. And the Israelite monarchs do little to curb it and much to encourage it. Table 13.2 presents my summary of the evaluation in *1 Kings* and *2 Kings* of sixteen of the Israelite monarchs (all but Ahaziah, Elah, and Shallum). Only Jehu is credited with suppressing the worship of Baal; most are judged very harshly.

Omri and Ahab are both strongly condemned. The story of Naboth's vineyard is well worth examining. Naboth the Jezreelite owns a vineyard near the king's palace, and Ahab wants it for a vegetable garden. He offers to give Naboth a better vineyard in return, or to pay him for his vineyard. But Naboth refuses since it is his ancestral inheritance.

Ahab is depressed, but his consort Jezebel tells him, "Do you now govern Israel? Get up, eat some food, and be cheerful; I will give you the vineyard of Naboth the Jezreelite" (1 Kings 21:7). She writes letters in Ahab's name and seals them with his seal. The letters ask the elders to proclaim a fast before judging Naboth. She finds "two scoundrels" to testify that Naboth has cursed God and the king, and Naboth is stoned to death. Ahab takes Naboth's garden. Ahab has coveted his neighbor's vineyard, and Jezebel has suborned perjury. Jezebel has committed murder, from which her husband profits. God tells the prophet Elijah, whom many Jews believe will herald the future Messiah, to condemn Ahab. "Go down to meet King Ahab of Israel, who rules in Samaria; he is now in the vineyard of Naboth, where he has gone to take possession. You shall say to him, 'Thus says the LORD: Have you killed, and also taken possession?' You shall say to him, 'Thus says the LORD: In the place where dogs licked up the blood of Naboth, dogs will also lick up your blood'" (1 Kings 21:18–19). Hoshea, the last king of Israel, receives a relatively perfunctory rebuke.

But by this stage, God is no longer willing to support the kingdom. Faced with a far stronger power of the emerging Assyrian Empire, and finding no allies to protect it, Israel falls. *2 Kings* explains the fall of Israel in moral terms: "This occurred because the people of Israel had sinned against the LORD their God, who had brought them up out

**Table 13.2   Assessments of the Kings of Israel, according to *1 Kings* and
*2 Kings***

Kings:

Jeroboam:
The prophet Ahijah tells Jeroboam's wife, "The LORD will strike Israel, as a
reed is shaken in the water; he will root up Israel out of this good land that he
gave to their ancestors, and scatter them beyond the Euphrates, because they
have made sacred poles, provoking the LORD to anger. He will give Israel up
because of the sins of Jeroboam, which he sinned and which he caused Israel
to commit" (1 Kings 14:15–16).

Nadab:
"He did what was evil in the sight of the LORD, walking in the way of his
ancestor and in the sin that he caused Israel to commit" (1 Kings 15:26).

Baasha:
"He did what was evil in the sight of the LORD, walking in the way of
Jeroboam and in the sin that he caused Israel to commit" (1 Kings 15:34).

Elah:
No assessment. He was assassinated by Zimri, while "drinking himself drunk"
(1 Kings 16:9), after reigning only two years.

Zimri:
"When Zimri saw the city was taken, he went into the citadel of the king's
house; he burned down the king's house over himself with fire and he died—
because of the sins that he committed, doing evil in the sight of the LORD,
walking in the way of Jeroboam, and for the sin that he committed, causing
Israel to sin" (1 Kings 16:18–19).

Omri:
"Omri did what was evil in the sight of the LORD; he did more evil than all
who were before him. For he walked in all the way of Jeroboam son of Nebat,
and in the sins that he caused Israel to commit, provoking the LORD, the
God of Israel, to anger by their idols" (1 Kings 16:25–26).

Ahab:
Ahab and his Phoenician wife Jezebel are among the most evil characters in
the *Hebrew Bible*, a notch less evil than the Pharaoh who attempts to kill all
Israelite males, or Haman, who tries to annihilate all the Jews in the Persian
Empire. As we saw, Ahab sins by coveting Naboth's vineyard, Jezebel suborns
perjury, violating the injunction against bearing false witness, and leading
to judicial murder and theft. On God's order, Elijah condemns him. *1 Kings*
21:17–24 concludes: "Indeed, there was no one like Ahab, who sold himself
to do what was evil in the sight of the LORD, urged on by his wife Jezebel. He
acted most abominably in going after idols, as the Amorites had done, whom
the LORD drove out before the Israelites."

(continued)

Table 13.2 (*continued*)

Ahaziah:
When he is injured, he tells his messengers to ask Baal whether he will
recover. But Elijah tells him, "Thus says the LORD: Is it because there is no
God in Israel that you are sending to inquire of Baal-zebub, the god of Ekron?"
(2 Kings 1:6). There is no summary assessment.

Jehoram:
"He did what was evil in the sight of the LORD, though not like his father
and mother, for he removed the pillar of Baal that his father had made.
Nevertheless he clung to the sin of Jeroboam son of Nebat, which he caused
Israel to commit; he did not depart from it" (2 Kings 3:2–3).

Jehu:
"Thus Jehu wiped out Baal from Israel. But Jehu did not turn aside from the
sins of Jeroboam son of Nebat, which he caused Israel to commit—the golden
calves that were in Bethel and in Dan" (2 Kings 10:28–29). For this, God tells
him that four generations of his descendants will occupy the throne of Israel.
Even so, "Jehu was not careful to follow the law of the LORD the God of
Israel with all his heart; he did not turn from the sins of Jeroboam, which he
caused Israel to commit" (2 Kings 10:31).

Jehoahaz:
"He did what was evil in the sight of the LORD, and followed the sins of
Jeroboam son of Nebat, which he caused Israel to sin; he did not depart from
them. The anger of the LORD was kindled against Israel, so that he gave
them repeatedly into the hand of King Hazael of Aram, then into the hand of
Benhadad son of Hazael" (2 Kings 13:2–3). Jehoahaz asks God for help, and
He sends a savior to protect Israel, but Israel continues to sin.

Jehoash (Joash):
"He also did what was evil in the sight of the LORD; he did not depart from
all the sins of Jeroboam son of Nebat, which he caused Israel to sin" (2 Kings
13:11).

Jeroboam II:
"He did what was evil in the sight of the LORD; he did not depart from all the
sins of Jeroboam son of Nebat, which caused Israel to sin" (2 Kings 14:24).
But God saves Israel partly because of the actions of Jonah the son of Amatti,
who is best known for saving the Assyrian city of Nineveh.

Zechariah:
"He did what was evil in the sight of the LORD, as his ancestors had done.
He did not depart from the sins of Jeroboam son of Nebat, which he caused
Israel to sin" (2 Kings 15:9).

Shallum:
No assessment. Was king only for one month.

Menahem:
"He did what was evil in the sight of the Lord; he did not depart all his days from any of the sins of Jeroboam son of Nebat, which he caused Israel to sin" (2 Kings 15:18).

Pekahiah:
"He did what was evil in the sight of the LORD; he did not turn away from any of the sins of Jeroboam son of Nabat, which he caused Israel to sin" (2 Kings 15:24).

Pekah:
"He did what was evil in the sight of the LORD; he did not turn away from the sins of Jeroboam son of Nebat, which he caused Israel to sin" (2 Kings 15:28).

Hoshea:
"He did what was evil in the sight of the LORD, yet not like the kings of Israel who were before him" (2 Kings 17:2).

Sources: 1 Kings and *2 Kings.*

of the land of Egypt from under the hand of Pharaoh king of Egypt. They had worshipped other gods and walked in the customs of the nations whom the LORD drove out before the people of Israel, and in the customs that the kings of Israel had introduced. The people of Israel secretly did things that were not right against the LORD their God. They built for themselves high places at all their towns, from watchtowers to fortified city; they set up for themselves pillars and sacred poles on every high hill and under every green tree; there they made offerings on all the high places, as the nations did whom the LORD carried away before them. . . . Yet the LORD warned Israel and Judah by every prophet and every seer, saying, 'Turn from your evil ways and follow my commandments and my statutes, in accordance with all the law that I commanded your ancestors and that I sent you by my servants the prophets'" (2 Kings 17:7–13).

In the *KJV*, "For *so* it was, that the children of Israel had sinned against the LORD their God, which had brought them up out of the land of Egypt, from under the hand of Pharaoh king of Egypt, and had feared other gods, [a]nd walked in the statutes of the heathen, whom the LORD cast out from before the children of Israel and of the kings of Israel, which they had made. And the children of Israel did secretly *those* things that *were* not right against the LORD their God, and they built them high places in all their cities, from the tower of the watchmen to the fenced city. And they set them up images and groves in every high hill, and under every green tree: And there they burnt incense in all the high places, as *did* the heathen whom the LORD carried away before them; and wrought wicked things to provoke the LORD to anger: For they served idols, whereof the LORD said unto them, Ye shall not do this thing. Yet the LORD testified against Israel, and against Judah, by all the prophets, *and by* all the seers, saying, Turn ye from your evil ways, and keep my commandments *and* my statutes, according to which I commanded your fathers, and which I sent to you by my servants the prophets."

Political Implications: Is this explanation for Israel's downfall correct? Or should its demise be explained by its foreign policy failures that led the Assyrian leader, Shalmaneser V, to crush it, as Norman Gelb (2010: 87) argues. These explanations are not mutually exclusive, and, even if they were, there is no crucial test between them. Hoshea tried to take advantage of a period of temporary instability caused by the death of King Tiglath-Pileser III of Assyria (727 BCE) and was encouraged by Egypt. Hoshea ceased paying tribute to Assyria. It was an act of rebellion that the new Assyrian king could not tolerate, and for Hoshea, "It was an act of national suicide" (Gelb, 2010: 87). Unfortunately, King Hoshea did not have the opportunity to read the Athenian advice to the Melians, recorded by Thucydides (5:89) nearly three hundred years later: "you know as well as we do that right, as the world goes, is only in question between equals in power, while the strong do what they can, and the weak suffer what they must."

The Chronology of the Kings of Judah

Basic Text: The chronology of the kings of Judah is of far more religious interest than that of the kings of Israel. Many Christians believe that Jesus, or at least Joseph of Nazareth, was descended from this line, and many Jews believe that the Messiah will descend from David. Except for the six-year reign of Queen Athalia, all of the monarchs of Judah are lineal descendants of King David (see Table 13.3), which begins with the divided kingdom. As King Josiah is the father of Jehoahaz, Jehoiakim, and Zedekiah, Table 13.3 shows sixteen generations between Solomon and Zedekiah.[1] Adding David produces seventeen generations, three more than Matthew's fourteen, fourteen, and fourteen generational formula allows for (Matt. 1:17) (see chapter 18).

Table 13.3 Kings of Judah

Name	Father	According to who was the king of Israel	Dates of reign (all dates are BCE)	Length of reign according to *Kings*	Mentioned in Matthew's genealogy
Rehoboam	Solomon	After King Solomon's death	931–914	17	Yes (1:7)
Abijah	Rehoboam	Eighteenth year of King Jeroboam	914–911	3	Yes (1:7)
Asa	Abijah	Twentieth year of King Jeroboam	911–871	41	Yes (1:8) (translated as Asaph)
Jehosophat	Asa	Fourth year of King Ahab	871–848	25	Yes (1:8)
Jehoram (Joram)	Jehosophat	Fifth year of King Jehoram	848–841	8	Yes (1:8) (translated as Joram)
Ahaziah	Jehoram (Joram)	Same year as King Jehu begins to reign	841–840	1	No
Queen Athalia	Unclear	First year of King Jehu	840–835	6	No
Joash (Jehoash)	Ahaziah	Seventh year of King Jehu	835–796	40	No
Amaziah	Joash (Jehoash)	Second year of King Jehoash	796–767	29	No
Uzziah (Azariah)	Amaziah	Twenty-seventh year of King Jeroboam II	767–739	52	Yes (1:8)
Jotham	Uzziah (Azariah)	Second year of King Pekah	739–734	16	Yes (1:9)
Ahaz	Jotham	Seventeenth year of King Pekah	734–728	16	Yes (1:9)

(continued)

Table 13.3 *(continued)*

Hezekiah	Ahaz	Third year of King Hoshea	728–698	29	Yes (1:9)
Manasseh	Hezekiah		698–643	55	Yes (1:10)
Amon	Manasseh		642–641	2	Yes (1:10) (translated as Asos
Josiah	Amon		641–609	31	Yes (1:10)
Jehoahaz	Josiah		609	3 months	No
Jehoiakim	Josiah		609–598	11	No
Jehoiachin	Jehoiakim		598–597	3 months	Yes (1:11) (translated as Jechoniah)
Zedekiah	Josiah		597–587	11	No

Fall of Jerusalem to Babylon and the beginning of early deportations, 597–538

[a] Except for Queen Athalia, all are from the House of Judah.
Sources: See Table 13.1.
Notes: See Table 13.1. There are also some ambiguities with Matthew's genealogy.

However, the dynasty ends with Zedekiah because after the Babylonians capture him, "They slaughtered the sons of Zedekiah before his eyes, then put out the eyes of Zedekiah; they bound him in fetters and took him to Babylon" (2 Kings 25:7). (In the *KJV*, "And they slew the sons of Zedekiah before his eyes, and put out the eyes of Zedekiah, and bound him with fetters of brass, and carried him to Babylon.")

The Davidic dynasty lasts from about 1000 BCE to 587 BCE, 413 years. During that period, it had twenty-two monarchs.

King Ahaziah had been killed on the orders of King Jehu of Israel (2 Kings 9:27), her palace guards assassinated Queen Athalia (2 Kings 11:15–16), and his servants assassinated King Amon (2 Kings 21:23). King Josiah was killed at (2 Kings 23:29) or mortally wounded (2 Chron. 35:20–24) at a battle against the Egyptians at Megiddo. The divided monarchy lasted between 931 BCE and 587 BCE, about 344 years. If we take the entire period between the consolidation of David's rule to the end of Zedekiah's kingship, the average reign was nearly nineteen years; if we begin with the divided monarchy, the average reign was seventeen years. Either average contrasts favorably with the average reign of eleven years in the Kingdom of Israel.

Political Implications: Even though Judah was smaller than Israel, having a divinely established dynasty had two major advantages. First, it gave the monarch greater legitimacy. Second, it helped reduce the conflicts that often arise when the elites, and sometimes the mass public, choose a new political leader. Having Jerusalem as its capital was another advantage. It occupies high ground and is easily fortified. Yet even during the divided monarchy, it was conquered by King Shishak of Egypt and by King Jehoash of Israel before being destroyed by the Babylonians. And in 70 CE, the Romans destroyed it again.

Evaluating the Kings of Judah

Basic Text: 1 *Kings* and 2 *Kings* pass moral assessments on the kings of Judah. But whereas the Israelite kings are rated from very, very bad to bad, the kings of Judah are rated from very, very bad to very, very good. I present my summary evaluations of 1 *Kings* and 2 *Kings* in Table 13.4. Even most of the monarchs who "did right in the sight of the LORD," did not remove the "high places" where people worshipped idols. Only Kings Hezekiah and Josiah receive unqualified praise. Josiah even has the people renew their covenant with God. But an especially evil son, Manasseh, followed Hezekiah and two evil

Table 13.4   Assessments of the Kings of Judah, according to *1 Kings* and *2 Kings*

Kings:

Rehoboam:

In his reign "Judah did what was evil in the sight of the LORD; they provoked him to jealousy with their sins that they committed, more than all that their ancestors had done. For they also built for themselves high places, pillars, and sacred poles on every high hill and under every green tree; there were also male temple prostitutes in the land. They committed all the abominations of the nations that the LORD drove out before the people of Israel" (1 Kings 14:22–24).

Abijah:

"He committed all the sins that his father did before him; his heart was not true to the LORD his God like the heart of his father David. Nevertheless for David's sake the LORD his God gave him a lamp in Jerusalem; setting up his son after him, and establishing Jerusalem; because David did what was right in the sight of the LORD, and did not turn aside from him in anything that he commanded all the days of his life, except in the matter of Uriah the Hittite" (1 Kings 15:3–5).

Asa:

"Asa did what was right in the sight of the LORD, as his father David had done. He put away the male temple prostitutes out of the land, and removed all the idols that his ancestors had made. . . . But the high places were not taken away. Nevertheless the heart of Asa was true to the LORD all of his days" (1 Kings 15:11–14). There is a more extensive discussion of Asa in *2 Chronicles* (14–16), which also evaluates him favorably, although Carl D. Evans, who wrote the *Anchor Bible Dictionary* entry on Asa, thinks it is of "debated historical worth" (1992, vol. 1, 468).

Jehosophat:

"He walked in the ways of his father Asa; he did not turn aside from it, doing what was right in the sight of the LORD; yet the high places were not taken away, and the people still sacrificed and offered incense on the high places" (1 Kings 22:43).

Jehoram (Joram):

"He walked in the way of the kings of Israel, as the house of Ahab had done, for the daughter of Ahab was his wife. He did what was evil in the sight of the LORD" (2 Kings 8:18).

Ahaziah:

"He also walked in the way of the House of Ahab, doing what was evil in the sight of the LORD, as the house of Ahab had done, for he was son-in-law to the house of Ahab" (2 Kings 8:27).

Queen Athalia:
When Athalia saw her son was dead, "she set about to destroy all the royal family" (2 Kings 11:1). In 2 Chronicles 22:10, "she set about to destroy the royal family of the house of Judah." However, Joash is saved. In her seventh year, the priest Jehoiada urges the palace guard to slay her, which it does. Joash becomes king. However, there is no summary judgment evaluating her reign.

Joash:
"Joash did what was right in the sight of the LORD all his days because the priest Jehoiada instructed him. Nevertheless the high places were not taken away; the people continued to sacrifice and make offerings on the high places" (2 Kings 12:2–3).

Amaziah:
"He did what was right in the sight of the LORD, yet not like his ancestor David; in all things he did as his father Joash had done. But the high places were not removed; the people still sacrificed and made offerings on the high places" (2 Kings 14:3–4).

Uzziah (Azariah):
"He did what was right in the sight of the LORD, just as his father Amaziah had done. Nevertheless the high places were not taken away; the people still sacrificed and made offerings on the high places" (2 Kings 15:3–4).

Jotham:
"He did what was right in the sight of the LORD, just as his father Uzzaiah had done. Nevertheless the high paces were not removed; the people still sacrificed and made offerings on the high places" (2 Kings 15:34–35).

Ahaz:
"He did not do right in the sight of the LORD his God, as his ancestor David had done, but he walked in the way of the kings of Israel. He even made his son pass through the fire, according to the abominable practices of the nations the LORD drove out before the people Israel" (2 Kings 16:2–3).

Hezekiah:
"He did what was right in the sight of the LORD just as his ancestor David had done. He removed the high places, broke down the pillars, and cut down the sacred pole. He broke in pieces the bronze serpent that Moses had made, for until those days the people of Israel had made offerings to it; it was called Nehushtan. He trusted in the LORD the God of Israel; so that there was no one like him among all the kings of Judah after him, or among those who were before him. For he held fast to the LORD; he did not depart from following him but kept the commandments that the LORD had commanded Moses" (2 Kings 18:3–6).

(continued)

Table 13.4   (*continued*)

Manasseh:

"He did what was evil in the sight of the LORD, following the abominable practices of the nations that the LORD drove out before the people of Israel. For he rebuilt the high places that his father Hezekiah had destroyed; he erected altars for Baal, made a sacred pole, as King Ahab of Israel had done, worshipped all the host of heaven, and served them. . . . He made his son pass through the fire; he practiced soothsaying and augury, and dealt with mediums and wizards. He did much evil in the sight of the LORD, provoking him to anger"(2 Kings 21:2–6).

Amon:

"He did what was evil in the sight of the Lord, as his father Manasseh had done. He walked in all the way in which his father walked, and served the idols that his father served, and worshipped them; he abandoned the LORD, the God of his ancestors, and did not walk the way of the LORD" (2 Kings 21:20–21).

Josiah:

"He did what was right in the sight of the LORD, and walked in all the way of his father David; he did not turn to the right or to the left" (2 Kings 22:2). He went up to the house of the LORD, gathered the people and read the book of the covenant. "All the people joined in the covenant" (2 Kings 23:3). He commanded the people to celebrate Passover, and "No such passover had been kept since the days of the judges who judged Israel, even during all the days of the Kings of Israel and of the Kings of Judah" (2 Kings 23:22). He "put away the mediums, wizards, teraphim, idols, and all the abominations that were seen in the land of Judah and in Jerusalem" (2 Kings 23:24). "Before him there was no king like him, who turned to the LORD with all his heart and with all his soul, and with all his might (see Deut. 6:4–5) according to the law of Moses; nor did any arise after him" (2 Kings 23:25).

Jehoahaz:

"He did what was evil in the sight of the LORD, just as his ancestors had done" (2 Kings 23:32).

Jehoiakim:

"He did evil in the sight of the LORD, just as all his ancestors had done" (2 Kings 23:37).

Jehoiachin:

"He did what was evil in the sight of the LORD, just as his father had done" (2 Kings 24:9).

Zedekiah:

"He did what was evil in the sight of the LORD, just as Jehoiakim had done" (2 Kings 24:19).

Sources: 1 Kings and 2 Kings.

sons, Jehoahaz and Jehoiakim, followed Josiah. Granted, God may have abandoned Judah. According to *2 Kings* 24:20, "Indeed, Jerusalem and Judah so angered the LORD that he expelled them from his presence. Zedekiah rebelled against the king of Babylon." (In the *KJV*, "For through the anger of the LORD it came to pass in Jerusalem and Judah, until he had cast them out from his presence, that Zedekiah rebelled against the king of Babylon."[2])

The *Jewish Study Bible* argues that based upon *Jeremiah* and *Ezekiel*, it appears that Zedekiah was planning a revolt with the Phoenician and Transjordan kingdoms, but that the revolt was aborted by Nebuchadnezzar,[3] who then moved to punish Judah. In their translation and commentary of *II Kings* for the *Anchor Bible* series, Mordechai Cogan and Hayim Tadmor (1988: 322) argue that there was a "meeting in Jerusalem of representatives of Edom, Moab, Ammon, Tyre, and Sidon . . . to plan revolt. . . . But this rebellion died at birth." They base their conclusion upon *Jeremiah* 27:3.[4] Both *2 Kings* 24:20 and *2 Chronicles* 36:13 report Zedekiah rebelled against Babylon. Jerusalem was besieged in the ninth year of his reign and fell in the eleventh year (587 BCE).

By Zedekiah's time Judah was already severely weakened, and, according to Gelb (2010: 137) by the reign of Jehoahaz (609 BCE), "Judah was drifting inexorably toward extinction." Deportations to Babylon had already begun at the end of his predecessor's reign in 597 BCE. Although the Babylonians need a lengthy siege to take the city, they succeed and destroy Solomon's Temple, and carry off more captives.

Political Implications: The sins that weakened the kingdom of Judah may well have played a major role in its downfall. But the Bible also suggests that its kings did not understand the changing nature of power politics in the region. Babylon was emerging as the regional superpower, whereas the kings of Judah were hoping for protection from Egypt. Some prophets, most notably Jeremiah, argued against relying on Egypt and against rebelling against Babylon. Zedekiah, like Hoshea, might have profited had he been able to read Thucydides.

Perhaps because the transgressions of the kingdoms of Israel and Judah were so egregious, great prophets emerged during these reigns, and we will turn to two of them to study the political implications of their preachings.[5]

Notes

1. Not including the generation between Jehoiakim and Jehoiachin.
2. The *KJV* seems to suggest that God may have encouraged Zedekiah to revolt against Nebuchadnezzar, the king of Babylon. My reading of the Hebrew suggests this is misleading, as do more recent English translations.
3. More specifically, Nebuchadnezzar II, who lived between approximately 642 BCE and 562 BCE and reigned between approximately 605 BCE and 562 BCE.
4. In my view, the passage from *Jeremiah* is thin evidence that any such revolt was planned.
5. According to Jewish tradition, the age of prophecy ended with Malachi. According to Andrew E. Hill in the *Anchor Bible Dictionary* (vol. 4, 487–79), his prophecies suggest that his career was from 515 BCE to 548 BCE. Christians see Jesus as the Messiah, not a mere prophet. Islam sees Jesus as a prophet, but rejects any supernatural status. It sees Muhammad, whose prophetic career lasted from 613 CE to 632 CE, as "The Seal of the Prophets." As Huston Smith (p. 223) writes, according to Islam, "No valid prophets will follow him."

14

Isaiah

First Isaiah

Basic Text: The Book of Isaiah contains some of the most beautiful language of the *Hebrew Bible*. As Klaus Koch (1983: 106) writes, "Of all the prophets known to us, Isaiah is the most powerful in his language. The wealth of images he uses and the impressive force of his prophecies have continually elicited cries of admiration even from scholars who are otherwise sparing in their praise." *The Book of Isaiah* plays a major role in Jewish Liturgy.[1]

It is difficult to summarize *Isaiah*'s contents because the prophecy covers a long time period and uses different styles.[2] In the *Anchor Bible Dictionary*, Christopher R. Seitz (vol. 3, 472), divides the book into four sections. Chapters 1–39 are classified as *First Isaiah*, which include four chapters 24–27, sometimes labeled "The Little (or Isaiac) Apocalypse;" chapters 40–55 are labeled *Second Isaiah* (often called *Deutero-Isaiah*); and chapters 56–66 are labeled *Third Isaiah*. The *Anchor Bible* (2000a, 2000b, 2003) series translates Isaiah in three books, conforming to these divisions, except that "The Little Apocalypse" is included in the volume for chapters 1–39.

According to estimates by A. S. Herbert (1973: xiii) in his *Cambridge Bible Commentary* on *The Book of Prophet Isaiah, 1–39* of *The New English Bible*, First Isaiah may have been active from the last years of King Uzziah of Judah to the beginning of the reign of King Manasseh of Judah (see Table 13.3). His religious significance is far greater than his political importance. In a statement that seems to foretell Jesus's miraculous birth, he proclaims, "Therefore the LORD himself will give you a sign. Look, the young woman is with child and shall bear a son, and shall name him Immanuel" (Isa. 7:14). But this prophecy is much stronger in the *KJV*, "Therefore the Lord himself shall give you a sign; Behold, a virgin shall conceive, and bear a son, and shall call his name Immanuel."[3]

Isaiah is also known for a prophecy that might also be seen as heralding the Messiah. In 1:18, he proclaims:

> Come now, let us argue it out,
> says the LORD:
> though your sins are like scarlet,
> they shall be like snow;
> though they are red like crimson,
> they shall become like wool.

In the far more poetic language of the *KJV*:

> Come now, and let us reason together, saith the LORD:
> though your sins be as scarlet, they shall be as white as snow;
> though they be red like crimson, they shall be as wool.

First Isaiah makes two important political predictions. He warns both Israel and Judah against relying on Egypt (Isa. 31:1):

> Alas for those who go down to Egypt for help
> and who rely on horses,
> who trust in chariots because they are many
> and in horsemen because they are very strong,
> but do not look to the Holy One of Israel
> or consult the LORD!

This is solid advice, similar to warnings issued by Jeremiah.

But Isaiah's most famous political prediction concerns a change "in days to come" (Isa. 2:2), when Isaiah proclaims (Isa. 2:3–4):

> For out of Zion shall go forth instruction,
> and the word of the LORD from Jerusalem.
> He shall judge between the nations,
> and shall arbitrate for many peoples;
> they shall beat their swords into plowshares,
> and their spears into pruning hooks;
> nation shall not lift up sword against nation,
> neither shall they learn war any more.

(In the *KJV*, this prophecy is to be fulfilled "in the last days," but the rest of the translation is similar.)

Political Implications: First Isaiah's predictions about the imminence of the Messiah go beyond the scope of this book. His advice about not relying upon Egypt was sound, and ignoring it was costly for the last kings of Israel and Judah. According to Abraham J. Heschel (2001: 91), Isaiah was fundamentally distrustful of alliances. "Isaiah could not accept politics as a solution, since politics itself, with its arrogance and disregard for justice, was a problem. When mankind is, as we would say, spiritually sick, something more radical than political sagacity is needed to solve the problem of security. For the moment a clever alignment of states may be of help. In the long run, it is bound to prove futile."

What of Isaiah's predictions of worldwide peace? The time frame for this prediction was imprecise, but war has not been abolished. True, most armies do not rely upon swords and spears, but in the mass genocide in Rwanda in 1994 (De Forges, 1999; Gourevitch, 1998), in which an estimated 800,000 people were killed, most Hutu militiamen were armed with machetes. But surely Isaiah was not merely hoping for an era when sword and spears would be replaced by rifles and bayonets. World War II was the costliest conflict in history, and although the total number of deaths in China is difficult to estimate, Gerald L. Weinberg (2005: 894) writes that "the total for the globe probably reached sixty million, a figure which includes the six million murdered because they were Jewish." As of this writing, the United States is engaged in three wars: Operation Enduring Freedom in Afghanistan, Operation New Dawn in Iraq (formerly Iraqi Freedom), and Operation Odyssey Dawn in Libya.

Isaiah recognizes that his own countrymen need to be prepared militarily. As Koch (1983: 125) writes, "There is no passage which suggests that Isaiah would have considered that an army and that the defence of the country were superfluous. . . . It is only in the Isaiah school which later looks forward to an eschatological period in which swords will be beaten into plowshares and spears into pruning hooks. But this is not going to happen because Yahweh himself takes over the military defence; it is because war among nations is going to cease forever (2:1–4)."

"The Little Apocalypse"

Basic Text: Although chapters 24–27 are included in the first thirty-nine books that are attributed to *The First Isaiah*, they are generally considered postexilic. However, many critics do not consider them to be apocalyptic. Herbert (1973: 143) argues that this is misleading, and Joseph Blenkinsopp (2000 : 346), the translator of all three *Anchor Bible* volumes of *Isaiah*, argues that these chapters have some of the attributes of an apocalypse, while lacking others.[4] These four chapters begin with a discussion of the earth and its inhabitants (Isa. 24:3–13), an ode to God's majesty and his ability to destroy (24:14–23), a banquet prepared by God (25:6–8), and three psalms of thanksgiving (25:1–9, 9–12, and 26:1–6). This is followed by what Blenkinsopp calls an "Eschatological Psalm" (27:1), that is, a psalm predicting the imminent end of the world, a vineyard revisited (27:2–6), and a discussion of the city and of God's people. Isaiah makes one optimistic prophecy: "In days to come Jacob shall take root, Israel shall blossom and put forth shoots, and fill the whole world with fruit" (Isa. 27:6). (In the *KJV*, "He shall cause them that come of Jacob to take root: Israel shall blossom and bud, and fill the face of the world with fruit.")

Political Implications: According to Herbert (1973: 144), these four chapters reflect the political conditions when they were written. "These chapters seem to indicate a world in confusion . . . in which the Jews were inevitably involved, yet in no way responsible." He continues, "It was in the fourth century that the struggle for supremacy between Persia and Greece was taking place, a struggle in which the political stability of the world was threatened. In many respects, the conditions of the postwar world of our own time would form a fitting context for these chapters. Where in the midst of confusion is there any ground for hope? What contribution has religion to offer? Clearly, the old nature-religions are ill-equipped to meet these strains, and religion deriving from national supremacy can hardly survive. It may be regarded as one of the triumphs of Israel's faith, mediated through prophet and cultus [a system of religion based on cultic practice], that in these chapters it could not only survive but prove victorious."

Second Isaiah Comforts the People

Basic Text: According to Richard J. Clifford, author of the *Anchor Bible Dictionary* entry on *Second Isaiah* (vol. 3, 490), "The historical context of chaps. 40–55 differs entirely from that of chaps. 1–39. The enemy of Israel is the Neo-Babylonian Empire (626–539 BC; cf. chaps. 46; 47; 48:20–21), not the Neo-Assyrian Empire of First Isaiah (935–612 BC; cf. chaps. 10; 14:24–27), which collapsed with the destruction of Nineveh in 612 BC. The gentile king in chaps. 40–55 is Cyrus of Persia (fl 560–530 BC; cf. 41:2–5; 25; 44:24–45:13; 48:14), not the Assyrian King of First Isaiah's eighth-century Jerusalem: the message is to leave Babylon; cross the desert, and return to Zion."

At the very outset, *Second Isaiah* begins by providing comfort to the exiled people (Isa. 40:1–2):

> Comfort, O comfort, my people,
> says your God.
> Speak tenderly to Jerusalem,
> and cry to her
> that she has served her term,
> that her penalty is paid,
> that she has received from the LORD's hand
> double for all her sins.

In the *KJV*:

> Comfort ye, comfort ye my people, saith your God.
> Speak you comfortably to Jerusalem, and cry unto her,
> that her warfare is accomplished, that her
> iniquity is pardoned:
> for she has received of the LORD's hand
> double for all her sins.

God reminds the people that nations are insignificant (Isa. 40:15–17):

> Even the nations are like a drop from
> a bucket,
> and are accounted for as dust on
> the scales;
> see, he takes up the isles like fine
> dust.
> Lebanon would not provide fuel
> enough,
> nor are its animals enough for a
> burnt offering.
> All the nations are as nothing before
> him;
> they are accounted by him as less
> than nothing and emptiness.

In the *KJV*:

> Behold, the nations *are* as a drop of a bucket, and are
> counted as the small dust of the balance:
> behold, he taketh up the isles as a very little thing.
> And Lebanon *is* not sufficient to burn, nor the beasts thereof

sufficient for a burnt offering.
All nations before him *are* as nothing; and they are counted to
   him
less than nothing, and vanity.

Political Implications: In his *Anchor Bible* translation of chapters
40–55, Blenkinsopp (190–91) argues that these verses "reveal the political point and purpose of this hyperbolic language: the measured-out
water of the world and the dust of the earth are contrasted with the
nations as drops from an empty bucket and dust left on the scales, and
the weighing of the mountains and hills links with the failure of Mount
Lebanon to provide enough wood and livestock for adequate sacrifice."
And in his *Cambridge Bible Commentary* of *The Book of the Prophet
Isaiah, 40–66* of the *New English Bible*, Herbert (1975: 23) points out
that these passages "describe God as the sole ruler of history. The verse
about Lebanon, he argues, may be regarded as a parenthesis which
describes even the most extravagant sacrifices as inadequate means
of expressing man's worship. The might of empires and the pomp of
kings are insignificant before the real majesty of God."

Second Isaiah and the Return to the Promised Land

Basic Text: Second Isaiah attempts to assure the Jewish people that
they, with God's aid, have the ability to return to the Promised Land.
They are growing stronger, while the nations that suppress them are
weakening. According to the prophet, "Listen to me, O Jacob, and
Israel, whom I called: I am He; I am the first, and I am the last" (Isa.
48:12). God promises them success (Isa. 48:20–22):

> Go out from Babylon, flee from Chaldea,
> declare this with a shout of joy, proclaim it,
> send it forth to the end of the earth;
> say, "The Lord has redeemed his servant Jacob!"
> They did not thirst when he led them through the deserts:
> he made water flow for them from the rock;
> he split open the rock and the water gushed out.
> "There is no peace," says the LORD, "for the wicked."

In the *KJV*:

> Go ye forth of Babylon, flee ye from the Chaldeans, with a
> voice of singing declare ye, tell this, utter it *even* to the
> end of the earth; say ye, The LORD hath redeemed his servant
> Jacob.

And they thirsted not *when* he led them through the deserts:
he caused the waters to flow out of the rock for them: he clave
the rock also, and the waters gushed out.
There is no peace, saith the LORD, unto the wicked.

Political Implications: Second Isaiah correctly predicts that
the Jews will be allowed to return to their homeland, but the
comparisons with the Exodus from Egypt are misleading. Instead
of a reluctant Pharaoh who resisted releasing the Israelite slaves
from bondage, the Jews were given the opportunity to return
to their homeland shortly after the Babylonian Empire fell to
Cyrus of Persia. Cyrus issued a decree in 538 BCE allowing Jews
to return to their native land. But the Jews knew that conditions
had deteriorated and that they would face many hardships if they
returned. Most did not. Herbert (1975: 85) argues that this exodus
from Babylon will be even more marvelous than the first exodus
from Egypt "since the divine work of salvation is good news for
all mankind."

Third Isaiah

Basic Text: Although scholars agree that chapters 56–66 are
postexilic, they are difficult to date because there are few references
to specific political events. The content can be easily summarized.
Chapters 56–58 contain prophecies and judgments against the resto-
ration community. Chapter 59 is a call for repentance, while chapters
60–62 contain promises of salvation. Chapters 63 and 64 provide a
lament for the community and report God's response. Finally, chapters 65 and 66 contain future prophesies of judgments and promises
of final salvation.[5]

The prophet reminds the people that God loves justice (Isa. 61:8):

> For I the LORD love justice,
> I hate robbery and wrongdoing;
> I will faithfully give them their
> recompense,
> and I will make an everlasting
> covenant with them.

In the *KJV*:

> For I the LORD love judgment, I hate robbery for burnt offering;
> and I will direct their work in truth, and I will make an everlasting
> covenant with them.

Moreover, God promises to protect Jerusalem (Isa. 62:6–7):

> Upon your walls, O Jerusalem,
> I have posted sentinels;
> all day and all night
> they shall never be silent.
> You who remind the LORD,
> take no rest
> and give him no rest
> until he establishes Jerusalem
> and makes it renowned throughout the earth.

Or, in the *KJV*:

> I have set watchmen upon thy walls, O Jerusalem,
> *which* shall never hold their peace day nor night:
> ye that make mention of the LORD, keep not silence.
> And give him no rest, till he establish, and till he make
> Jerusalem a praise in the earth.

Political Implications: In the first passage, God emphasizes the importance of justice, a value just below the importance of rejecting idolatry. One can argue that the verse shows God "declaring his hostility to all oppression and his activities on behalf of all his loyal worshippers" (Herbert, 1975: 164). In that case, Jews may have no special claim by virtue of physical descent (see Rom. 4:13–14). But one can also argue, as Blenkinsopp does in his *Anchor Bible* Commentary on *Isaiah* 56–66 (229), that the passage shows that, "since YHVH is a God of Justice (cf. Ps. 37:28) he opposes the rapine and wrongdoing from which Israel has suffered for so long."

"You who remind the Lord" or "Ye who mention the LORD" has been translated many ways. *The Jewish Publication Society* uses "O you, the LORD's remembrancers," the *Anchor Bible* translation employs, "O you who invoke YHVH's name," and the *New English Bible*, reads, "You who invoked the LORD's name." According to Herbert (1975: 168), the phrase "You who invoke the LORD's name" has much greater significance in Hebrew than the English translation suggests. He writes, "The word for *invoke* is the word used for one of David's court officials (2 Sam. 8:16; 'secretary of state') whose function appears to have been to keep the king constantly informed about events so that he might take appropriate action."

Perhaps the promise to guard Jerusalem is conditional, although *Third Isaiah* does not spell out those conditions. Although the

Second Temple was destroyed in 70 CE, there was a second rebellion against Rome led by Simon Bar Kakhba, which began in 132 CE and was quashed in 135 CE. The Emperor Hadrian (who reigned between 117 and 138) barred all Jews from Jerusalem and renamed the city Aella Capitolina, dedicating it to Jupiter. The city came under Islamic rule in 638, and Sunni Muslims consider the Al-Aqsa mosque their third holiest site. In 1090, some Jews fought with the Arabs against the Christians during the Crusades. Although there was always a Jewish presence in the Holy Land between the defeat of Bar Kokhba and the Israeli Declaration of Independence in 1948, large-scale immigration from Europe did not begin until the 1880s (see Martin Gilbert, 1993).[6] Asher Arian (2005: 20) reports that in 1882, the total population of Eretz Israel (the Land of Israel) was 600,000, of whom only 24,000 were Jews, only 4.0 percent. Although the Western half of Jerusalem came under Jewish control after the War of Independence (1948–49), Jordan controlled East Jerusalem, including the Jewish Quarter of the Old City, until the Six Day War in June 1967. Although Israel claims sovereignty over all of Jerusalem, other countries do not recognize this claim. Today, 469,300 Jews live in metropolitan Jerusalem, which has a total population of 706,400. Of these Jews, 180,000, some 38 percent of Jerusalem's Jews, live in East Jerusalem.[7] Arian estimates that in 2003, the total population of Israel was 6,631,000, of whom 5,094,000 were Jews, 76.8 percent. On the other hand, if one includes non-Jews living in the territories, the total population rises to 9,800,000, and Jews make up only 52.0 percent. In addition, Arian estimates that the total percentage of the Jews in the world living in Israel has risen dramatically. In 1882, it was only 0.3 percent. Between 1939 and 1954, as the result of the Holocaust and immigration to Israel,[8] the percentage of the world's Jews living in Israel rose from 2.8 percent to 12.8 percent. As of 2003, Arian estimates that 39.0 percent of the Jews in the world lived in Israel.

Notes

1. Perhaps indicative of its stature, the *Book of Isaiah* appears immediately after *2 Kings* in the *Hebrew Bible*. It is thus the twelfth book in the *Hebrew Bible*. In the *Christian Scriptures*, it appears in The Prophetic Books and is the twenty-third book in the Bible.

2. Between 1917 and 1919, Max Weber published articles that later appeared as *Das Antike Judentum* (1921), which appeared as *Ancient Judaism* in 1952. He has an extensive discussion of the Hebrew prophets (Chapters XI and XII), with a great deal of material about Isaiah and Jeremiah.

3. In his translation for the *Anchor Bible* series, Joseph Blenkinsopp (2000a) provides the following wording, "Wherefore, the Lord God himself will give you a sign: See, the young woman is pregnant and about to give birth to a son; she will give him the name Immanuel." I consulted five Jewish translations and all used the term "young woman." This is scarcely surprising since the Hebrew word *almah* used here means "young woman," not a "virgin." The Vulgate, which is the authoritative Catholic Bible, uses virgo, which *The New American Bible,* generally considered the best Roman Catholic English translation, reads, "Therefore the Lord himself will give you this sign: a virgin shall be with child, and bear a son, and shall name him Immanuel." Moreover, there are many Protestant translations that use the word virgin. See, for example, many of the translations available at http://www.biblegateway.com.

4. My discussion draws upon Blenkinsopp's discussion of *Isaiah, 1–39* (46–79).

5. This summary is based upon a summary of *The Book of Isaiah* in the *Harper Collins Bible Dictionary*, p. 464.

6. Martin Gilbert (1977: 37) estimates that there were more Jews than Muslims in Jerusalem in 1845. He reports that, according to the Prussian council, there were 7,120 Jews, 5,000 Muslims, 3,390 Christians, 800 Turkish Soldiers, and 100 Europeans. According to this count, 43 percent of the population of 16,410 was Jewish.

7. Most Jewish Israelis differentiate between Jewish "neighborhoods" in East Jerusalem and Jewish "settlements" in the West Bank. Israeli Prime Minister Benjamin Netanyahu underlined this distinction in a speech at the American Israel Public Affairs Committee (AIPAC) in March 2010. "The Jewish people were building in Jerusalem 3,000 years ago and the Jewish people are building Jerusalem today. Jerusalem is not a settlement. It is our capital." See: http://www.realclearworld.com/articles/2010/03/23/netanyahu_address_at_aipac_2010_98877.html, accessed on August 9, 2010.

8. Lucy S. Dawidowicz (1986: 403) estimates that 5,933,900 Jews were annihilated during the "Final Solution." She provides an extremely useful country-by-country discussion of the fate of European Jews (357–401). For an extensive compilation of evidence, see Raul Hilberg's (1985) three-volume study. For two outstanding studies, see Saul Friedländer (1997, 2007). Richard J. Evans (2009) discusses the Holocaust from a different point of view in his trilogy on the Third Reich. See especially, Chapters 1 and 3. Mark Mazower (2008) provides a comprehensive study of the Nazi occupation of Europe, including a great deal about their treatment of Jews. See Chapter 12 for his discussion of the Final Solution. The most famous book discussing the Holocaust is Hannah Arendt's (1963) *Eichmann in Jerusalem: A Report on the Banality of Evil*, which raised a firestorm of controversy by blaming Jewish leaders for cooperating with the Nazis. Her book has been republished several times, most recently in 2006 with an introduction by Amos Elon.

15

Jeremiah

Basic Text: Ira Sharkansky (1996: 129–49) provides an excellent summary of the political significance of Jeremiah's prophecy. As he writes (p. 129), "Along with Moses and Samuel, Jeremiah was among the most political of the prophets. He was also one of the most detailed characters in the Hebrew Bible. He was extreme in both the style and the substance of his prophecy. He threatened kings, priests and competing prophets with the end of their regime and urged capitulation in the face of a foreign army. His career occurred in a geopolitical setting that was among the most ominous in a national history that typically was under pressure." Sharkansky argues (p. 129), "There is no indication that he ever succeeded in changing the behaviors of elites or the people. However, he persisted in his intense public criticism of political leaders despite the national emergency and surpassed what the modern democracies have allowed to critics when they have been under stress." And, Sharkansky might have added, he even contributes his name to the English language.[1] *The Book of Jeremiah* also provides a substantial contribution to Jewish Liturgy.[2]

As Jack R. Lundbom, the translator and commentator of the three-volume *Anchor Bible* edition of *Jeremiah*, writes (1999: xv), the book "is the largest, and arguably most complex book, of the Hebrew Bible/Old Testament."[3] Some critics, such as Calvin, completed their commentaries, others such as St. Jerome (c347—420) did not.[4]

Jeremiah's prophetic career began in 627/626 BCE. As Klaus Koch (1984: 13) notes, "We can follow his activity for forty-five years, longer than for any other of the prophets. Once more a critical prophet appears on the stage at a moment when the wheels of world politics begin to turn." About the same time that Jeremiah began to prophesy, the Chaldaean prince Nabopolassar conquered Babylon from the Assyrians, and set up an independent state, fundamentally weakening the Assyrian state. As Koch writes (p. 13), "The moment of Jeremiah's prophetic entry on to the stage coincided with a mighty wave of expectation in his country. Had not Isaiah already prophesied the downfall of Assyrian power, linking this with the vision of a messianically reunited Israel? The fall was now immediately impending!"[5]

But Jeremiah is pessimistic. He sees Judah as sinful and vulnerable. The people have deserted God (Jer. 2:23–24):

> How can you say, "I am not defiled,
> I have not gone after the Baals"?
> Look at your way in the valley;
> know what you have done—
> a restive young camel interlacing her tracks,
> a wild ass at home in the wilderness,
> in her heat sniffing the wind!
> Who can restrain her lust?

And in (Jer. 3:1), he asks:

> If a man divorces his wife
>   and she goes from him
> and becomes another man's wife,
>   will he return to her?
> Would not such a land be greatly
> polluted?
> You have played the whore with
> many lovers;
> and would you return to me?
>   says the LORD.

Later he claims that he will pardon all of Jerusalem if he can find one just man (Jer. 5:1).[6]

Not only is Judah evil, but a new threat is emerging (Jer. 4:13):

> Look! He comes up like clouds,
> his chariots like the whirlwind;
> his horses are swifter than eagles—
> woe to us, for we are ruined!

He continues his prophecy, emphasizing that Judah faces a threat from the north.[7] (Jer. 5:15):

> I am going to bring upon you
> a nation from far away, O house of
> Israel

says the Lord,
It is an enduring nation,
it is an ancient nation,
a nation whose language you do not know,
nor can you understand what they say.

Political Implications: Although Sharkansky argues that *Jeremiah* is the most political of the prophets, he acknowledges that his prophecies are time-bound (p. 144).

As he is comparing ancient Israel to modern Israel, Sharkansky acknowledges that modern Israel, while small, is allied with a superpower, and I would add since 1991, it has been allied with the world's only superpower. Israel is among the wealthiest countries in the Middle East. And, as Sharkansky points out, modern Israel has nuclear weapons.

All the same, Jeremiah's early prophecies are politically relevant in so far as they caution against complacency. Whether moral weakness leads to national decline is problematic, although critics of the Weimar Republic and the French Third Republic made such arguments. They are made today. The threat from the "north" may have been difficult to foresee at the beginning of Jeremiah's prophetic career, but it became increasingly obvious during the last decade. By then Judah was a vassal state of Babylon, and the only two regional superpowers were Egypt and Babylon. Of course, although Egypt is mainly toward the west of Jerusalem, it is also to the south. Babylon, which is geographically equivalent to modern day Iraq, is mainly to the east of Jerusalem, but most of Iraq is north as well. However, the term "north" was much broader in Jeremiah's time. As Koch (1984: 19) explains, "The north, which for the Israelites stretched from Asia Minor to the Caspian Sea, had always, from time immemorial, been a political storm centre. Here, as elsewhere, the critical prophets show themselves to be close observers of world events. The level of practical politics within the metahistory is never overlooked."

Jeremiah Supports Babylon

Basic Text: Even though there were major religious reforms under King Josiah, these reforms ended and were reversed after he is killed or mortally wounded in a battle against the Egyptians at Megiddo in 609 BCE. After a three-month rule by Jehoahaz, he is removed by the Egyptians and replaced by Jehoiakim. But in 605 BCE, King Nebuchadnezzar defeats the Egyptians at Carchemish.[8] About

604 BCE, Jeremiah predicts that Babylon will conquer Jerusalem, but that Babylon itself will be destroyed seventy years later (Jer. 15:1–14). Since Jeremiah is not allowed to prophesy publicly, he dictates a scroll to his scribe Baruch. When it is read to King Jehoiakim, he orders it burned, but Jeremiah dictates a new scroll. Jehoiakim dies in 598 BCE and is followed by the three-month reign of King Jehoiachin (see Table 13.3). During his brief reign, Babylon invades, and he is taken into captivity along with leading citizens and craftsmen from Judah, although as the table shows he reemerges in Matthew's genealogy (Matt. 1:11).

Zedekiah becomes king, but he is a vassal of Babylon. Jeremiah advises that Judah accept Babylonian rule. Others disagree. Egypt was much closer. Sharkansky reports that a modern scholar estimates that an army could march from Egypt to Jerusalem in fifteen days, while it would take seventy-five days to march from Babylon to Jerusalem (Sharkansky, p. 131). But Babylon was the emerging power, as we saw above, and it had recently defeated Egypt.

Shortly after Zedekiah becomes king, Jeremiah puts on a wooden yoke to symbolize his prophecy that Judah must submit to Babylon. Another prophet, Hananiah breaks the yoke, but Jeremiah replaces it with an iron yoke. He predicts Hananiah's death, and he dies two months later.[9] Even though Jeremiah sees no hope for Jerusalem's chances if the king rebels against Babylon, he holds out hope for its future (Jer. 33:14–17):

> The days are surely coming, says the LORD, when I will fulfill the promise I made to the house of Israel and the house of Judah. In those days and at that time I will cause a righteous Branch to spring up for David; and he shall execute justice and righteousness in the land. In those days Judah will be saved and Jerusalem will live in safety. And this is the name by which it will be called: "The LORD is our righteousness."
>
> For thus says the LORD: David shall never lack a man to sit on the throne of the house of Israel.

In the *KJV*:

> Behold, the days come, saith the LORD, that I will perform that good thing which I have promised unto the house of Israel and to the house of Judah. In those days, and at that time, will I cause the Branch of righteousness to grow up unto David; and he shall execute judgment and righteousness in the land. In those days shall Judah be saved, and Jerusalem shall dwell safely; and this *is the name* wherewith she shall be called, the LORD our righteousness. For

thus saith the LORD; David shall never want a man to sit upon the throne of the house of Israel.

When Zedekiah rebels against Babylon, Nebuchadrezzar[10] and his army lay siege to Jerusalem, and the siege lasts one year and seven months. Jeremiah urges capitulation.

Zedekiah imprisons Jeremiah, but also seeks his counsel, which he refuses to accept. Several officials ask the king for permission to kill Jeremiah, and he agrees. They lower him by ropes into a waterless cistern, and he sinks into the mud. But he is rescued by Ebed-melech, an Ethiopian eunuch, who tells the king that it is unjust to kill the prophet. However, he is reimprisoned. When Jerusalem finally falls to the Babylonians, they treat Jeremiah well and do not take him into captivity. I have already reported Zedekiah's fate, (Chapter 13) but it is repeated in Jeremiah (Jer. 39:6–7, 52:31–34).

Gedalia, the member of a prominent Jerusalem family, is appointed as the Babylonian governor of Judea. He is assassinated, and many Jews fear severe reprisals and flee to Egypt.[11] Jeremiah urges them not to flee, but is forced to move with them to Egypt. Before leaving he dictates prophecies to his scribe about the fate of Egypt, the Philistines, Moab, Ammon, Edom, Damascus, Babylon, and of Israel and Judah. Except for Israel and Judah, all these prophecies foretell disaster. As for Israel and Judah (Jer. 50:19–20):

> I will restore Israel to its pasture, and it shall feed on Carmel and in Bashan, and on the hills of Ephraim and in Gilead its hunger shall be satisfied. In those days and at that time, says the LORD, the iniquity of Israel shall be sought, and there shall be none; and the sins of Judah, and none shall be found; for I will pardon the remnant that I have spared.

In the *KJV*:

> And I will bring Israel again to his habitation, and he shall feed on Carmel and and Bashan, and his soul shall be satisfied upon Mount Ephraim and Gilead. In those days, and in that time, saith the LORD, the iniquity of Israel shall be sought for, and *there shall be* none; and the sins of Judah, and they shall not be found; for I will pardon them whom I reserve.

Political Implications: With the benefit of 2,600 years worth of hindsight, it is easy to see that Zedekiah's policy of defying Babylon was suicidal and that his hopes that Egypt would provide sufficient aid were misguided. The Battle of Carchemish, fought only sixteen years before, clearly demonstrated Babylon's military superiority, and eight years earlier Babylon had occupied Jerusalem.

According to Abraham J. Heschel (p. 176), Jeremiah is not to be judged by his political foresight, since he was not a political prognosticator. "It is not political sagacity that explains Jeremiah's opposition to the stand of rulers of the kingdom, implying a reversal of the position taken by Isaiah that Judah should not capitulate to Assyria. The prophet does not see the world from the point of view of political theory; he is a person who sees the world from the point of view of God; he sees the world through the eyes of God. To Jeremiah, the relationship to Nebuchadnezzar was much less important than the relationship to God."

Notes

1. According to the Eleventh Edition of the *Merriam Webster's Collegiate Dictionary*, a jeremiad is "a prolonged lamentation or complaint" or "a cautionary and angry harangue."
2. In both the *Hebrew Bible* and the *Christian Scriptures, Jeremiah* comes directly after *Isaiah*. But, as we saw in Chapter 14, *Isaiah* is placed earlier in the *Hebrew Bible*. As a result, *Jeremiah* is the thirteenth book of the *Hebrew Bible* and the twenty-fourth book of the *Christian Scriptures*.
3. There is an earlier one-volume translation and commentary in the *Anchor Bible Series* by John Bright. Although published in 1965, it is still helpful in understanding the political implication of Jeremiah's prophecies.
4. In Jerome's case, his monastery was destroyed by fire in 416, three years before his death.
5. For an excellent summary of the historical conditions during Jeremiah's career, see Bright's (1965: xxviii–liv) one-volume *Anchor Bible* translation and commentary for the *Anchor Bible* series.
6. As Jack R. Lundrum reminds us in his *Anchor Bible* commentary of *Jeremiah 1–29* (376), Jeremiah seems to be anticipating by 250 years Diogenes's search for one honest man in the city of Athens.
7. According to my count, Jeremiah warns of a threat from the north in a total of twenty-five verses, in three verses (13, 14, and 15) in the first chapter alone.
8. In this battle, fought on the Euphrates River, a Babylonian army defeated a combined force of Egyptians and Assyrians.
9. This estimate of two months is based upon the *Soncino* commentary, 188.
10. This variation in spelling results from differences in the Masoretic (the authoritative Hebrew) text.
11. There is a fast day to commemorate Gedaliah which is usually observed after the second day of Rosh Hashanah (Head of the Year). The prophet Zechariah initiated it, although he does not specifically mention Gedaliah by name (Zech. 8:19).

16

Esther

Queen Vashti is Deposed

Basic Text: In the *Hebrew Bible*, the *Book of Esther* is the last of the five *Megillot* (scrolls) and thus part of the Writings. It comes after *Ecclesiastes* and before *Daniel*. It is the last of twelve Historical Books of the *Christian Scriptures*, coming after *Nehemiah* and before *Job*. It is the thirty-fourth book of the *Hebrew* Bible and the seventeenth book of the *Christian Scriptures*. Many readers of the Bible know that it does not mention God.[1] It is the only book of the *Hebrew Bible* for which not even a fragment is found in the Dead Sea scrolls. In his translation for the *Anchor Bible* series, Carey A. Moore writes (1971: xvi), "No other book of the Old Testament has received such mixed reviews by good, God-fearing men as the Book of Esther." The great Jewish scholar Maimonides (1135–1204) viewed it as second only to the *Pentateuch* in importance. On the other hand, Martin Luther (1483–1546) wrote, "I am so hostile to this book [II Maccabees] and to Esther that I could wish they did not exist at all" (quoted in Moore, 1971: xvi).

The story begins in the third year of the reign of the Persian King Xerxes I (486 BCE–465 BCE), who is referred to as "Ahasuerus" in most English translations, including the *KJV*. He first holds a banquet lasting 180 days for his nobles and provincial governors, and following that gives a seven-day banquet for all the men living in the citadel of his capital, Susa.[2] His Queen, Vashti, gives a banquet for the women in the palace. On the seventh day, "when the king was merry with wine" (Esther 1:10), he sent his seven eunuchs to order Vashti to appear "wearing the royal crown" (Esther 1:11).[3] Vashti refuses, and the king is enraged, but before acting he consults the seven officials most familiar with the laws of Persia and Medea. One argues that the queen's actions affront all of the men in the kingdom. When women learn of her disobedience, they will be contemptuous of their own husbands. The official recommends that Vashti be deposed. Moreover, there shall be a royal declaration that cannot be altered declaring that "every man should be master in his own house" (Esther 1:21). Ahasuerus is pleased with this advice and follows it, and letters are sent throughout his kingdom.

Political Implications: In his analysis of the political teachings of the *Book of Esther*, Yoram Hazony (1995: 11) argues that the goal of the lengthy banquet is to display the king's wealth. The banquet allows him "to create a setting in which the entire empire can see the immense financial and administrative power which he, the king, can muster and dissipate at whim." However, Hazony argues that despite his power, the monarch "never makes a decision of substance on his own in the entire book of Esther. . . . The result is that despite having vast powers at his disposal, Ahashverosh is at all times propelled by the pressures and manipulation of those around him—as is the state itself" (p. 15).

Avivah Gottlieb Zornberg (2009: 110) makes a similar observation. "Ahasuerus never issues an edict that has not been directly suggested to him. . . . Variously described in the midrash as a 'foolish king' and as a 'volatile king,' "he is a lord of misrule, tricked out in the panoply of majesty. Essentially no king at all. His ostentatious banquets, grotesquely extended through time (180 days), are to 'to show' a splendor and glory that lacks substance." "According to one midrashic tradition," she (p. 110) writes, "he has usurped the throne, on which he sits rather tentatively: a throne that is a close replica of the throne of King Solomon, which he coveted during the sack of Jerusalem."

Michael V. Fox argues that the book also introduces a totally unrealistic condition that rules once issued could not be repealed. He argues that the rule is referred to in *Daniel*, but not in any Persian or Greek source (1991: 22). As he correctly notes, a royal edict declaring that women must be subservient to their husbands is unenforceable.

Esther Becomes Queen

Basic Text: After Vashti is deposed, the king's anger abates. His servants suggest holding a contest to find a new queen. Beautiful young virgins should be selected throughout the kingdom, brought to his harem, turned over to his chief eunuch, Hegai, for beauty treatment, and the king should then select the virgin who pleases him most as his queen. Mordecai and Esther are now introduced to the story. Mordecai is a Benjaminite. His grandfather, Kish, was taken to Babylon at the time of the Babylonian captivity. Mordecai had brought up his cousin, whose Hebrew name is Hadassah (myrtle), but whose Persian name is Esther (Persian for star). When Esther is summoned to the beauty contest, Mordecai advises her not to reveal her background. Hegai favors Esther.

When Esther spends a night with the king, "she asked for nothing except what Hegai the king's eunuch, who had charge of the women, advised" (Esther 2:15). The king favors Esther, marries her, and holds a feast in her honor. After Esther becomes queen, Mordecai learns that two of the king's eunuchs plan to assassinate the king. He passes the news on to Esther, and she warns the king in Mordecai's name. The plot is investigated, found to be genuine, the men are hanged, and these events are recorded in the king's annals. After these things, Haman, the son of Hammedatha the Agagite, is named as the king's chief official.

Political Implications: Hazony argues that it was not necessarily Esther's beauty that leads Ahasuerus to select her, but her cleverness in following Hegai's advice about pleasing the king. Once chosen, she is in a position to pass on the information about the plot against the king's life. But, according to Hazony, once having executed the two plotters, the king does not reward Mordecai, whose report has saved his life. Up to now, the king has received counsel from eighteen named advisors (Hazony, p. 50). But he chooses an advisor who has not been mentioned at all until his appointment is reported, Haman.

We now have the setting for a confrontation that is a thousand years old: Haman appears to be the direct descendant of King Agag of the Amalekites, whom Saul defeats, but who Samuel kills (see Chapter 10), and Mordecai, although not a direct descendant of Saul, is from the same tribe and, apparently, the same family.

Haman Plots to Destroy the Jews

Basic Text: The king issues a command that all of his officials must bow to Haman. Mordecai refuses. When asked why he does not obey, he tells the king's servants that he is a Jew. Haman is furious, "But he thought it beneath him to lay hands on Mordecai alone" (Esther 3:6). Instead, he plots to kill all the Jews in Ahasuerus's kingdom. Haman and his colleagues cast lots to determine the day on which the Jews should be slaughtered, and the day chosen is the thirteenth day of the month of Adar. Haman then approaches the king and tells him, "There is a certain people scattered and separated among the peoples in all the provinces of your kingdom; their laws are different from those of every other people, and they do not keep the king's laws, so that it is not appropriate for the king to tolerate them" (Esther 3:8). Haman promises to pay ten thousand talents of silver to the king's treasury if he is authorized to eliminate them.

The king gives Haman his signet ring and tells him to forget about the payment. Haman drafts orders for destroying the Jews and sends them by royal messengers throughout the kingdom. The message sends orders "to destroy, to kill, and to annihilate all Jews, young and old, women and children, in one day, the thirteenth day of the twelfth month, which is the month of Adar, and to plunder their goods" (Esther 3:13).

Political Implications: The king has consolidated all power into the hands of a single advisor, Haman. The king's other servants must bow to him. Mordecai's refusal to comply is not explained. He says he is a Jew, but while that would preclude him from bowing to idols, it would not prevent him from bowing to royal officials. Haman does not restrict his desire for revenge to Mordecai, but to all Jews, including women and children. The hatred between the Amalekites and the Israelites goes back to the Exodus from Egypt. Haman's order "to destroy, to kill, and to annihilate" the Jews parallel God's order to "strike down the Amelek" and to put everything of his "under the ban," including women, children, and animals (1 Sam. 15:3).

Esther and Mordecai Plan to Save the Jews

Basic Text: Mordecai wears sackcloth and ashes and therefore is not allowed inside the king's gate. Esther quickly learns of Mordecai's symbolic mourning and sends one of her attendants to discover the problem. Mordecai sends her a copy of the king's decree. She sees Mordecai and he asks her to intervene. Esther reminds Mordecai that the penalty for appearing before the king unsummoned is death. Moreover, she has not been summoned for thirty days. One is spared only if the king holds out his golden scepter. But Mordecai replies, "Do not think that in the king's palace you will escape any more than all the other Jews. For if you keep silence at such a time as this, relief and deliverance will rise for the Jews from another quarter, but you and your father's family will perish. Who knows? Perhaps you have come to royal dignity for just such a time as this" (Esther 4:13–14).

Esther agrees to approach the king unsummoned, but asks that all the Jews of Susa fast for her for three days. She and her maids will also fast. "After that I will go to the king, though it is against the law;

and if I perish, I perish" (Esther 4: 16). Three days later, when Esther enters the inner court, the king holds out his golden scepter. He asks for her request, but she only asks that he attend a banquet she will arrange for him and for Haman that evening. He agrees. After the banquet, Ahasuerus again asks what she wishes, but she merely asks that the king and Haman come to another banquet the following evening. Haman returns home and sees Mordecai as he leaves. He tells his wife and his friends that despite all his wealth, his many sons, and his prominence, and even being invited to dinner with the king and queen, he can find no satisfaction in life when he sees Mordecai at the king's gate. His wife and friends suggest that he build a gallows fifty cubits (about seventy feet) high, and he sets out to ask the king's permission to hang Mordecai.

Political Implication: Haman appears to have accumulated all the political power in the kingdom. However, he lacks the authority to order an execution, so he is now on his way to ask the king's permission to hang Mordecai.

Haman is Undone and the Jews Saved

Basic Text: The king cannot sleep, so he orders the royal records read. The annals record how Mordecai saved the king's life, and Ahasuerus asks what reward he has received. The records show that he received none, and the king asks who is in the court. Haman has just entered to request permission to hang Mordecai. The king summons Haman and asks him, "What shall be done for the man whom the king wishes to honor?" (Esther 6:6). (In the *KJV*, "What shall be done unto the man whom the king delighteth to honour?")

"Haman said to himself, Whom would the king wish to honor more than me?" (Esther 6:6). (In the *KJV*, "Now Haman thought in his heart, To whom would the king delight to do honour more than to myself?") He suggests that the person be given royal robes that the king has worn, be placed upon a horse the king has ridden, and that the royal crown be placed upon his head. Then a leading official should conduct the man throughout the city proclaiming, "Thus shall it be done for the man whom the king wishes to honor" (Esther 6:9). The king commands Haman to do exactly what he has proposed to Mordecai. Haman complies and returns home crestfallen. His wife says, "If Mordecai, before whom your downfall has begun, is of the Jewish people, you will not prevail against him, but will surely fall before him" (Esther 6:13).

As they are talking, Haman is summoned to the second banquet. For the third time, Ahasuerus asks Esther what she requests. She replies, "If I have won your favor, O king, and if it pleases the king, let my life be given to me—that is my petition—and the lives of my people—that is my request. For we have been sold, I and my people, to be destroyed, to be killed, and to be annihilated. If we had been sold merely as slaves, men and women, I would have held my peace; but no enemy can compensate for this damage to the king" (Esther 7:3–4). The king asks who the evildoer is, and Esther replies, "A foe and enemy, this wicked Haman!" (Esther 7:6). The king, very angry, storms into the royal garden, and Haman falls upon Esther's couch to plead with her. But when the king returns and sees Haman on the same couch as Esther, he says, "Will he even assault the queen in my presence; in my own house?" (Esther 7:8).

At this point, Harbona, one of the eunuchs, speaks up, "Look, the very gallows that Haman has prepared for Mordecai, whose word saved the king, stands at Haman's house, fifty cubits high" (Esther 7:9). The king immediately orders that Haman himself be hanged on the gallows he built to hang Mordecai.

On the same day, Ahasuerus the king gives Haman's house to Esther and gives his royal ring to Mordecai. But his original orders to destroy the Jews cannot be rescinded. He will allow Mordecai to prevent their destruction. Mordecai instead issues orders allowing Jews to organize and defend themselves and to attack their enemies. Moreover, many officials throughout the kingdom support the Jews (Esther 9:3). On the day planned for their destruction, in the city of Susa, the Jews kill five hundred of their enemies, including Haman's ten sons. Esther asks the king for an additional day for the Jews to attack their enemies in Susa, during which another three hundred are killed. She also asks for permission to have the bodies of Haman's sons publicly impaled, and, this, too, is granted. Throughout all the king's provinces, 75,000 of the Jews' enemies are killed. Esther and Mordecai issue letters decreeing that a new holiday, Purim, be established, to celebrate their victory.[4] Moreover, Mordecai continues to be the king's advisor and issues tax reforms that improve the kingdom's finances.

Political Implications: As Hazony argues (1995: 191), Mordecai protects the Jews by (a) helping them organize militarily, (b) gaining the support of provincial and local administrators, and (c) building his own reputation. There is a great deal of coincidence that aids the Jews, not the least of which is the choice of Esther as queen, as well as the king being reminded of Mordecai's help in preventing his assassination.

A great deal of credit must go to Esther, who risks her life in entering the king's inner chamber without being summoned, as well as the timing of her actual request. On the second night, she is asked for her request a third time, and Ahasuerus promises for the third time to grant it even if it is half his kingdom. She knows she cannot delay again and condemns Haman. Purim is celebrated with great festivity in Israel, whereas in the United States, most Gentiles are not aware that it is being celebrated. But Julius Streicher, the editor of the Nazi anti-Semitic journal, *Der Stürmer* was aware of this festival. Among his last words to his hangman were, "Purim Festival of 1946!"(Giles MacDonogh, 2007: 450).

Richard Bauckham (1989: 130) argues that the *Book of Esther* must be read in light of the Holocaust. "Esther's relevance for Christians ought to derive, in the first place, from the fact that, while becoming less of a Christian book than almost any other book of the Old Testament, Esther has remained a Jewish book, whose annual reading at Purim, throughout the centuries of persecution, needed no interpretation to make it relevant to contemporary experience. In light of this history, Christians would do well to read the book of Esther precisely as a Jewish book whose presence in the Christian Bible claims Christian attention. They should read Esther as the book which Jewish inmates of the Nazi death-camps were forbidden to read, but wrote out from memory and read in secret on Purim."

Notes

1. On the other hand, when Esther decides to risk her life by appearing before the king without being summoned, she asks Mordecai to have the Jews of Susa fast on her behalf, and she says that she and her maids will fast (Esther 4:16).
2. According to the *Masoretic Text*, the banquet is held at Shushan, the winter capital of Persia. All five Jewish translations I consulted give the location as Shushan.
3. Some rabbis argue this means wearing only her crown. See the *Soncino* edition of *The Five Meggiloth*, 141.
4. The name takes the Persian word for "lot" and gives it a Hebrew masculine plural form.

17

Daniel

Daniel Advises Nebuchadnezzar

Basic Text: In the *Hebrew Bible, Daniel* is part of the Writings, coming after *Esther* and before *Ezra*, whereas in the *Christian Scriptures* it is among the Prophetic Books, coming after *Ezekiel* and before *Hosea*. It is the thirty-fifth book of the *Hebrew Bible* and the twenty-seventh book of the *Christian Scriptures.*

In the third year of King Jehoiakim's reign as King of Judah, Daniel, Hananiah, Mishael, and Azariah, all of the tribe of Judah, are deported to Babylon. They are chosen for they are handsome, wise, well educated, and knowledgeable. They are to be educated so that they can serve King Nebuchadnezzar. Each is given a new name. Daniel is called Belteshazzar; Hananiah, Shadrach; Mishael, Meshach; and Azariah, Abednego. Even though they refuse to eat meat or drink wine, they appeared healthier and fatter than those on the royal diet. They gain a great deal of knowledge, and when their training period is over the king tests them and finds them "ten times better than all the magicians and enchanters in his whole kingdom" (Dan. 1:20).

Nebuchadnezzar has a dream and demands that it be interpreted. But he refuses to reveal its content, and his advisors complain that no one can interpret a dream unless they know what it was. The king flies into a rage and orders that all the wise men of Babylon be destroyed. When Daniel and his fellow Jews are to be killed, he asks God to aid him.

Daniel appears before Nebuchadnezzar and explains that he himself cannot interpret the dream, "but there is a God in heaven who reveals mysteries, and he has disclosed to King Nebuchadnezzar what will happen at the end of days" (Dan. 2:28). Daniel not only reveals its content, but interprets it. He explains that after Nebuchadnezzar's reign, there will be an inferior kingdom; after that, a third kingdom will rule over the entire earth; and after that there will be a fourth kingdom that will be as strong as iron, but which will be divided. The king accepts Daniel's interpretation, rewards him, and promotes him to rule over the province of Babylon. Daniel asks that his friends be promoted and King Nebuchadnezzar complies.

Political Implications: Parallels between Joseph and Daniel are obvious. Both are foreigners, and both rise to prominence because they can interpret dreams. Moreover, both claim that God is the true interpreter.

As Wildavsky (1993: 126–29) argues, Joseph is much more assimilated to Egyptian society than Daniel is to Babylonian. Moreover, when he needs aid, Daniel turns to prayer, whereas there is no indication that Joseph asks for divine help.

Joseph's correct interpretations of Pharaoh's dreams leads to saving the Egyptian people as well as his own family, whereas Daniel's interpretations merely satisfy his monarchs' curiosity and save the lives of the king's counselors. Finally, it is worth noting that half of *Daniel* is written in Hebrew (1:1 through 2:4a and 8:1 through 12:13) and half in Aramaic (2:4b through 7:28), and that commentators consider the Aramaic to be superior in literary style to the Hebrew (see Raymond Hammer [1976: 83—84], on *Daniel* in the *Cambridge Bible Commentary* in *The New English Bible*, suggesting that the author's native language was Aramaic).

King Nebuchadnezzar's Madness

Basic Text: Chapter 3, in which Shadrach, Meshach, and Abednego are thrown into a fiery furnace for refusing to worship a specially constructed idol, does not mention Daniel, nor does it contain a political message. That they are delivered from this ordeal has a religious message, and even leads Nebuchadnezzar to issue a decree against blaspheming against their God. In the next chapter, the king has another dream; only now he reports its content. He dreams about a great tree that reaches to heaven, with abundant foliage, in which animals find shade, and in which birds nest. But the branches are cut down and its foliage and fruit scattered. A stump remains. A "holy watcher" (Dan. 4:13) decreed that "let seven times pass over him" (Dan. 4:16). None of the wise men is able to interpret the dream, so the king turns to Daniel.

Daniel is frightened by the dream and tells the king that perhaps it was intended for his enemies. But if it is meant to warn the king, the tree represents the monarch and the dream shows that he will be brought down and will live like an animal for seven years. That a stump remains shows that his kingdom will be reestablished. He advises the king to atone for his sins. But apparently the king does not atone, and a year later, he is seized by madness for seven years. After seven years, his sanity is restored.

Political Implications: Daniel is willing to take great risks to provide a true interpretation. Granted, he hedges his bets somewhat by saying that the dream may reveal the future for the king's enemies, but by advising Nebuchadnezzar to repent, he obviously shows that he believes the dream foretells the king's fate. Daniel does not appear to be rewarded for giving the correct interpretation, but he is not punished either.

Daniel Advises Belshazzar

Basic Text: King Belshazzar holds a great festival and "under the influence of the wine" (Dan. 5:2) he calls for the golden vessels that his father had taken from Jerusalem; and the king, his lords, his wives, and his concubines use them to drink wine. Immediately, the fingers of a human hand appear and write on the palace wall. But none of his enchanters, Chaldeans, or diviners can read the writing.

The queen (probably the queen mother) suggests that he summon Daniel. The king summons Daniel and asks him to read and interpret the writing. He promises to promote Daniel to the third rank in the kingdom if he can do so. Daniel tells the king that he may keep his gifts. He reminds the king that his father was punished by madness for his pride, but that despite this example, Belshazzar has acted pridefully. "You have exalted yourself against the LORD of heaven!" (Dan. 5:23). He took vessels from the temple to use in a banquet praising gods made of metal, wood, and stone.

Daniel tells him that the writings say "MENE, MENE, TEKEL, PARSIN" (Dan. 5: 25). These words mean, "MENE, God has numbered the days of your kingdom and brought it to an end; TEKEL, you have been weighed on the scales and found wanting; PERES, your kingdom is divided and given to the Medes and Persians" (Dan. 5:26–28). Belshazzar commands that Daniel be clothed in purple, that a gold chain be placed around his neck, and he issues a proclamation that he should be ranked third in the kingdom. That very night Belshazzar is killed. Darius the Mede becomes king.

Political Implications: Even though Daniel has proved an able interpreter of dreams for his father, Belshazzar does not summon him until the queen suggests that he do so. Granted, reading and interpreting strange writing should not be as difficult as interpreting unreported dreams. Nonetheless, the reader should be confident that Daniel will succeed. However, Daniel once again takes great risks in reporting such a negative dream to Belshazzaar. Not only is his kingdom to end, but he is chastised for his prideful behavior and specifically for using the vessels taken from the temple in Jerusalem. Despite this, Belshazzar gives Daniel his promised reward.

Daniel and the Lions' Den

Basic Text: Chapter 6 recounts the most famous episode in Daniel's life—his escape from the lions' den. Daniel holds a high position under King Darius, but other leaders jealous of him can find no reason for bringing about his downfall. They say, "We shall not find any ground for complaint against this Daniel unless we find it in connection with the law of his God" (Dan. 6:5). So these advisors propose that the king establish a law that for thirty days anyone who prays to anyone, divine or human, except to the king himself will be thrown into a den of lions. The king is asked to sign a document so that it cannot be revoked. Despite this law, Daniel continues to pray to his God from the upper rooms of his house in a room facing Jerusalem with the windows open.

The conspirators against Daniel find him praying and approach the king, reminding him of his decree, pointing out that it cannot be revoked. King Darius is greatly distressed, but has to throw Daniel into the den of lions. However, he tells Daniel that, "May your God, whom you faithfully serve, deliver you!" (Dan. 6:16). The king prays for Daniel, and at daybreak he rushes down to see how he is faring. Daniel is still alive and tells the king that God has sent an angel to shut the lions' mouths. The king is very glad and commands that Daniel be taken from the den. He orders that Daniel's accusers, along with their wives and their children, be thrown into the den. They are all killed before they reach the bottom. The king then writes a decree which he sends to his entire kingdom that people should "tremble and fear before the God of Daniel" (Dan. 6:26).

Political Implications: This mentions the rule that royal edicts could not be revoked, an edict that played an important role in the *Book of Esther* (see Chapter 16). It plays a role here as well since Darius does not want to execute Daniel. Few readers will expect Daniel to be devoured. It seems reasonable that Darius will punish the conspirators against Daniel. Yet, as Louis F. Hartman and Alexander A. Di Lella point out in their *Anchor Bible* translation (1978: 200), "That the wives and children of these men had to share their gruesome fate seems repugnant to modern ideas of justice. But in Old Testament times the concept of family solidarity often caused a man's whole family to pay the penalty for his crime." Of course, there are twentieth century examples of dictators punishing their opponents' relatives.

Daniel's Prophecies

Basic Text: The last six chapters report visions that Daniel experiences, which have usually been interpreted as visions of future kingdoms. Most Christian scholars consider Chapter 7 to be the most important of these chapters, if not the most important in the entire book. Daniel sees four beasts emerging from the sea. The first is a lion with eagle's wings. The wings are plucked off and the beast is lifted from the ground. Next Daniel sees a bear with fangs in its mouth. After this, he sees a beast, a leopard with four wings on its back. The fourth beast is the most fearsome of all. It has iron teeth and devours the remains of the first three beasts. But this beast too is killed. Daniel receives an interpretation of his vision. The beasts represent four kingdoms that will rule the earth. Then "the holy ones of the Most High shall receive the kingdom and possess the kingdom forever—forever and ever" (Dan. 7:18). According to *Daniel* 7:27:

> The kingship and dominion
> and the greatness of the kingdoms
> under the whole heaven
> shall be given to the people of the
> holy ones of the Most High;
> their kingdom shall be an everlasting
> kingdom,
> and all dominions shall serve and
> obey them.

Political Implications: The political significance of this vision depends on what these beasts signify and when this vision occurred. Some Christian scholars argue that these beasts refer to Babylon, Medeo-Persia, Greece, and Rome. The destruction of the last beast leads to the everlasting kingdom and refers to Christ. If one attributes the dream to Daniel himself, since the Babylonian captivity began in the sixth century BCE, Daniel would have needed great prophetic ability to foresee the dominance of Greece and the Roman Empire.

On the other hand, in their *Anchor Bible* translation, Hartman and Di Lella argue that these beasts represent Babylon, the Medes, the Persians, and the Greek Kingdom of the Seleucids. Nor do they believe there is any reference to Christ. Moreover, they argue that the book was finalized in the second century BCE. The *Jewish Study Bible* agrees with the *Anchor Bible* translators about the meaning of the four beasts and concludes that the book was finalized in 164 BCE.

Hammer (1976: 119–20), in his *Cambridge Bible Commentary*, provides an excellent summary of *Daniel's* meaning:

> The book of Daniel, like the book of Revelation, also written in an age of persecution, asserts that the unseen reality can challenge all appearances. Appearance is only transient. The empires come and go. They may be powerful and fearful, but their destruction is seen as inevitable. The abiding reality is God himself, and God is concerned with this world. He is represented as having his plan and purpose for the world, a plan and purpose which are universal in their scope, embracing all nations.

18

The Gospels

The Genealogy of Jesus

Basic Text: The Gospels present two genealogies of Jesus.[1] The most famous comes at the beginning of *Matthew* 1:1–17, the first of the four gospels. It presents, "An account of the genealogy of Jesus the Messiah, the son of David, the son of Abraham" (1:1). (In the *KJV*, "The book of the generation of Jesus Christ, the son of David, the son of Abraham.") It relates fourteen generations from Abraham to David, fourteen from David to the deportation to Babylon, and fourteen from the deportation to the birth of the Messiah. It notes that Joseph was "the husband of Mary, of whom Jesus was born, who is called the Messiah" (Matt. 1:16). "So all the generations from Abraham to David are fourteen generations; and from David to the deportation to Babylon, fourteen generations; and from the deportation to Babylon to the Messiah, fourteen generations" (Matt. 1:17). In addition to Mary, three other women are named—Tamar (1:3), Rahab (1:5), and Ruth (1:5), and one is mentioned but unnamed—"the wife of Uriah" (1:6). (In the *KJV*, "of her *that had been the wife* of Urias."[2])

Luke's genealogy begins in his third chapter. He reports that, "Jesus was about thirty years of age when he began his work. He was the son (as was thought) of Joseph" (Luke 3:23). In the *KJV*, "And Jesus himself began to be about thirty years of age, being (as was supposed) the son of Joseph." Luke continues backwards to "Seth, son of Adam, son of God" (Luke 3:38). Luke mentions no women in his genealogy, but he earlier reports Mary's miraculous conception (Luke 1:26–35).

Based upon both biblical and extra-biblical sources, it seems likely that Jesus was born about 5 BCE, began his public ministry when he was about thirty, and was executed in either 28 CE or 29 CE (*Harper Collins Bible Dictionary* 510–23], and Ben F. Meyer's entry on Jesus Christ in *The Anchor Bible Dictionary* [vol. 3: 773–96].)

Political Implications: The genealogies are important because they help to establish that Jesus is the Messiah. This is especially true of Matthew's genealogy. In their *Anchor Bible* translation and commentary of *Matthew*, W. F. Albright and C. S. Mann (1971: 5) argue that "Matthew's purpose is to demonstrate who Jesus is: the Messiah.... He is also son of David, of the royal house of Judah by descent. Finally, he is son of Abraham, through whom God had promised that he would bless all the families of the earth.'" Most scholars agree that there are too many discrepancies between the Matthean and Lukan genealogies for them to be reconciled. For example, they do not even agree on the name of Jesus's grandfather, whom *Matthew* (1:15) names as Jacob and whom *Luke* (3:23) names as Heli. They follow different lines after King David's death, with *Matthew* (1:7) naming Solomon, whereas *Luke* (3:31) names Nathan, a son of David who never becomes king. In fact, in tracking Jesus's genealogy from Solomon through the Babylonian captivity all twenty of Judah's kings are descended from David and, *Matthew* lists fourteen of them (for the list between Rehoboam and Zekekiah, see Table 13.3). *Luke* does not name a single one. On the other hand, *Luke* lists more ancestors. *Matthew* includes only forty men tracing Jesus's lineage from Abraham through Joseph; if we end *Luke*'s backward genealogy with Abraham, fifty-five men are named.

Granted, Jesus later states that his descent from David is of little importance (Matt. 22:41–44). "Now, while the Pharisees were gathered together, Jesus asked them the question: 'What do you think of the Messiah? Whose son is he?' They said to him, 'The son of David.' He said to them, 'How is it then that David by the Spirit calls him the Lord, saying:

> The Lord said to my Lord,
> "Sit at my right hand,
> until I put your enemies under your feet."

In my view this statement is ambiguous and does not dispel the widely accepted belief that the Messiah would arise from the Davidic line. Why is it important to establish that Jesus has descended from the House of David? As Christians were attempting to convert non-Christian Jews, it was important to develop appeals that would attract them. The *Hebrew Bible* suggests that the Messiah would emerge from the line of David. God directs the prophet Nathan to declare that David's kingdom would be everlasting. God tells David, through Nathan (2 Sam. 7:15–16): "My loyalty shall not swerve from him [David] as I made it swerve from Saul whom I removed from before you. And your house and your kingship shall be steadfast forever, your throne unshaken forever." The importance of the Davidic kingdom is illustrated in *Psalm* 89:4–5:

> I have sealed a pact with my chosen one,
> I have sworn to David My servant.
> Forevermore I shall make your seed stand firm,
> and make your throne stand strong for all generations.

There are passages in *Isaiah, Jeremiah,* and *Ezekiel* that suggest the future importance of the "stump of Jesse" (Isa. 11:1), "David a righteous Branch" (Jer. 23:5), and "my servant David" (Ezek. 34:23).

The *Synoptic Gospels* refer to the "Son of David" in twenty-one verses: eleven in *Matthew* 1:1; 1:20; 9:27; 12:23; 15:22; 20:30; 20:31; 21:9; 21:15; 22:42; and 22:45; four in *Mark* 10:47; 10:48; 12:35; and 12:37; and six in *Luke* 1:32; 3:31; 18:38; 18:39; 20:41; and 20:44.

As Albright and Mann (1971: 6) maintain, "What is being established in both genealogies is a claim to legitimate Davidic ancestry, even though later Jesus himself is represented as dismissing the Davidic ancestry as of little moment." They note that both *Matthew* and *Luke* claim that Jesus has Davidic ancestry while at the same time they accept the doctrine of virginal conception and birth. But, they conclude (p. 6), "Allowing for the very tenacious traditions with respect to ancestry among Jews at the time of Jesus, we are certainly entitled to say that both evangelists were faithfully recording the traditions they had received."

Augustus' Census

Basic Text: Luke is the only Gospel to mention the census that leads Joseph to take Mary to Bethlehem. "In those days a decree went out from Emperor Augustus that all the world should be registered" (Luke 2:1). (In the *KJV*, "And It came to pass in those days, that there went out a decree from Cæsar Augustus, that all the world should be taxed.") To register, people need to return to their own town. "Joseph also went from the town of Nazareth in Galilee to Judea, to the city of David called Bethlehem, because he was descended from the house and family of David" (Luke 2:4). He goes "with Mary, to whom he was engaged, and who was expecting a child" (Luke 2:5). (In the *KJV*, "with Mary, his espoused wife, being great with child.") She gives birth to a son in a manger, for there is no room at the inn. An angel appears to shepherds and tells them that "to you is born this day in the city of David a Savior, who is the Messiah, the Lord" (Luke 2:11), and tells them where to find him. Then the angel and a heavenly host sings (Luke 2:14):

> "Glory to God in the highest heaven,
> and on earth peace among those
> whom he favors!"

The shepherds go to Bethlehem, find Joseph, Mary, and the child and tell them what they had heard. "Mary treasured all these words and pondered them in her heart" (Luke 2:19) and the shepherds returned home and told people what they saw. On the eighth day, the child was circumcised.

Political Implications: As Joseph A. Fitzmyer, the translator for the *Anchor Bible* editions of *Luke* (1970: 393) argues, "It is clear that the census is a purely literary device used by him to associate Mary and Joseph, residents of Nazareth, with Bethlehem, the town of David, because he knows of a tradition, also attested in *Matthew* 2, that Jesus was born in Bethlehem." Readers would know that David was a Bethlehemite, thus further establishing Jesus's Davidic credentials.

However, as Philip C. Schmitz writes in the *Anchor Bible Dictionary* (vol. 1: 884), "Classical scholars are convinced that there is no evidence for a simultaneous census of every province of the empire." Fitzmyer (p. 393) also concludes "there is no extra-Lucan evidence for such a worldwide census under Augustus."

However, Fitzmyer (p. 394) also notes that by referring to Caesar Augustus, *Luke* depicts the emperor as God's agent in assuring that Jesus is born in the town of David's youth. Fitzmyer writes, "Jesus's Davidic connection is thus dramatically emphasized." Moreover, writing from a somewhat later period than Jesus's lifetime, Luke knows that Augustus was viewed as a highly successful emperor who brought peace to the Roman world. "Thus," Fitzmyer argues, "Luke . . . associates the birth of Jesus with a famous Roman emperor and suggests that the real bearer of peace and salvation to the whole world is the one whose birth occurred in the town of David and was made known by angels of heaven." He concludes, "The child thus born under *Pax Augusta* will eventually be hailed as 'the king, the One Who is to come in the name of the Lord'—and the result will be 'peace in heaven and glory in the highest heaven!'" (Luke 19:38).

Jesus and the Legion of Demons

Basic Text: Mark 5:1–20 and *Luke* 8:26–39 relate the story of Jesus exorcizing multiple demons from a man across the Sea of Galilee from the region of Gerasenes. The man is restrained with chains, but he breaks them. Although people cannot subdue him, he spends most of his time living in tombs. But when he sees Jesus, he runs toward him, bows, and asks Jesus to help him, pleading with Jesus to cleanse him. Jesus asks the spirit his name, but instead of providing their names, the spirits reply, "My name is Legion; for we are many" (Mark 5:9). In *Mark,* the demons beg Jesus not to send them out of the country, and Jesus forces them to enter about two thousand swine (Mark 5:10–13). In *Luke,* the demons beg Jesus not to send them into the abyss. Jesus forces them into an unspecified number of swine (Luke 8:32). In both accounts the swine run into the lake and drown (Mark 5:13; Luke 8:33), and the man is told to return home and tell people what Jesus has done for him (Mark 5:19; Luke 8:39).

Political Implications: As Virgil reminds his readers, Aeneas founds Rome with the aid of the gods. The Romans have a goddess of justice, Justitia, and established courts of justice throughout their empire. The Romans claim to bring peace and commerce, but also to provide justice.

The story of "Legion" presents a not-too-thinly veiled suggestion that the Roman Empire is demonic. As Joel Marcus (2000: 351) argues in his *Anchor Bible* translation of *Mark, 1–8,* "The demon's self-identification may also have a political nuance, since the 'legion' was a Latin military term . . . and the narrative may have originally been a satire on the Roman military presence in the east. The demonic, unclean Romans, like imperialists elsewhere, do not want to be dislodged from the land they have occupied (5:10), and 'the story symbolically satisfies the desire to drive them into the sea like pigs.'" He (p. 351) continues, "This interpretation is aided by the fact that the wild boar was the emblem of the Roman legion stationed in Palestine, and Jewish sources as old as *1 Enoch* 89:12 identify the boar with Esau, who became a symbol of Rome. . . ."

Referring to the same story, Warren Carter (2006: 121) is even more direct. "Mark's Jesus identifies Rome and the military power of its legions as demonic. . . . He anticipates God's powerful destruction of Rome by casting the demons called Legion into the sea."

Paying Taxes

Basic Text: All three Synoptic Gospels relate the story of Jesus being asked whether one should pay taxes to the emperor (see Matt. 22:15–22; Mark 12:13–17; and Luke 20:20–26). In his translations of the *Anchor Bible* edition of *Mark*, Marcus (2009: 819–21) presents a figure that outlines these passages in all three Gospels, as well as in three noncanonical texts. All are similar, although *Mark* and *Luke* provide the greatest detail. I will draw on *Mark*.

The chief priests, scribes, and elders send some Pharisees[3] and some Herodians[4] to trap Jesus by getting him to make a treasonous statement. "Teacher, we know that you are sincere and show deference to no one; for you do not regard people with partiality, but teach the way of God in accordance with truth. Is it lawful to pay taxes to the emperor, or not? Should we pay them, or should we not?" (Mark 12:14). Jesus recognizes the hypocrisy behind the question, and asks, "Why are you putting me to the test?" (Mark 12:15). He asks them to bring him a denarius, a Roman silver coin, and then asks them, "Whose head is this, and whose title?" (Mark 12:16) They answer that it is the emperor's. Jesus tells them to "give to the emperor the things that are the emperor's, and to God the things that are God's" (Mark 12:17). (In the *KJV*, "Render to Cæsar the things that are Cæsar's, and to God the things that are God's.") And his questioners were amazed.

Political Implications: Jesus cleverly turns the question around by asking the Pharisees to produce the Roman coin. The denarius very likely bore the image of Tiberius Caesar, bearing the inscription, "TI[BERIVS] CAESAR DIVI AVG[VSTI] F[ILIUS] AVGVSTVS," ("Tiberius Caesar, son of the deified Augustus [himself] Augustus"). As Marcus (2009: 824) points out in his *Anchor Bible* translation of *Mark, 9–16*, "There would be good reasons for Jews to be outraged at the requirement that they pay their taxes with this sort of coin." But the Pharisees carry these coins, whereas Jesus himself apparently does not (Carter, p. 29).

In his *Anchor Bible* commentaries on *Luke*, Fitzmyer (1985) argues that there are three ways of interpreting Jesus's reply (1292–93). First, it might represent a two-kingdoms view. The kingdom of God does not yet supplant the political kingdoms of the world. Secondly, the reply could be ironic. Fitzmyer writes, "Some commentators have understood the words of Jesus as irony. Jesus would not have been really interested in the tribute to Caesar; so his recommendation to, 'Pay to Caesar

what is Caesar's is a flash of wit, devoid of any serious import.'" There
is a third possibility. Fitzmyer argues, Jesus may simply have been
cautioning Jewish Zealots.[5] "Jesus would be openly opposing the
refusal to pay the Roman tribute, but his pronouncement would have
no real bearing on the problem of the state." Fitzmyer (1293) concludes,
"The kingdom which Jesus preaches does not call into question
Caesar's rightful kingship; but that is not the all-important aspect of
human life. A human being belongs to God, whose image he/she bears.
God has not only a right to possession over human beings, but also a
claim to a basic recognition of his lordship." Richard Bauckham (1989:
81) argues that Jesus's reply was aimed against Zealots and that, once
we realize this, "it is clear that he is making only a limited point."

Carter (pp. 28–29) notes the cleverness of Jesus's answer:

> Paying taxes expressed submission to Rome's and the elite's sovereign-
> ty while nonpayment was regarded as rebellion. Given this power dif-
> ferential, hostile intent, and imperial context, Jesus answers in a way
> that subordinated people often do. . . . He cleverly combines loyalty
> and deference with his own subversive agenda. He employs ambigu-
> ous, coded, and self-protective speech to uphold payment of a coin
> bearing the emperor's image, while also asserting overriding loyalty
> to God. He balances apparent compliance with hidden resistance.

Pope Benedict XVI (2007:12) maintains that Jesus's reply was a
way of expressing the comparability between the secular and religious
spheres. But he also quotes *Acts* (5:29), "We must obey God rather
than any human authority."

The Trial of Jesus

Basic Text: All four Gospels relate the story of Jesus's arrest, his hearing
before the chief priests, his trial before Pontius Pilate, the Roman governor,
his sentence by Pilate, and his execution (see Matt. 26:1–29, 47–54;
Mark 14:1–15:39; Luke 22:1–23:47; John 18:1–19:37). In his translation
of the 1986 *Anchor Bible* edition of *Mark*, Mann presents two tables
that outline the stories as told in each of the Gospels (544–50; 603–05.)
I will summarize his tables, drawing mainly upon his outline of the
story in *Mark*. Where I draw upon the other Gospels, I will indicate
the source. In one instance, I believe that Mann omits relevant material
from *Matthew*, and I will indicate clearly where I have added it.[6]

In *Mark*, the story begins with the chief priests and scribes plot-
ting to kill Jesus (Mark 14:1–2), but they do not want to arrest him

on a festival day to avoid risking a possible riot. Judas goes to the high priests offering to betray Jesus, and they offer him money (Mark 14:10–11.) (In *Matthew* 26:15 he is paid thirty pieces of silver.) Jesus meets with his disciples for the first day of the Feast of Unleavened Bread. He tells them that his time has come and announces that one of them will betray him. He gives them bread saying, "Take; this is my body" (Mark 14:22), and serves them wine saying, "This is my blood of the covenant, which is poured out for many" (Mark 14:24).

Jesus predicts that all his apostles will stumble, but Peter says he will not. But Jesus says that before the cock crows Peter will deny him three times. Jesus and his disciples go to the garden of Gethsemane, which is at the western base of the Mount of Olives. Jesus is arrested and taken to the high priest's house. Peter secretly follows, but as Jesus predicts, he denies knowing Jesus three times before the cock crows. The chief priests and elders seek witnesses against Jesus, but their testimony is contradictory. Jesus is asked whether he is the Messiah, and he answers that he is "the Son of Man" (Mark 14:62). The high priest declares that this is blasphemy, and all agreed that he is guilty. The high priests and elders agree to bind Jesus and take him before Pilate.

Pilate asks Jesus if he is the king of the Jews. Jesus answers, "You say so" (Mark 15:2). Jesus answers none of the charges against him and Pilate is amazed. According to *Luke*, Pilate sends Jesus to Herod, who questions him at length, but Jesus does not reply. Herod says he finds no charges against Jesus and returns him to Pilate. The Passover custom allows the Jews to request that one condemned prisoner be released. Pilate gives the people the choice of the "King of the Jews," or Barabas, a rebel who had committed murder in an insurrection. The people demand that Barabas be released. In *John*, Pilate tells the crowd, "Here is your King ... Shall I crucify your King?" (John 19:14–15).

The chief priests say they have loyalty only to Caesar. "We have no king but the emperor" (John 19:15). There is one important exchange in *Matthew* that Mann does not report. When Pilate reluctantly concludes that he cannot spare Jesus in the face of popular protest, "Then the people as a whole answer, 'His blood be on us and on our children!'" (Matt. 27:25).[7]

Political Implications: Even the Roman governor of Judea does not find adequate grounds for convicting Jesus. On the other hand, he responds to the demands of the mob demanding Jesus's crucifixion rather than risk a riot. But a few days before, Jesus has been welcomed enthusiastically when he enters Jerusalem, and the priests are careful to arrest him at night in a remote location. It seems very unlikely that the crowd demanding Jesus's death represented the Jewish population. Like most colonial governors, Pilate probably has limited knowledge of local events. He knew Latin and probably Greek, but it seems highly unlikely that he knew Aramaic, the language spoken by most Judeans, including Jesus.

The story of the hearing and trial as related in the Gospels is probably inaccurate. Haim Hermann Cohn (1971), who served as a Justice on the Israeli Supreme Court, analyzes both the hearing before Jewish leaders and the trial before Pilate, and finds these accounts inconsistent with what we know about Jewish and Roman law. Clearly, the Gospels are designed to cast as much blame on the Jews as possible, and to do as much as possible to absolve the Roman authorities. As Gerard S. Sloyan (2006: 92) writes, "Because Pilate's consistent finding of no cause (John 18:38) in him [Jesus] suited an approach of disciples of Jesus to the empire that could have been developed very early if the empire continued to harass them after his death as a group suspect of insurgency."

Although scholars recognize that the statement of Jews to have "His blood be on us and on our children!" (Matt. 27:25) was not an eternal acceptance of guilt, the belief that Jews are responsible for Jesus's death persists. A scene from Claude Lanzmann's 1985 film, *Shoah*, provides a graphic illustration. A group of Poles in the 1980s are standing in front of Simon Srebnic, who was a Jewish teenage boy from Chelmo who survived the Holocaust. A Polish woman speaks of events she alleges occurred in 1942 (99–100):

> "The Jews there were gathered in a square. The rabbi asked an SS man: 'Can I talk to them?' The SS man said yes. So the rabbi said that around two thousand years ago the Jews condemned the innocent Christ to death. And when they did that, they cried out: "Let his blood fall on our heads and on our sons' heads." Then rabbi told them: 'Perhaps the time has come for that, so let us do nothing, let us go, and do what we're asked.'"

Of course the account of a Polish woman in the1980s speaking about events that supposedly occurred forty years earlier are not the official Catholic position about the guilt of modern-day Jews. The doctrine of "Nostra Aetate," published in 1965 in reaction to Vatican Council II

(1962–65), modified the Church's position making it clear the actions of Jews during Jesus's trial cannot be blamed on all Jews alive at the time, let alone on Jews today. And in the second book of his planned trilogy on the life of Jesus, Pope Benedict XVI (2011: 184–88) goes even further to absolve Jews.

Josephus' Account

In his *The Antiquities of the Jews* (18:3), Flavius Josephus (37/38 CE–c100 CE) presents an account of Jesus's life, including his crucifixion. Here is his full account:

> Now, there was about this time Jesus, a wise man, if it be lawful to call him a man, for he was a doer of wonderful works—a teacher of such men as revere the truth with pleasure. He drew over to him many of the Jews, and many of the Gentiles. He was [the] Christ, and when Pilate, at the suggestion of the principal men amongst us, had condemned him to the cross, those of us who loved him at the first did not forsake him, for he appeared to them alive again the third day, as the divine prophets had foretold these and ten thousand other wonderful things concerning him and the tribe of Christians so named from him are not extinct at this day.

Josephus's account does not clearly establish the responsibility for Jesus's execution. His account is far less detailed than any of the Gospels, and it would be difficult to assess who was responsible for the execution.

Notes

1. The first three Gospels, *Matthew, Mark,* and *Luke,* are known as the Synoptic Gospels because they can be viewed side-by-side using a synopsis. They have a great deal of overlapping content not found in *John,* whereas *John* includes material not found in the first three. For my purposes, however, it is better to discuss all four Gospels in one chapter. It will be apparent that two of the three Synoptic Gospels (*Matthew and Luke*) present genealogies of Jesus, that only one Synoptic Gospel (*Luke*) discusses Augustus' census, that two of the three Synoptic Gospels (*Mark and Luke*) discuss the exorcism of the "Legion" of demons, and that all three of the Synoptic Gospels discuss Jesus's response about paying taxes. *John* is silent about all these subjects. Only *John* reports Jesus's first miracle, transforming water into wine. But all four Gospels discuss Jesus's arrest, hearing, trial, and crucifixion, and each presents a somewhat different account.
2. In this instance the *KJV* is in line with the report in *2 Samuel* (11–12), but takes substantial liberty with the Greek text (see *The Interlinear NASB-NIV Parallel New Testament in Greek and English*). The boy conceived while Bathsheba was Uriah's wife dies shortly after being born. When Solomon is conceived, Uriah is dead, and Bathsheba is King David's wife.

3. The Pharisees were observant Jews who were influential, especially in Palestine, between the second century BCE to the first century CE. They were noted for their religious learning.
4. The Herodians were a faction that may have been supporters of Herod Antipas.
5. There appear to be many interpretations of who should be considered as Zealots. The term is usually associated with Jews who were strongly opposed to Roman rule of Judea.
6. Ron E. Hassner (2003) presents a game theoretic analysis of Jesus's trial and crucifixion.
7. Although *Matthew* makes the strongest condemnation of the Jews in relation to the story of Jesus's trial, many scholars argue that *The Gospel of John* is more negative toward Jews than the three Synoptic Gospels. For the most influential statement of this thesis, see Rosemary Ruether (1997). For a summary of early Christian anti-Semitism, see John G. Gager (1983:

19

Acts, Romans, 1 Corinthians, 2 Corinthians, Galatians, Philippians, 1 Thessalonians, and Philemon (The Career and Epistles of Paul)

Paul's Conversion and Career

Basic Text: Although entitled *The Acts of the Apostles*, Peter is the only apostle discussed in detail. Saul of Tarsus, whose Greek name is Paul, is the major character. He was probably born between 5 CE and 10 CE, and claims to be a Roman citizen (Acts 16:37; 22:25–27). Saul begins as a circumcised Jew from the tribe of Benjamin, who is a Pharisee well versed in Jewish law. In his early career, he persecutes followers of Jesus.

On his way to Damascus, he sees a light from heaven and hears a voice saying, "Saul, Saul, why do you persecute me?" (Acts 9:4). (In the *KJV*, "Saul, Saul, why persecutest thou me?") Paul asks who is speaking, and the voice says he is Jesus. After his epiphany, Paul continues to Damascus and he begins his ministry. The book describes Paul's missionary activity in Asia Minor and Greece. He returns to Jerusalem, where he is arrested. Eventually, he is transported to Rome to be tried directly by the Emperor. The voyage to Rome is described in considerable detail. However, *Acts* describes neither his trial nor his execution. There are neither biblical nor historical records of his death, but if he were a Roman citizen, he would have been beheaded rather than crucified. He probably died in 67 CE during the reign of Nero (54 CE–68 CE).

As Michael White (2004: 145) writes, despite appearing to provide a great deal of information about Paul's voyages, it is difficult to reconstruct Paul's career from the biblical account. In chapters 7 and 8 of his book, White presents his own recounting of Paul's ministry.

Political Implications: Paul is the most successful missionary of early Christianity, and is sometimes seen as its first theologian.[1] Thirteen of the twenty-seven writings of the *New Testament* are attributed to Paul. According to Terence L. Donaldson (2010: 27), these letters make up one quarter of the *New Testament*. Granted, most modern scholars conclude that only seven of the epistles were definitely written by Paul: *Romans, 1 Corinthians, 2 Corinthians, Galatians, Philippians, 1 Thessalonians,* and *Philemon* (see *The Pauline Epistles,* passim), and these are the only Pauline Epistles that I discuss. That Jesus directly converts Paul enhances his credentials. But his importance rests on his writings. As Craig C. Hill (2010: 64) points out, "Paul is not the founder of Roman Christianity and so cannot assume charge over it. It is worth noting, however, that even in Paul's own churches, he had no real power. Paul could exercise authority only in so far as he could persuade his audience of his right to do so."

Rodney Stark (1996: 45), a sociologist who studies religion, argues that the early church was more successful among the "solid citizens of the empire." But he acknowledges that he cannot "prove" his thesis. "Had Paul sent out not simply letters but also questionnaires, such proof might be forthcoming" (pp. 45–46). He argues (p.46) that whether early Christianity drew its support from "the relatively privileged" or the "downtrodden" makes a great deal of difference. "Had Christianity actually been a proletarian movement, it strikes me that the state necessarily would have responded to it as a *political* threat rather than simply as an illicit religion." He estimates (1996, 7) that as of 40 CE there were only 1,000 Christians, making up only 0.0017 percent of the population of the Roman Empire (which he estimates at 60,000,000). Even by 100 CE, there were only 7,530 Christians, 0.0126 percent. A hundred years later (200 CE), there were 217,795 Christians, 0.36 percent of the Empire. By 300 CE there were 6,299,382 Christians, 10.5 percent of the Empire, and by 311 CE, the Emperor Galerius excused Christians from worshipping Roman gods. After winning the Battle of Milvian Bridge (312 CE), Constantine (c280 CE–337 CE; reigned with others from 311 CE and as sole ruler from 314 CE–337 CE) converted to Christianity in 313 CE. Stark estimates that by 350 CE, there were 33,882,008 Christians and that they made up 56.5 percent of the Empire.[2]

Paul and Jewish Law

Basic Text: In Acts, Peter argues that Gentiles do not need to be circumcised (15:1–4) and that they do not need to obey Mosaic dietary laws. But it is Paul who develops an extensive rationale for these reforms. There appear to be changes in Paul's views about circumcision during his ministry. In *Acts* he discovers a disciple, Timothy, who had a Greek father and a Jewish mother. Paul takes him on his journeys, but has him circumcised since Jews knew that his father was Greek (Acts 16:3). But in *Galatians* he reports journeying with Titus, who is also a Greek, and he does not require Titus to be circumcised (Gal. 2:3). In Galatians he once again speaks of the insignificance of circumcision:

> Listen! I, Paul, am telling you that if you let yourself be circumcised, Christ will be of no benefit to you. Once again I testify to every man who lets himself be circumcised that he is obliged to obey the entire law. You who want to be justified by the law have cut yourself off from Christ; you have fallen away from grace. For through the Spirit, by faith, we eagerly wait for the hope of righteousness. For in Christ Jesus neither circumcision nor uncircumcision counts for anything; the only thing that counts is faith working through love. (Gal. 5:2–6)

In *Romans*, rightly considered by Hill (p. 57) to be "one of the eminent texts of Western history" and which is "commonly regarded as Paul's supreme work, the consummate expression of his mature theology," Paul presents an extensive argument that circumcision is unnecessary (Rom. 2:25–29; 3:1–4; 4:9–12). The clearest statement from the first passage:

> Circumcision indeed is of value if you obey the law; but if you break the law, your circumcision has become uncircumcision. So, if those who are uncircumcised keep the requirements of the law, will not their uncircumcision be regarded as circumcision? Then those who are physically uncircumcised but keep the law will condemn you that have the written code and circumcision but break the law. For a person is not a Jew who is one outwardly, nor is true circumcision something external and physical. Rather, a person is a Jew who is one inwardly, and real circumcision is a matter of the heart—it

145

is spiritual and not literal. Such a person receives praise not from others but from God.

In *Romans* 14 Paul also argues that people should not be criticized for ignoring the Mosaic dietary laws:

> I know and am persuaded in the Lord Jesus that nothing is unclean in itself; but it is unclean for anyone who thinks it is unclean. If your brother or sister is being injured by what you eat, you are no longer walking in love. Do not let what you eat cause the ruin of one for whom Christ died. So do not let your good be spoken of as evil. For the kingdom of God is not food and drink but righteousness and peace and joy in the Holy Spirit. (Rom. 14:14–17)

In *Galatians* 2:12, Paul condemns the actions of James, who "used to eat with the Gentiles. But after they came, he drew back and kept himself separate for fear of the circumcision faction." Paul adds, "We ourselves are Jews by birth and not Gentile sinners; yet we know that a person is justified not by the works of the law but through faith in Jesus Christ" (Gal. 2:15–16). (In the *KJV*, "We *who are* Jews by nature, and not sinners of the Gentiles, knowing that a man is not justified by the works of the law, but by the faith of Jesus Christ.") Believing in Jesus is obviously much more important than obeying the Mosaic dietary laws.

Political Implications: These arguments about circumcision and dietary laws are politically important because they drive a wedge between Christianity and Judaism. Circumcision is basic to the covenant between God and Abraham, and many Jews will view the covenant as abrogated if it is abandoned. The dietary laws were probably instituted to make it more difficult for Israelites and the inhabitants of Canaan to interact. As Hill (p. 59) observes, "Paul sanctioned disobedience by Jews of certain Jewish (particularly food) laws . . . an attitude that did not endear himself to many in Israel, Christian or otherwise." On the other hand, dispensing with circumcision and dietary restrictions may have aided Christianity gain converts.[3] Of course, Christianity had other appeals, especially its promise of eternal salvation. However, the triumph of Christianity as the state religion of the Roman Empire, and ultimately the dominant religion of Europe, had immense political consequences.

Freud (1939: 111–112) views Paul's doctrines of salvation and his views about circumcision as a crucial religious development.

The Mosaic religion had been a Father religion; Christianity became a Son religion. The Old God, the Father, took second place; Christ, the Son, stood in his stead, just as in those dark times every son had longed to do. Paul, by developing the Jewish religion further, became its destroyer. His success was certainly due mainly to the fact that through the idea of salvation he laid the ghost of the feelings of guilt. It was also due to giving up the idea of the chosen people and its visible sign—circumcision. This is how the new religion could become all-embracing, universal.

Paul and Sexual Morality

Basic Text: Paul was apparently unmarried, at least during his ministry, and he recommended celibacy. "To the unmarried and the widows I say that it is well for them to remain unmarried as I am. But if they are not practicing self-control, they should marry. For it is better to marry than to be aflame with passion" (1 Cor. 7:8–9). (In the *KJV*, "I say therefore to the unmarried and widows, It is good for them if they abide even as I. But if they cannot contain, let them marry: for it is better to marry than to burn.")

He advises men who are not yet married not to seek a wife (1 Cor. 7:25–31), and for unmarried women to remain unmarried (1 Cor. 7:34–35). But Paul does not advocate dissolving marriages. He stresses that a husband has authority over his wife's body, but a wife has authority over her husband's body (1 Cor. 7:3–4). In none of the epistles that I review does he endorse monogamy, although in other writings he may endorse monogamy for church leaders (1 Tim. 3:2; 3:12; Titus 1:6).

Paul repeats the injunction against homosexuality but extends it to women. As for the ungodly, Paul writes (Rom. 1:26–27), "God gave them up to degrading passions. Their women exchanged natural intercourse for unnatural, and in the same way also the men, giving up natural intercourse with women, were consumed with passion for one another. Men committed shameless acts with men and received in their own persons the due penalty for their error." (In the *KJV*, "God gave them up into vile affections: for even their women did change the natural use into that which is against nature. And likewise also the men, leaving the natural use of the woman, burned in their lust one toward another; men with men working that which is unseemly, and receiving in themselves that recompense of their error which was meet.")

Political Implications: God's first command to humans is, "Be fruitful and multiply and fill the earth and conquer it" (Gen. 1:28). (In the

147

KJV, "Be fruitful, and multiply, and replenish the earth, and subdue it.") Paul's recommendation of celibacy seems to contradict God's fundamental commandment. Granted, there is little danger of universal celibacy among humans, so there is little danger of the human population expiring through lack of sexual activity. And if the world is about to end, there is no need for humans to reproduce.

But the first *Anchor Bible* translators of *1 Corinthians*, William F. Orr and James Arthur Walther (1976: 221–22), see little connection between Paul's preference for chastity and his eschatological views, that is to say, his views about the imminent end of the world. And, as John Barclay (2010: 105) writes in his discussion of *1 Corinthians*, "The lack of enthusiasm for marriage in its own right, for the procreation of children, or for the establishment of a Christian family (contrast Eph. 5:21; 6:4) is notable." (*Ephesians* is an epistle attributed to Paul but whose authorship is questioned.)[4]

The condemnation of homosexuality is politically important since, as noted above, these controversies about same-sex marriage have become an important part of the political discourse in the United States, Western Europe, and even in Latin America. Likewise, the Congressional ban against homosexuals serving openly in the U.S. military is a contentious political issue. Although one of Barack Obama's 2008 campaign promises was to end the ban on military service by men and women who are openly homosexual, Congress passed legislation removing this ban during the lame-duck session of the 111th Congress held after the 2010 midterm election. As of this writing, however, the ban remains in effect.[5]

Paul and Slavery

Basis Text: In *Philemon*, Paul is in prison. Onesimus, a runaway slave who belongs to Philemon, is attending Paul. Paul writes to Philemon, but does not ask him to free Onesimus. Rather, Paul asks if he can continue to use his services (1:13). In *1 Corinthians* 7:21–24, he argues that Christians should not change their status:

> Were you a slave when called? Do not be concerned about it. Even if you can gain your freedom, make use of your present condition now more than ever. For whosoever was called in the Lord as a slave is a freed person belonging to the Lord, just as whoever was free when called is a slave of Christ. You were bought with a price; do not become slaves of human masters. In whatever condition you were called, brothers and sisters, there remain with God.

In *Galatians* (3:27–29), Paul writes, "As many of you were baptized into Christ have clothed yourself with Christ. There is no longer Jew or Greek, there is no longer slave or free, there is no longer male and female; for all of you are one in Christ Jesus. And if you belong to Christ, then you are Abraham's offspring, heirs according to the promise." (According to the *KJV*, "For as many of you as have been baptized into Christ have put on Christ. There is neither Jew nor Greek, there is neither bond nor free, there is neither male nor female: for ye are all one in Christ Jesus. And if ye *be* Christ's, then are ye Abraham's seed, and heirs according to the promise.")

Political Implications: Slavery became a major political issue in the nineteenth century, lasting longer in the United States than in most Western societies. For example, the United Kingdom had outlawed the slave trade in 1807 and outlawed slavery throughout its empire in 1833. Slavery was abolished in French colonies during the Revolution in 1794, although as First Consul Napoleon partially reintroduced it in 1802. But in 1835, France and Britain signed a treaty abolishing the slave trade. Britain abolished slavery in most of its Empire in 1832, and France abolished slavery in its colonies in 1848. Mexico abolished slavery in 1829. But in the United States, slavery persisted as the major political issue. In the 1790 Census, the total U.S. population was 3,893,635, of whom 694,280 were slaves—18 percent of the total. In the 1860 Census, conducted on the eve of the Civil War, the U.S. population was 31,443,321, among whom 3,953,761 were slaves—13 percent of the total. Slavery was not abolished until 1865 with the ratification of the Thirteenth Amendment.

Given how well read American political elites were in the Bible, biblical arguments were made both for and against this "peculiar institution." Joseph A. Fitzmyer (2000: 19), in the *Anchor Bible* edition of *Philemon*, points out, the epistle was used to both defend and attack slavery. Pro-slavery advocates viewed the epistle as "the Pauline Mandate" on slavery. On the other hand, antebellum abolitionists argued that there was no evidence that Onesimus was a slave. Biblical arguments were made both for and against slavery. Controversies about slavery split several Protestant denominations.

In his outstanding summary of antebellum pro and antislavery arguments, Mason I. Lowance Jr. (2003) shows how biblical arguments were used to both support (pp. 51–87) and oppose (pp. 88–115) slavery. As he notes (p. 51), "Early Americans took the Bible very seriously.... As a source of revealed authority governing human history, the Bible was rivaled only by the rapid rise of science as a means of perceiving truth." There were arguments sanctioning slavery in the *Hebrew Bible* as well, but Paul's arguments, especially his letter to Philemon, were often used to support it. One of the weakest proslavery arguments based on the Bible was that Negroes, as descendants of Ham, were condemned to subjugation by virtue of Noah's curse. "Cursed be Canaan [a son of Ham], the lowliest slave shall he be to his brothers" (Gen. 9:25). (In the *KJV*, "Cursed *be* Canaan, a servant of servants shall he be unto his brethren.") As Lowance (p. 59) reports, "The narrative assumes that both Ham and Noah's grandson, Canaan, were guilty of seeing their father's nakedness; the curse placed on Canaan was used to explain the presumed inferiority of the African, which was designated by his blackness, a sign of this curse."

It was more difficult for opponents of slavery to draw upon the Bible. As Lowance (2003, 88) writes, "While abolitionists and anti-slavery advocates both used the Bible as an antislavery resource, they were less able to turn to Scripture for precedent and example than the proslavery writers because the Old Testament, and some parts of the New Testament, offered historical precedents for the divine sanction of slavery." But, Lowance argues, they often attacked the arguments based upon Noah's curse. Theodore Dwight Weld (1803–95) made a strong argument in his essay, *The Bible Against Slavery* (1837):

> This prophecy of Noah is the *vade mecum* of slaveholders, and they never venture abroad without it. It is a pocket-piece for sudden occasion, a keepsake to dote over, a charm to spell-bind opposition, and a magnet to attract whatsoever worketh abomination, or maketh a lie. But closely as they cling to it, cursed be Canaan is a poor drug to stupefy a throbbing conscience—a mocking lullaby, vainly wooing slumber to unquiet tossing, and crying. Peace, be still, where God makes war, and breaks his thunders. (Quoted in Lowance, 2003: 95.)

Paul's writings, in particular, were of little aid to opponents of slavery. However, as the Marxist historian Eugene D. Genovese (1974: 165) points out, Paul's views could be used to remind slaves that their owners were also subject to a higher authority.

It is unreasonable to judge Paul's views about slavery by twenty-first century standards, or even the way his writings were used in the nineteenth century. At the time Paul wrote, the population of the Roman Empire was probably between fifty-five and sixty-five million, of whom between a fourth and a third were slaves. Slavery was an accepted institution among both Jews and their Roman masters.

To propose the abolition of slavery nearly two thousand years ago would have doomed an upstart religion to repression and likely extinction. In any event, Paul may well have thought that the world was facing an imminent end, in which case differences between free men and slaves would be irrelevant. (For a summary of the history of slavery from about 1450 to the end of World War II, see Seymour Drescher 2009; and for information about de facto slavery today, see the website of the Anti-Slavery Society, http://anti-slaverysociety. addr.com/index.htm.)

Paul and Political Authority

Basic Text: I am quoting in full Paul's views on the way Christians should respond to political authority (Rom. 13:1–7):

> Let every person be subject to governing authorities; for there is no authority except from God, and those authorities that exist have been instituted by God. Therefore whoever resists authority resists what God has appointed, and those who resist will incur judgment. For rulers are not a terror to good conduct, but to bad. Do you wish to have no fear of the authority? Then do what is good, and you will receive its approval; for it is God's servant for your good. But if you do what is wrong, you should be afraid, for the authority does not bear the sword in vain! It is the servant of God to execute wrath on the wrongdoer. Therefore one must be subject, not only because of wrath but also because of conscience. For the same reason you also pay taxes, for the authorities are God's servants, busy with this very thing. Pay to all what is due them—taxes to whom taxes are due, revenue to whom revenue is due, respect to whom respect is due, honor to whom honor is due.

In the *KJV*:

> Let every soul be subject unto the higher powers. For there is no power but of God: the powers that be are ordained of God. Whosoever therefore resisteth the power, resisteth the ordinance of God: and they that resist shall receive to themselves damnation. For rulers are not a terror to good works, but to evil. Wilt thou then not be afraid of the power? do that which is good, and thou shalt have praise of the same: For he is the minister of God to thee for good. But if thou do that which is evil, be afraid; for he beareth not the sword in vain: for he is the minister of God, a revenger to *execute* wrath upon him that doeth evil. Wherefore *ye* must needs be subject,

151

not only for wrath, but also for conscience sake. For this cause pay ye tribute also: for they are God's ministers, attending continually upon this very thing. Render therefore to all their dues: tribute to whom tribute *is due;* custom to whom custom; fear to whom fear; honour to whom honour.

Political Implications: Paul strongly opposes active resistance to political authority, and even passive resistance is questionable. Consider American colonists who refused to pay the Stamp Tax in 1765, Indians who participated in the Salt March led by Gandhi in 1930, or the African Americans who supported the Montgomery Bus Boycott led by Martin Luther King Jr. in 1955. Did these nonviolent actions violate Paul's injunction to obey political authority? And what of violent political actions? Are we to condemn the Anglican leaders who, along with William of Orange, overthrew James II in 1688 (a revolution which, as Steve Pincus [2009] shows, involved a great deal of violence), the American patriots who called upon Nature's God to break American ties with Britain, or the numerous men who attempted to assassinate Adolph Hitler (Roger Moorhouse, 2006)?

Especially, in light of the atrocities committed during World War II, modern Christian scholars have reevaluated *Romans* 13. For example, Hill (p. 85) writes:

> Few if any passages in the Pauline corpus have been more subject to abuse than vv. 1–7 [in Rom. 13]. Paul does *not* indicate that one is required to obey public officials in all circumstances, nor does he say that every exercise of civil authority is sanctioned by God. No particular government is authorized; no universal authority is legitimated. Instead, Paul reiterates the common Jewish view that human governance operates under God's superintendency.

Fitzmyer, in his translation *Romans* for the *Anchor Bible* series (1993: 662), cautions that in a post-World War II era, we must be especially careful in reading *Romans* 13:1–7. "Although this passage of Romans is often spoken of as that in which Paul discusses the relationship of Christians to the 'state,' there is no mention in it of 'state.' Such a view of this passage reflects a modern problem that especially came to the fore in the period of Hitler and Mussolini and after the Second World War. Nor is there any mention of 'Rome,' the important and pervasive civil authority in the world in the time in which Paul lived and wrote." Fitzmyer notes that when this letter was written, the Empire had not begun to officially persecute Christians, although for local reasons the Emperor Claudius had expelled Jews (and some Jewish Christians (Acts 18:1–2)) from Rome. He notes that some scholars find no eschatological considerations in Paul's argument, although he thinks the word "wrath" suggests that Paul may have had such considerations in mind (p. 663). He concludes, "The passage emphasizes order, authority, civil obedience, payment of taxes or revenue, and honor for civil authorities, regarded as 'God's servants.'"[6]

Notes

1. For a contrary view see John G. Gager (2000).
2. Stark (1996: 7) reminds us that although he is presenting absolute numbers, his results are actually estimates. But he shows that they are consistent with many other sources.
3. Islam spread quickly despite demanding that male converts be circumcised and that Muslims follow dietary restrictions. But the early spread of Islam resulted from military conquest.
4. For a more recent *Anchor Bible* commentary on *First Corinthians*, see Joseph A. Fitzmyer (2008). Fitzmyer discusses Paul's views on celibacy on 273–87.
5. In *1 Thessalonians* (4:1–5) Paul warns Christians against fornication, although this does not add to Jewish law.
6. Whatever Paul writes about obedience in *Romans*, he assures his readers in *Philippians* (3:20) that "our citizenship is in heaven, and it is from there that we are expecting a Savior, the Lord Jesus Christ."

20

The First and
Second Epistles of John

The Antichrist

Basic Text: John's three epistles have been summarized briefly by
Judith Lieu (1991: 71–79) and Raymond E. Brown (1988: 105–26),
and discussed extensively in Brown's (1982) *Anchor Bible* translation
and the sources cited therein. The first and second epistles include
the only four verses in the Bible where the term "antichrist" is used,
three times in *1 John* 2:18; 2:22; 4:1–3, and once in *2 John* 1:7. The full
warnings about the dangers of the antichrist(s) are as follows:

"Children, it is the last hour! As you have heard that antichrist is
coming, so now many antichrists have come. From this we know that
this is the last hour" (1 John 2:18).

"Who is the liar but that one who denies that Jesus is the Christ?
This is the antichrist, the one who denies the Father and the Son"
(1 John 2:22).

"Beloved, do not believe every spirit, but test the spirits to see
whether they are from God; for many false prophets have gone out
into the world. By this you know the Spirit of God: every spirit that
confesses that Jesus Christ has come in the flesh is from God, and
every spirit that does not confess Jesus is not from God. And this is
the spirit of the antichrist, of which you have heard that it is coming;
and now it is already in the world" (1 John 4:1–3).

Finally, as noted above, John's second epistle has one reference to
the antichrist:

> Many deceivers have gone out into the world, those who do not
> confess that Jesus Christ has come in the flesh; any such person is
> the deceiver and the antichrist! Be on your guard, so that you do
> not lose what we have worked for, but may receive a full reward.
> Everyone who does not abide in the teaching of Christ, but goes
> beyond it, does not have God; whosoever abides in the teaching

has both the Father and the Son. Do not receive into the house or welcome anyone who comes to you and does not bring this teaching. (2 John 1:7–10)

Political Implications: According to Brown (1988), John's discussion of the antichrist must be seen in light of his belief that the world is in its final hour. There will be a struggle between Satan and Christ, and in this apocalyptic conflict, antichrists will deny Christ and ally themselves with Satan.

As I read these epistles, there can be many antichrists, but in common usage the antichrist is often thought of as a single person. For example, in the opening paragraph of *War and Peace*, Anna Pavlovna Scherer affirms her belief that Buonaparte, as she calls him, is the Antichrist.

The term has relevance in contemporary American politics because some believe that President Barack Obama is the antichrist. For example, a Harris poll conducted in March 2010 showed that 14 percent of Americans said that President Obama "may be the Anti-Christ" (*LiveScience*, March 25, 2010) http://www.livescience.com/8160. Opinions were divided by party: only six percent of the Democrats held this view, while 24 percent of Republicans did. As the antichrist (or as antichrists) probably does (do) not advertise his, her, or their identity or identities, Obama may be the antichrist. A Google search shows that there are many sites claiming that he is the antichrist. In his attack on what he calls the "lunatic fringe" (which is much more critical of the far right than the far left), John Avalon (2010), one of the founders of *The Daily Beast*, documents numerous attempts to label Obama as the antichrist. He cites a *Scripps-Howard* poll showing that twenty-five percent of Americans have heard the rumor that Obama is the Antichrist (p. 69).

Avalon notes that there are many e-mail chains claiming that Obama is the antichrist. Citing one chain e-mail message, he reports (p. 70), "According to The Book of Revelations [sic] . . . the Anti-Christ will be a man, in his 40s, of MUSLIM descent, who will deceive the nations with persuasive language, and have a MASSIVE Christ-like appeal . . . the prophecy says people will flock to him and he will promise false hope and world peace, and when he is in power, he will destroy everything." Avalon points out that (pp. 71–2), *Revelation* was complete by the end of the second century and Islam did not develop until about four hundred years later. As he points out, it is implausible to argue that *Revelation* uses the term Muslim (p. 72). It doesn't. In fact, most scholars think that *Revelation* was written in 95 or 96 CE (see Adela Yarba Collins in the *Anchor Bible Dictionary*, vol. 5: 700). Muhammad was born in 570 CE and the Islamic era dates from 622 CE. Avalon could have also noted that *Revelation* never uses the term "antichrist" either. But John could never know how the term "antichrist" would be used nearly two thousand years later. But it seems likely he would be amazed.

However, the John who wrote *Revelation* reports that he is transmitting a revelation from Jesus (Rev. 1:1–2). Jesus could have known about the future development of Islam. But if the prophecy mentioned a Muslim, it would have been incomprehensible to its readers.

21

Revelation

The Apocalypse

Basic Text: The Revelation to John is the last book of the *New Testament*, and many regard it as its most enigmatic (see Bernard McGinn, 1997: 523). It is addressed as a serial letter to seven churches in Roman provinces in Asia, probably in 95 or 96 CE. Little is known about John, but he was a Jewish Christian writing from the Mediterranean Island Patmos, where he was apparently in exile. He reports a revelation from Jesus predicting conflicts between forces of good and evil, in which the forces of good will eventually triumph. At the outset, God announces "I am the Alpha and the Omega" (Rev. 1:8), that is to say, the beginning and the end. Drawing heavily upon J. M. Massynberde Ford's (1975: 46–50) translation and commentary for *The Anchor Bible* edition, we can see that John relies heavily upon numerical patterns, especially by using the number seven, which scholars identify as representing "completeness" or "perfection" in the *Hebrew Bible* (see, e.g., Järad Friberg in the *Anchor Bible Dictionary*, vol. 4: 1143–44; R. A. H. Gunner, 1962: 898; J. Edwin Hartill, 1947: 115–16; *Harper Collins Bible Dictionary*, 1996: 764).

The letter, as noted above, is addressed to seven churches. In chapter 6, there are seven seals. Each time a seal is broken, a new event occurs: there is a white horse (6:1–2), a red horse (6:3–4), a black horse (6:5–6), a yellow-greenish horse (6:7–8), souls under an altar (6:9–11), and a massive earthquake (6:12–13). When the seventh seal is broken, there is silence for half an hour (8:1). In chapters 8, 9, and 11, there are seven angels, each of whom is given a trumpet. Once again, blowing these trumpets heralds new events: the earth is set on fire (8:7), the sea turns to blood (8:8–9), rivers and springs become bitter (8:10–11), heavenly bodies become dim (8:12–13), there are locusts (9:1–2), and there are horsemen (9:13–11:14).

When the seventh angel blows his trumpet, loud voices in heaven proclaim (11:15):

> The kingdom of the world has
> become the kingdom of
> our Lord
> and of his Messiah,
> and he will reign forever and ever.

In the *KJV*:

> The kingdoms of this world are become *the kingdoms* of our Lord, and of his Christ; and he shall reign for ever and ever.

In chapters 12–15, seven more signs appear: a woman giving birth (12:1–2), Satan being cast down to the earth (12:7–12), a dragon (12:13–17), a beast rising from the sea (13:1–10), a beast rising from the earth (13:11–18), 144,000 people with his Father's name on their foreheads (14:1–5), three angels proclaiming judgment (14:6–13), and seven angels reaping a harvest (14:14–20). As for the beast rising from the earth, John tells us, "Let anyone with understanding calculate the number of the beast, for it is the number of a person. Its number is six-hundred and sixty-six" (13:18). (In the *KJV*, "Let him that hath understanding count the number of the beast: for it is the number of a man; and his number *is* Six hundred threescore *and* six.")

In chapter 15, John introduces angels with seven bowls, and they pour out the contents of their bowls on the earth (16:2), the sea (16:3), on the waters (16:4), on the sun (16:5), and on the beast's throne (16:10–11). When the sixth angel pours the contents of his bowl into the Euphrates, he warns, "See, I am coming as a thief! Blessed is the one who stays awake and is clothed, not going about naked and exposed to shame" (16:15). When the seventh angel spills his bowl into the air, there is a great earthquake, and Babylon splits into three parts (16:19). In chapters 17–19, John discusses the end of Babylon. First, he describes Babylon (17:1–6) and explains its iniquity (17:7–18). He describes its fall (18:1–8), the mourning for its destruction (18:9–20), its final ruin (18:21–24), and the song of a great multitude in heaven praising its fall (19:1–2):

> Hallelujah!
> Salvation and glory and power to our God,

for his judgments are true and just;
he has judged the great whore
who corrupted the earth with her fornication,
and he has avenged on her the blood of his servants.

In the *KJV*:

Alleluia; Salvation, and glory, and honour, and power, unto the Lord our God. For true and righteous *are* his judgments: for he hath judged the great whore, which did corrupt the earth with her fornication, and hath avenged the blood of his servants at her hand.

In chapters 19 and 20, John describes a rider on a white horse (19:11–16), a supper with God (19:17–18), capturing two beasts (19:19–21), the angels who throw Satan into an abyss (20:1–3), the first resurrection (20:4–10), Satan's release from prison (20:7), and the final judgment (20:11–15).

Political Implications: There are scholars who claim to have decoded *Revelation*, but I think humility is needed to evaluate its meaning. The author was a learned scholar and his letter is filled with allusions to the *Hebrew Bible*, so much so that some scholars have criticized it for being overly Jewish. The work is clearly enigmatic, and Dionysius, the Bishop of Alexandria in the Third Century, acknowledged that he could not understand it (Adela Yarbo Collins in the *Anchor Bible Dictionary*, vol. 5: 706). Neither John nor his audience would have been interested in a prophecy announcing Babylon's destruction since the Babylonian Empire fell to Cyrus the Great of Persia in 538 BCE. Rather, Babylon is a thinly veiled disguise to describe the Roman Empire. As Richard Bauckham (1993: 156) argues, John includes so many parallels between Babylon and Rome as "to make the reference unmistakable." For example, like Rome, Babylon was built on seven hills, and John lists the goods traded by Rome (18:11–13) with enough accuracy as to make its identity clear to his readers.[1] Chapter 13, one of the harshest criticisms of the "beast" has been seen as a balance to *Romans* 13, in which Paul makes his strongest argument for obeying civil authority (Craig C. Hill, p. 86). Indeed, Christopher Bryan (2005: 107) argues that "The seer of Revelation . . . is surely the one obvious and explicit enemy of Rome in the New Testament."

Who or what does the "number of the beast" refer to? The famous number 666 has been identified as the Emperor Nero, mainly by using gematria, which uses the numerical values of letters to derive hidden meanings.[2] Suetonius (*Lives of the Caesers*, Book VI, 39:2) reports that one Greek graffito during Nero's reign was "A calculation new. Nero his mother slew." In his translation of *Revelation*, Ford (p. 226) points out, "The numerical value of the letters in the name Nero is equal to that of the letters in the rest of the sentence." According to T. F. Glasson's (1965: 83) *Cambridge Bible Commentary* on *The New English Bible* version of *The Revelation of John*, "The most widely accepted interpretation is that this number stands for 'Nero Caesar.' If these two names are written in Hebrew the numerical value comes to 666." However, he concludes (p. 83), "The number 666 alone would be far from conclusive in indicating Nero, but strong support given by the fact that so many other factors in these chapters point to him." However, there are many other interpretations, and Ford's careful evaluation suggests that there is no way to know who John had in mind.

Bauckham argues that John expects Christians to play an active role in the struggle between the forces of good and evil. As he (1993: 161) writes: "Revelation does not respond to the dominant ideology by promoting Christian withdrawal into a sectarian enclave that leaves the world to its judgment while consoling itself with millennial dreams. Since this is the standard caricature of the apocalyptic mentality, it must be strongly emphasized that it is the opposite of Revelation's outlook, which is oriented to the coming of God's kingdom in the whole world and calls Christians to active participation in this coming of the kingdom."

Others disagree. As Bryan argues (2005: 111), "not even the author of Revelation . . . counsels resistance to the empire. Even John is clear that if Rome serves Satan, it is God, not Christians, who will overthrow Satan and Rome alike."

The New Jerusalem

Basic Text: In Chapter 21 John relates his vision of "the holy city, the new Jerusalem" (21:2). The city comes down from heaven "as a bride adorned for her husband" (21:2). A loud voice proclaims from a throne (21:3–4):

> See, the home of God is among the mortals.
> He will dwell with them;

they will be his peoples,
and God himself will be with them;
he will wipe every tear from
their eyes.
Death will be no more;
mourning and crying and pain will be
no more,
for the first things have passed away.

In the *KJV*:

> Behold, the tabernacle of God *is* with men, and he will dwell with them, and they shall be his people, and God himself shall be with them, *and be* their God.
>
> And God shall wipe out away all tears from their eyes; and there shall be no more death, neither sorrow, nor crying, neither shall there be any more pain: for the former things are passed away.

The one on the throne repeats, "I am the Alpha and the Omega, the beginning and the end" (21:6). "To the thirsty, I will give water as a gift from the spring of the water of life. Those who conquer will inherit these things, and I will be their God and they will be my children" (21:6–7). The wicked, however, will be punished (21:8). One of the seven angels who had the seven bowls full of the last seven plagues speaks to the people who are to be spared: "Come, I will show you the bride, the wife of the Lamb" (21:9). The city of Jerusalem comes down from heaven and the city is built of gold, and adorned with jewels. It will have twelve gates. There will be no temple, for "the temple is the Lord God almighty and the Lamb" (21:22). The city will have no need of the sun or moon, for God is the light and the Lamb is the lamp. "Its gates will never be shut by day—and there will be no night there. People will bring into it the glory and the honor of the nations. But nothing unclean will enter it, nor anyone who practices abomination or falsehood, but only those who are written in the Lamb's book of life" (21:25–27). (In the *KJV*: "And the gates of it shall not be shut at all by day: for there shall be no night there. And they shall bring the glory and honour of the nations into it. And they shall in no wise enter into it any thing that is defileth, neither *whatsoever* worketh abomination, or *maketh* a lie: but they which are written into the Lamb's book of life.")

In Chapter 22, "The angel showed me the river of the water of life, bright as crystal, flowing from the throne of God" (22:1). In this single chapter, Jesus promises three times that his return will be soon. "See, I am coming soon! Blessed is the one who keeps the words of the prophecy of this book" (7); "See, I am coming soon; my reward is with me; to repay anything according to everyone's work. I am the Alpha and the Omega, the first and the last, the beginning and the end" (12–13); and "The one who testifies these things says, 'Surely I am coming soon'" (20). In the *KJV*: "Behold, I come quickly: blessed *is* he who keeps the prophecy of this book" (7); "And, behold, I come quickly; and my reward *is* with me, to give every man according as his work shall be. I am the Alpha and the Omega, the beginning and the end, the first and the last" (12–13); and "He which testifies these things saith, Surely I come quickly" (20).

Political Implications: The final chapter of *Revelation* emphasizes a highly eschatological view; that is to say, the author believed that the world as he knows it will end soon. Was the Parousia (Second Coming) imminent? *Revelation* was written 1900 years ago, and Jesus has not returned. Should we still view his coming as imminent? As Adela Yarbro Collins writes in her *Anchor Bible Encyclopedia* (vol. 5, 706–07) entry on *Revelation*, there has been ongoing controversy about this issue. As *Revelation* predicts that Satan would be imprisoned for 1,000 years, Christians did not expect the apocalypse until about 1000 CE. Collins notes that apocalyptic concerns never died out and became prominent in the twelfth century. Martin Luther argued that the end time was near and that the events predicted in *Revelation* corresponded with events in his own time. He also identified the papacy with the Antichrist. Collins notes that millenarian reading of *Revelation* became prominent in seventeenth century England. Such readings once again became prominent in the late twentieth century and are prominent in the early twenty-first century.

According to Collins (*Anchor Bible Dictionary*, vol. 5: 707), "The historical-critical approach has evoked two major reactions. One is the aesthetic literary mode of interpretation that emphasizes the qualities of Revelation that characterize it as a work of art and imagination. The other is the fundamentalist approach that insists on the literal truth of Revelation's images, usually as predictions of future events." Bauckham (1993: 152–53) argues that the prophecy in *Revelation* was fulfilled, in as much as the Roman Empire fell, but that it did not fall in the manner predicted, nor was it replaced by a New Jerusalem.

But, he argues, "fundamentalist interpretation, which finds in biblical prophecy coded predictions of specific events many centuries later than the prophet, misunderstands prophecy's continuing relevance by neglecting to ask what it meant to its hearers. It is important . . . to understand how John's prophecy addressed his contemporaries, since they are the only readers it explicitly addresses."

Eschatological views may affect politics today. If the Parousia is imminent, for example, we have little need to worry about global warming, as God should be able to easily solve environmental problems. A study by James L. Guth et al. (1995), which relies upon several surveys conducted in the late 1980s and early 1990s, reveals that Protestants with conservative eschatological views (Biblical literalism and End Times thinking), traditional religious views, and high levels of religious commitment were less likely to support protecting the environment than Protestants with more liberal views. In an analysis that analyzed the effects of all of these variables, conservative eschatological views were the strongest predictor of negative attitudes toward environmentalism. As Robert Booth Fowler (1995: 45) writes, "Indifference toward the environment, or at least toward claims of environmental crisis abounds among fundamentalist Protestant writings. Thus, while environmentalists worry about the ozone layer or about toxic waste, many fundamentalist Protestants sound other alarms, especially over end times. In fundamentalist analysis, the arrival of end times is more than a prophecy about the distant future; end times are imminent. By this view, nobody can save the earth; that is for God to do. What people *can* do is prepare for the impending apocalypse."

As Kenneth D. Wald and Allison Calhoun-Brown (2011: 194) argue, there are many views toward environmentalism among Christians because "the Bible itself can be used to support both proenvironmental and antienvironmental stances." But, they argue, research suggests that opposition to environmentalism is concentrated among Christians (194) who perceive the end of the world to be imminent.

According to Fowler (1995: 54), "End time Protestant writings invariably identify the re-creation of Israel as a nation in 1948 as the most significant sign of the coming end." In the United States, Christian fundamentalists are among the strongest supporters of Israel. As Gabriel A. Almond, R. Scott Appleby, and Emmanuel Sivan (2003: 73) argue, American fundamentalists view the Middle East and the Holy Land as the center of "the war theater of the Apocalypse." "The prophetic landscape predicted in the Books of Ezekiel, Daniel, and Revelation saw its veracity confirmed by the strategic role of the Middle East in the international arena over the last quarter century. Cosmology has suddenly been endowed with a down-to-earth significance."

Notes

1. For an additional discussion of these parallels by Richard Bauckham, see (1989: 85–102).
2. Tolstoy provides an example of gematria by showing how Pierre Bezúkhov was able to convince himself that "*l'empereur Napoléon*" was the beast referred to in *Revelation* 13:18. By creating a spelling error in French, Pierre finds that "*L'russe Besuhof*" also equals 666, convincing himself that he is linked to Napoleon (see *War and Peace*, vol. III, Part One, Chapter XIX).

22

Conclusions

This book examines the political implications of stories in eighteen of the thirty-nine books of the *Hebrew Bible* and fifteen of the twenty-seven books of the *New Testament*. There are many other great literary works that may also be mined for political insights, such as the *Iliad*, the *Aeneid*, and Shakespeare's tragedies and histories. Great novels, especially historical novels, also provide insight. And reading history is essential to understanding contemporary politics. Most contemporary issues in the United States have historical parallels. For example, one cannot understand restrictions on civil liberties following the September 11, 2001 terrorist attacks without understanding the conflict over the Alien and Sedition Acts of 1798–1802, the suspension of the writ of habeas corpus by Abraham Lincoln during the Civil War, the restrictions on civil liberties during both World Wars, the Red Scare after World War I, and McCarthyism after World War II (see Darren W. Davis, 2007: 2–3). And one cannot understand the current controversy over "birthright citizenship" without reading about the reaction to foreign immigration in the 1840s.[1] Ira Sharkansky (1991) clearly demonstrates that there are many parallels between ancient and modern Israel.

As I said at the outset, my goal was to help readers think critically about politics and the way that ancient texts can illuminate our understanding of politics and justice. I trust that goal has been accomplished. But what lessons have we learned?

Reading the Bible politically leads to four basic conclusions. Admittedly, these conclusions can be learned from other sources, but the Bible provides lucid examples.

Of course, the main theme of the *Hebrew Bible* is religious, not political. From Exodus 20 onward it emphasizes, "You shall have no other gods beside Me" (Exod. 20:2). The fundamental message of the *New Testament* is to accept Jesus as Christ. The message of accepting

Jesus has political implications, but it it is not fundamentally political. Accepting Jesus may affect political behavior. Certainly views about religion are important politically, including views in non-Christian societies, as Pippa Norris and Ronald Inglehart (2004) convincingly demonstrate. In our analyses of presidential elections between 1992 and 2008, John Aldrich, David Rohde, and I find (Abramson, Aldrich, and Rohde, 1995: 134–35, 1999: 94–95, 2003: 99–100, 2007: 110, 2012: 119) that white Evangelicals are more likely to vote Republican for president than white Mainline Protestants, and that white Protestants with a high level of religious commitment are more likely to vote Republican than those with lower levels. But neither the *Hebrew Bible*'s message against polytheism nor[2] the *New Testament*'s message that Jesus is the savior is fundamentally political.

Pursue Justice: The basic political message of the Bible is that leaders must pursue justice. In *Deuteronomy* 16:20, Moses tells the people:

> "Justice, justice, shall you pursue, so that you may live and take hold of the land that the LORD your God is about to give to you."

The prophets continually emphasize the need for justice, and Isaiah makes eloquent appeals. For example, he proclaims:

> "Learn to do good;
> seek justice,
> rescue the oppressed,
> defend the orphan,
> plead for the widow" (Isa. 1:17).
> "Thus says the LORD:
> Maintain justice, and do what
> is right,
> for my salvation will come,
> and my deliverance be revealed" (Isa. 56:1).
> "For I the LORD love justice,
> I hate robbery and wrongdoing" (Isa. 61:8).

Solomon is remembered for his temple, his many wives, and his legendary wisdom. But he is best remembered for his judgment in determining which of two prostitutes is the true mother of a baby boy (1 Kings 3:16–28). The final verse reads:

> All Israel heard of the judgment that the king had rendered; and they stood in awe of the king, because they perceived that the wisdom of God was in him, to execute justice. (1 Kings 3:28)

The story of Jesus driving out the demons named "Legion" (Mark 5:1–20; Luke 8:26–39) strongly suggests that despite its claims of providing justice, the Roman Empire was demonic.

And Jesus speaks of his love for justice. In confronting some Pharisees, he tells them (Luke 11:42):[3]

> But woe to you Pharisees! For you tithe mint and rue and of herbs of all kinds, and neglect justice and the love of God; it is those you ought to have practiced, without neglecting the others.

Political Leaders are Flawed: The Bible teaches that leaders are flawed. Moses, the greatest leader of the *Hebrew Bible*, has a fierce temper, which contributes to his downfall at the waters of Meribah. He also finds it difficult to accept that he is not the appropriate man to lead the Children of Israel to conquer Canaan. Eventually, God tells him, "Do not speak more to Me of this matter" (Deut. 3:26). David, the greatest biblical king, commits adultery and murder and fails to respond to the misdeeds of his sons. But whatever his faults, he realizes that he must step down from the kingship or accept Adonijah's coup (1 Kings 1:32–37).[4] Solomon is endowed with great wisdom, but refuses to obey the injunction in *Deuteronomy* 17:17 not to have many wives (1 Kings 11:1–3) and serves other gods (1 Kings 11:4–8), and God decides to divide his kingdom after he dies (1 Kings 11: 11–13).

And ineffective leaders make remarkable blunders. Rehoboam should have realized that he did not have the military resources to "chastise" Israel, and his harsh response to their demands leads to a divided kingdom (1 Kings 12:16–20). Zedekiah should have realized that he could not challenge Babylon and that he could not expect meaningful help from Egypt. His rebellion destroys the kingdom of Judah and leads to the destruction of Solomon's temple and Jerusalem (2 Kings 25:8–17).

Even great political leaders in relatively recent times have been flawed. Abraham Lincoln suppressed civil rights, and although he became a great self-taught military leader (see James M. McPherson, 2008), he was initially slow to replace Union generals who were reluctant to fight. Franklin D. Roosevelt also trampled on the rights of Japanese Americans. Like Lincoln, he was also an active wartime leader, but he was naïve about Joseph Stalin's postwar intentions (Andrew Roberts, 2009: 557–58).

Evil leaders are deeply flawed. Through his purges Stalin weakened the Soviet military (Robert Conquest, 2008: 182–213), and he refused to accept compelling evidence that Germany was about to invade (Chris Bellamy, 2007: 36–63). Adolph Hitler's catastrophic misjudgment that Germany, along with Italy and Japan, could defeat Britain and her Empire, the Soviet Union, and the United States was more costly in human lives than any previous political miscalculation (Ian Kershaw, 2000: 393–457; Gerald L. Weinberg, 2005: 894).

It is Easier to Mislead than to Lead: When political leaders mislead, it is often easy for them to gain followers. Many people in the kingdom of Israel were idolaters and were eager to worship Baal and other deities. Among all the monarchs of Israel, only Jehu discouraged Baal worship (see Table 13.2). The people were all too willing to be led by monarchs who encouraged idolatry. In Judah, idolatry was weaker, and two of the kings, Hezekiah and Josiah, did their best to crush it (see Table 13.4). Most of the kings were more tolerant, and under their reigns idolatry flourished.

The *New Testament* provides an example of misleading the people. In this case, the leaders are heads of the Jerusalem priesthood. The Gospels relate that Jesus received a tumultuous welcome as he entered Jerusalem (Matt. 21:9; Mark 11:9; Luke 19:35–38; John 12:13). But when Pilate judges him, the high priests appear to have no difficulty in finding a crowd willing to condemn him (Matt. 27:15–23; Mark 15:6–14; Luke 23:17–23; John 18:33–44).

The people are not necessarily evil. Sometimes people take great risks to remove tyrannical leaders. But many times in world history, political leaders have successfully resorted to racism, xenophobia, and, in Germany during the Weimer Republic (1919–33), to anti-Semitism, to gain political power.

Limited Government is Best: Daniel Elazar (1989, 1995) and Aaron Wildavsky (1984) both emphasize the way God's covenant with the Children of Israel established limits on leaders. The Council of Elders (Num. 11:24–26) is consulted, and the Levites are given religious authority as hereditary priests (Deut. 17:18), although they receive no tribal allotment (Lev. 18:23). *Deuteronomy* sets limits on kingship, since kings must consult the priests (17:18), and may not have many horses or wives (17:16–17).

According to Elazar, chapter 27 of *Deuteronomy* moves Israel from having a covenant to having a constitution. He writes (1995: 210):

> In an appropriate conclusion for a covenant, chapter 27 provides for writing down the entire constitutional corpus once the Israelites are in the land and for a ceremony evoking curses on any violators of its provisions. The blessings and curses receive greater elaboration in chapter 28 . . . Moses then makes a summation of the covenant with its promises and obligations (chapters 29–31), concluding with formal designation of his successor, the writing of the constitution and its placement in the Ark of the Covenant, and the provision for a public ceremony to renew the covenant every seven years at the end of a sabbatical year during Succot [the Feast of the Tabernacles].[5]

Elazar (1989) also summarizes these constitutional principles in his monograph on *The Book of Joshua*.

However, even if one is willing to accept the thesis that both *Deuteronomy* and *Joshua* make a case for decentralized government, there is no evidence that these ideas were institutionalized. Granted, during the rule of the judges, the tribes were highly decentralized, and there is a period of relatively centralized leadership between the time David conquered Jerusalem through the end of Solomon's reign. David's key officials are named in *2 Samuel* (8:16–18) and Solomon's officials are named in *1 Kings* (4:2–19) We also know that David listened to the prophet Nathan (2 Sam. 12; 1 Kings 1:22–27). But we have very little idea about how the kingdoms of Judah and Israel were governed under their kingships.

The *New Testament* has little to say about how governments should be run, perhaps because its authors never envisaged a day when Christians would be running a worldly government. There is no need to know how to run a government after the Parousia. All the same, Christian monarchs could quote from the *New Testament* because it clearly states that people should obey civil authority. But their opponents could and did quote from the Bible to oppose monarchs.

Limiting leaders is important because leaders are likely to be flawed. As James Madison reminds us men are not governed by angels (Federalist Number 51). If we were governed by angels, politics would be a remarkably dull subject.

Today, most political leaders are elected, and most face elections if they wish to retain office. But they must still be limited, because elected leaders can still do substantial damage in a four- or five-year term. The biblical authors knew nothing about elections, although, on rare occasions, elites do respond to popular demands, such as Samuel appointing a monarch against his misgivings. But even elected leaders must be limited. There are many sources that teach the need to limit leaders, including Aristotle, Locke and Montesquieu *The Federalist Papers*. The Bible teaches this message with powerful examples and often with great literary power.

Recommended Editions of the Bible

My translations are from some of the best editions available (see the Introduction) including the *KJV*. But there are many other translations.

Many translations of the Bible are available online at: http://www.biblegateway.com.

This site provides access to twenty-three English translations, six of which are available in audio versions. It also provides access to the *Hebrew Bible* in Hebrew and the *New Testament* in Ancient Greek. It provides access to the Latin version of the Catholic Bible, eight Spanish translations, as well as translations in forty-nine other languages.

For readers who want the most literary translation of the Bible into English, see *The Bible, Authorized King James Version with Apocrypha.* [1611]. New York: Oxford University Press, 2008.

For readers with some command of biblical Hebrew, see *JPS Hebrew-English Tanakh: The Traditional Hebrew Text and the New JPS Translation—Second Edition.* Philadelphia: The Jewish Publication Society, 2003.

However, the typeface for the paperback edition is quite small, so readers may want to invest in the hard copy edition.

There is also an interlinear Hebrew and English version: *The Interlinear NIV Hebrew-English Old Testament.* Interlinear translation by John Kohlenberger III. Grand Rapids, MI: Zondervan, 1987.

Readers who do not know Hebrew, but who want a standard Jewish translation of The Hebrew Bible, may consult *Tanakh: The Holy Scriptures—The New JPS Translation According to the Traditional Hebrew Text.* Philadelphia, PA: The Jewish Publication Society, 1985. (pocket edition).

For readers with some command of Ancient Greek, see *The Interlinear NASB-NIV Parallel New Testament in Greek and English*, interlinear translation by Alfred Marshall. Grand Rapids, MI: Zondervan, 1987.

Readers who prefer a Catholic translation may wish to purchase either

*The New American Bible (With the Revised Book of Psalms and the Revised New Testament).*Totowa, NJ: World Catholic Press, 1987.

or

The Catholic Study Bible: The New American Bible, 2nd ed., edited by Donald Senior and John J. Collins. New York: Oxford University Press, 1990, 2006.

The authoritative Catholic version of the Bible is the Latin Vulgate. The best edition of the Vulgate is: *Biblia Sacra Vulgata*, 5th ed. Prepared by Robert Weber and Roger Gryson. Stuttgart, Germany: German Bible Society, 1987.

I could not find a Latin-English parallel translation, except on Kindle.

Notes

1. The Fourteenth Amendment to the U.S. Constitution, ratified in 1868, states that, "All persons born or naturalized in the United States and subject to the jurisdiction thereof, are citizens of the United States and of the State wherein they reside." This Amendment was passed to protect newly enfranchised slaves from state efforts to deprive them of citizenship. Americans who want to restrict immigration to the United States would like to deny U.S. citizenship to the children of parents who are in the United States illegally.

2. In their study of the Israeli Jews in the eight Knesset elections between 1969 and 2006, Michal Shamir and Asher Arian (1999) found that self-reported religious observance had a strong and growing relationship to the vote. More observant Jews were likely to vote for the right-of-center Likud (Unity) Party; whereas less observant Jews were more likely to vote for the right-of-center Labor Party.

3. See also, Matt. 23:23.

4. Of course, despite his age, Moses was perfectly healthy until just before his death (see Deut. 34:7); David was old and could not get warm (1 Kings 1:1).

5. The more common transliteration is Sukkot.

Bibliography

Abramson, Paul R. "Generations and Political Change in the United States." *Research in Political Sociology* 4 (1989): 235–80.

_____. "Review of Ira Sharkansky, *Israel and Its Bible: A Political Analysis.*" *American Political Science Review* 91 (June 1997): 490–91.

_____. "Generations: Political." In *International Encyclopedia of the Social and Behavioral Sciences,* edited by Neil J. Smelser and Paul B. Baltes, 6050–53.Amsterdam: Elsevier, 2001.

_____ "Critiques and Counter-Critiques of the Postmaterialism Thesis: Thirty-four Years of Debate." Paper available online at the Center for the Study of Democracy, University of California at Irvine. http://www.escholarship.org/uc/item/3f72v9q4.

Abramson, Paul R., John H. Aldrich, and David W. Rohde. *Change and Continuity in the 1992 Elections.* Rev. ed. Washington, DC: CQ Press, 1995.

_____. *Change and Continuity in the 1996 and 1998 Elections.* Washington, DC: CQ Press, 1999.

_____. *Change and Continuity in the 2000 and 2002 Elections.* Washington, DC: CQ Press, 2003.

_____. *Change and Continuity in the 2004 and 2006 Elections.* Washington, DC: CQ Press, 2007.

_____. *Change and Continuity in the 2008 and 2010 Elections.* Washington, DC: CQ Press, 2012.

Abramson, Paul R., and Ronald Inglehart. *Value Change in Global Perspective.* Ann Arbor, MI: University of Michigan Press, 1995.

The Aeneid of Virgil. Translated by Robert Fagles. New York, NY: Penguin, 2006.

Almond, Gabriel A. "Political Science: The History of the Discipline." In *A New Handbook of Political Science,* edited by Robert E. Goodin and Hans-Dieter Klingemann, 50–96. New York, NY: Oxford University Press, 1996.

Almond, Gabriel A., R. Scott Appleby, and Emmanuel Sivan. *Strong Religion: The Rise of Fundamentalists around the World.* Chicago, IL: University of Chicago Press, 2003.

Almond, Gabriel A., and Sidney Verba. *The Civic Culture: Political Attitudes and Democracy in Five Nations.* Princeton, NJ: Princeton University Press, 1963.

Alter, Robert. *The Art of Biblical Narrative*. New York, NY: Basic Books, 1981.

_____. *Pen of Iron: American Prose and the King James Bible*. Princeton, NJ: Princeton University Press, 2010a.

_____. *The Wisdom Books: Job, Proverbs, and Ecclesiastes: A Translation with Commentary*. New York, NY: Norton, 2010b.

The Anchor Yale Bible Dictionary, 6 volumes. Editor-in-Chief David Noel Freedman. New Haven, CT: Yale University Press, 1992, 2008.

Arendt, Hannah. *Eichmann in Jerusalem: A Report on the Banality of Evil*. New York: Viking, 1963.

_____. *Eichmann in Jerusalem: A Report on the Banality of Evil*. Rev. and enlarged ed. New York: Penguin, 2006.

Arian, Asher. *Politics in Israel: The Second Republic*. 2nd ed. Washington, DC: CQ Press, 2005.

Augustine of Hippo [Saint Augustine]. [413, 415, 417, 418, 425, 427] 1972, 1984, 2003. *Concerning the City of God against the Pagans*. Translated by Henry Bettenson. London: Penguin.

Avalon, John. *Wingnuts: How the Lunatic Fringe is Hijacking America*. New York, NY: Beast Books, 2010.

Barclay, John. "1 Corinthians." In *The Pauline Epistles: The Oxford Commentary*. Updated selection, edited by John Muddiman and John Barton, 91–126. New York, NY: Oxford University Press, 2010.

Bauckham, Richard. *The Bible in Politics: How to Read the Bible Politically*. Louisville, KY: Westminster/John Knox Press, 1989.

_____. *The Theology of the Book of Revelation*. Cambridge: Cambridge University Press, 1993.

Bellamy, Chris. *Absolute War: Soviet Russia in the Second World War*. New York, NY: Vintage Books, 2007.

Benedict XVI (Pope) [Joseph Ratzinger]. *Jesus of Nazareth: From the Baptism in the Jordan to the Transfiguration*. Translated by Adrian J. Walzer. Vatican City: Liberia Editrice Vaticana, 2007.

_____. *Jesus of Nazareth, Part Two: Holy Week: From the Entrance into Jerusalem to the Resurrection*. Translated by Philip J. Whitmore. Vatican City: Liberia Editrice Vaticana, 2011,

Berman, Joshua A. *Created Equal: How the Bible Broke With Ancient Political Thought*. New York, NY: Oxford University Press, 2008.

The Bible: Hebrew and English. Tel Aviv. Sinai Publishing, 1996.

The Jerusalem Bible. Jerusalem: Koren Publishers, 1992.

The New American Bible (With the Revised Book of Psalms and the Revised New Testament). Totowa, NJ: World Catholic Press, 1987.

The Bible: Authorized King James Version with Apocrypha. New York, NY: Oxford University Press, [1611] 2008.

The New Oxford Annotated Bible: New Revised Standard Version With the Apocrypha. Fully revised 4th ed. New York, NY: Oxford University Press, 2010.

Borgman, Paul. *David, Saul, and God: Rediscovering an Ancient Story.* New York, NY: Oxford University Press, 2008.

Brams, Steven J. *Biblical Games: Game Theory and the Hebrew Bible.* 2nd ed. Cambridge, MA: MIT Press, 2003.

_____. *Game Theory and the Humanities: Bridging Two Worlds.* Cambridge, MA: MIT Press, 2011.

Brams, Steven J., and D. Marc Kilgour. "How Democracy Resolves Conflict in Difficult Games." In *Games, Groups, and the Global Goods,* edited by Simon A. Levin, 229–42. New York, NY: Springer, 2009.

Brown, Raymond E. *The Gospel and Epistles of John: A Concise Commentary.* Collegeville, MN: The Liturgical Press, 1988.

Bryan, Christopher. *Render to Caesar: Jesus, the Early Church, and the Roman Superpower.* New York, NY: Oxford University Press, 2005.

Carter, Warren. *The Roman Empire and the New Testament: An Essential Guide.* Nashville, TN: Abingdon Press, 2006.

The Catholic Study Bible: The New American Bible. 2nd ed. Edited by Donald Senior and John J. Collins. New York, NY: Oxford University Press, 1990, 2000.

Charlesworth, James H. ed. "Joseph and Aseneth." In *The Old Testament Pseudepigrapha,* Vol. 2. C. Burchard translator. Doubleday Anchor Bible Reference Library, 177–247. Peabody, MA: Hendrickson, 1985.

Chronicles: Hebrew Text and English Translation with an Introduction and Commentary. Introduction and commentary by I. W. Slotki. London: Soncino Press, 1985.

I Chronicles. Translated with an introduction and notes by Jacob M. Myers. Garden City, NY: The Anchor Bible, Doubleday, 1965.

II Chronicles. Translated with an introduction and notes by Jacob M. Myers. Garden City, NY: The Anchor Bible, Doubleday, 1965.

Cohn, Haim Hermann. *The Trial and Death of Jesus.* Old Saybrook, CT: Konecky and Konecky, 1971.

Connolly, William E. *The Augustinian Imperative: A Reflection on Political Morality.* New edition. Lanham, MD: Rowman and Littlefield, 2002.

Conquest, Robert. *The Great Terror: A Reassessment,* 40th anniversary ed. New York: Oxford University Press, 2008.

I Corinthians. A new translation, introduction with a study of the life of Paul. Notes and commentary by William Orr and James Arthur Walther. Garden City, NY: The Anchor Bible, Doubleday, 1976.

First Corinthians. A new translation with introduction and commentary by Joseph A. Fitzmyer. New Haven, CT: The Anchor Yale Bible, Yale University Press, 2008.

II Corinthians. A new translation with introduction and commentary by Victor Paul Furnish. Garden City, NY: The Anchor Bible, Doubleday, 1984.

Cross, Frank Moore. *Canaanite Myth and Hebrew Epic: Essays in the History of the Religion of Israel.* Cambridge, MA: Harvard University Press, 1973.

The Book of Daniel. A new translation with introduction and commentary by Louis F. Hartman and Alexander A. Di Lella. New York, NY: Anchor Bible, Doubleday, 1978.

The Book of Daniel: The Cambridge Bible Commentary on the New English Bible. Commentary by Raymond Hammer. Cambridge: Cambridge University Press, 1976.

Daniel, Ezra, Nehemia: Hebrew Text and English Translation. Introductions and commentary by Judah J. Slotki. London: Soncino Books, 1985.

The David Story: A Translation and Commentary of 1 Samuel and Samuel. Translation and commentary by Robert Alter. New York, NY: Norton, 1999.

Davis, Darren W. *Negative Liberty: Public Opinion and the Terrorist Attacks on America.* New York, NY: Russell Sage, 2007.

Dawidowicz, Lucy S. *The War Against the Jews: 1933–1945.* 10th anniversary ed. New York, NY: Holt, Rinehart, and Winston, 1986.

The Dead Sea Scrolls Bible: The Oldest Known Bible Translated for the First Time into English. Translated with commentary by Martin Abegg Jr., Peter Flint, and Eugene Ulrich. New York, NY: HarperOne, 1999.

De Forges, Alison. *"Leave None to Tell the Story": Genocide in Rwanda.* New York, NY: Human Rights Watch, 1999.

Deuteronomy, 1–11. A new translation with introduction and commentary by Moshe Weinfeld. New York, NY: The Anchor Bible, Doubleday, 1991.

The JPS Torah Commentary, Deuteronomy: The Traditional Hebrew Text with the New JPS Translation. Commentary by Jeffrey H. Tigay. Philadelphia, PA: Jewish Publication Society, 1996.

Dever, William G. *Who Were the Early Israelites and Where Did They Come From?* Grand Rapids, MI: Eerdmans, 2003.

Diamant, Anita. *The Red Tent.* New York, NY: St. Martin's Press, 1997.

Donaldson, Terence L. "Introduction to the Pauline Corpus." In *The Pauline Epistles: The Oxford Bible Commentary.* Updated selection, edited by John Muddiman and John Barton, 27–56. New York, NY: Oxford University Press, 2010.

Douglas, Mary. *Leviticus as Literature.* New York, NY: Oxford University Press, 1999.

Drescher, Seymour. *Abolition: A History of Slavery and Antislavery.* Cambridge, MA: Cambridge University Press, 2009.

Ecclesiastes. A new translation with introduction and commentary by Choon-Leong Seow. New York, NY: The Anchor Bible, Doubleday, 1997.

Elazar, Daniel J. *The Book of Joshua as a Political Classic.* Jerusalem: Jerusalem Center for Public Affairs, 1989. http://www.jcpa.org/dje/articles2/joshua.htm.

_____. *Covenant and Polity in Biblical Israel: Biblical Foundations and Jewish Expressions, Volume 1 of the Covenant Tradition in Politics.* New Brunswick, NJ: Transaction Publishers, 1995.

The Epistles of John. A new translation with introduction and commentary by Raymond E. Brown. New York, NY: The Anchor Bible, Doubleday, 1982.

Esther. A new translation with introduction and commentary by Carey A. Moore. New York, NY: The Anchor Bible, Doubleday, 1971.

The JPS Bible Commentary: Esther. The Traditional Hebrew Text with the New JPS Translation. Commentary by Adele Berlin. Philadelphia, PA: The Jewish Publication Society, 2001.

Etz Hayim: Torah and Commentary. Senior Editor David L. Lieber. Philadelphia, PA: The Jewish Publication Society, 1999, 2001.

Evans, Richard J. *The Third Reich at War.* New York, NY: Penguin, 2009.

Exodus, 1–18. A new translation with introduction and commentary by William H. C. Propp. New York, NY: The Anchor Bible, Doubleday, 1999.

Exodus, 19–40. A new translation with introduction and commentary by William H. C. Propp. New York, NY: The Anchor Bible, Doubleday, 2006.

The JPS Torah Commentary, Exodus: The Traditional Hebrew Text with the New JPS Translation. Commentary by Nahum M. Sarna. Philadelphia, PA: The Jewish Publication Society, 1991.

The Federalist Papers. Alexander Hamilton, James Madison, and John Jay. Edited by Clinton Rossiter. New York, NY: Penguin, [1787, 1788], 2003.

Finkelstein, Israel, and Neil Asher Silberman. *The Bible Unearthed: Archeology's New Vision of Ancient Israel and the Origins of Its Sacred Texts.* New York, NY: Simon and Schuster, 2002.

_____. *David and Solomon: In Search of The Bible's Sacred Kings and the Roots of the Western Tradition.* New York, NY: Free Press, 2006.

Fiorina, Morris P., with Samuel J. Abrams, and Jeremy C. Pope. *Culture War? The Myth of a Polarized America*, 3rd ed. Boston, MA: Longman, 2006.

The Five Books of Moses: A Translation with Commentary. Translation and commentary by Robert Alter. New York, NY: Norton, 2004.

The Five Books of Moses: Genesis, Exodus, Leviticus, Numbers, and Deuteronomy. A new translation with introductions, commentary, and notes by Everett Fox. New York, NY: Schocken, 1983, 1986, 1990, 1995, and 1997.

The Five Megilloth: Hebrew Text and English Translation with an Introduction and Commentary. Introduction and commentary by A. Cohen and A. J. Rosenberg. London: Soncino Press, 1984.

Fowler, Robert Booth. *The Greening of Protestant Thought.* Chapel Hill, NC: University of North Carolina Press, 1995.

Fox, Michael V. *Character and Ideology in the Book of Esther.* 2nd ed. Columbia, SC: University of South Carolina Press, 1991.

Freud, Sigmund. *Moses and Monotheism.* Translated by Katherine Jones. New York, NY: Vintage Books, [1937] 1939.

Friedländer, Saul. *Nazi Germany and the Jews: Volume 1, The Years of Persecution, 1933–1939.* New York, NY: HarperCollins, 1997.

_____. *Nazi Germany and the Jews, 1939–1945: The Years of Extermination.* New York, NY: HarperCollins, 2007.

Friedman, Richard Elliott. *Who Wrote the Bible?* San Francisco, CA: HarperOne, 1989.

_____. *The Bible with Sources Revealed: A New View into the Five Books of Moses.* San Francisco, CA: HarperOne, 2003.

Friedrich, Carl J. *Constitutional Government and Democracy: Theory and Practice in Europe and America.* Rev. ed. Waltham, MA: Blaisdell, 1950.

Frymer-Kensky, Tikva. *Reading the Women of the Bible: A New Interpretation of Their Stories.* New York, NY: Schoeken, 2002.

Fukuyama, Francis. *The Origins of Political Order: From Prehuman Times to the French Revolution.* New York, NY: Farrar, Straus, and Giroux, 2011.

Gager, John G. *The Origins of Anti-Semitism: Attitudes Toward Judaism in Pagan and Christian Antiquity.* New York, NY: Oxford University Press, 1983.

_____. *Reinventing Paul.* New York, NY: Oxford University Press, 2000.

Galatians. A new translation with introduction and commentary by J. Louis Martyn. Garden City, NY: The Anchor Bible, Doubleday, 1997.

Gates of Freedom Haggadah. Rev. ed. Edited by Chaim Stern. Springfield, NJ: Behrman House, 1999.

Gelb, Norman. *Kings of the Jews: The Origins of the Jewish Nation.* Philadelphia, PA: The Jewish Publication Society, 2010.

Genesis. A new translation with introduction and commentary by E. A. Speiser. New York, NY: The Anchor Bible, Doubleday, 1962.

The JPS Torah Commentary, Genesis: The Traditional Hebrew Text with the New JPS Translation. Commentary by Nahum M. Sarna. Philadelphia, PA: The Jewish Publication Society, 1989.

Genesis: A Living Conversation: Companion to the Public Television Series. Narrated by Bill Moyers. New York, NY: Doubleday, 1966.

Genovese, Eugene D. *Roll Jordan Roll: The World the Slaves Made.* New York, NY: Pantheon Books, 1974.

Gilbert, Martin. *Jerusalem: Illustrated History Atlas.* Rev. ed. Tel Aviv: Steimatzky, 1977.

_____. *The Dent Atlas of the Arab–Israeli Conflict.* 6th ed. London: Dent, 1993.

Ginzberg, Louis. *The Legends of the Jews, Volume Three: Moses in the Wilderness.* Translated by Paul Radin. Baltimore, MD: Johns Hopkins University Press, [1911, 1939] 1998a.

_____. *The Legends of the Jews: Volume Six: From Moses to Esther.* Baltimore, MD: Johns Hopkins University Press, [1928, 1956] 1998b.

_____. *The Legends of the Jews, Volume I: From the Creation to Jacob.* New York, NY: Cosimo, [1909] 2005.

_____. *The Legends of the Jews, Volumes I and II.* Republished By Forgotten Books, [1909] 2008. http://www.forgottenbooks.org.

Give Us a King! Samuel, Saul, and David. A new translation of Samuel I and II with an introduction and notes by Everett Fox. New York, NY: Schocken, 1999.

Golding, William. *Lord of the Flies: A Novel.* New York, NY: Berkley, 1954.

Gourevitch, Philip. *We Wish to Inform You That Tomorrow We Will Be Killed With Our Families: Stories From Rwanda.* New York, NY: Farrar, Straus, and Giroux, 1998.

Green, Adam. *King Saul: The True History of the First Messiah.* Cambridge, England: The Lutterworth Press, 2007.

Gunner, R. A. H. "Number." In *The New Bible Dictionary.* Organizing Editor J. D. Douglas, 895–98. Grand Rapids, MI: Eerdmans, 1962.

Guth, James L., John C. Green, Lyman A. Kellstedt, and Corwin E. Smidt. "Faith and the Environment: Religious Beliefs and Attitudes on Environmental Policy." *American Journal of Political Science* 39 (May 1995): 364–82.

The Haftarah Commentary. Commentary by W. Gunther Plautt and Chaim Stern. New York, NY: UAHC Press, 1996.

Harper Collins Bible Dictionary. General Editor Paul J. Achtemeier. New York, NY: HarperCollins, 1996.

Hartill, Edwin J. *Principles of Biblical Hermeneutics.* Grand Rapids, MI: Zondervan, 1947.

Hassner, Ron E. "The Trial and Crucifixion of Jesus: A Modest Proposal." *Theory and Decision* 54 (February 2003): 1–32.

Hazony, Yoram. *The Dawn: Political Teachings of the Book of Esther.* Jerusalem: Genesis Press, 1995.

Heller, Joseph. *God Knows.* New York, NY: Knopf, 1984.

Herzog, Chaim. *Heroes of Israel: Profiles of Jewish Courage.* Boston, MA: Little, Brown, 1989.

Herzog, Chaim, and Mordechai Gichon. *Battles of the Bible.* Rev. ed. London: Greenhill Books, 1997.

Heschel, Abraham J. *The Prophets.* New York, NY: HarperCollins, [1982] 2001.

Hilberg, Raul. *The Destruction of the European Jews*, Rev. ed., 3 volumes. New York, NY: Holmes and Meier, 1985.

Hill, Craig C. "Romans." In *The Pauline Epistles: The Oxford Commentary*. Updated selection, edited by John Muddiman and John Barton, 57–91. New York, NY: Oxford University Press, 2010.

Hobbes, Thomas. *Leviathan*. Edited by J. E. A. Gaskin. Oxford: Oxford University Press, [1651] 1996.

Holy Bible. New International Version. Grand Rapids, MI: Zonderhavan, 1984.

The Holy Scriptures: A Jewish Bible According to the Masoretic Text, Hebrew and English. Tel Aviv: Sinai Publishing, [1881], 1996.

The Holy Scriptures According to the Masoretic Text: A New Translation. Philadelphia, PA: The Jewish Publication Society, 1917.

Honig, Bonnie. "Ruth, The Model Emigrée: Meaning and the Symbolic Politics of Immigration." *Political Theory* 25 (February 1997): 112–36.

_____. *Democracy and the Foreigner*. Princeton, NJ: Princeton University Press, 2001.

The Iliad of Homer. Translated by Roger Fagles. New York, NY: Penguin, 1990.

Inglehart, Ronald, and Paul R. Abramson. "Measuring Postmaterialism." *American Political Science Review* 93 (September 1999): 665–77.

Inglehart, Ronald, Miguel Basañez, and Alejandro Moreno, eds., *Human Values and Beliefs: A Cross-Cultural Sourcebook, Political, Religious, Sexual, and Economic Norms in 43 Societies: Findings from the 1990–93 World Values Survey*. Ann Arbor, MI: University of Michigan Press, 1998.

Inglehart, Ronald, Miguel Basañez, Jaime Diez-Medrano, Loek Halman, and Rudd Luijkx, eds., *Human Beliefs and Values: A Cross-Cultural Sourcebook Based on the 1999–2002 World Values Surveys*. México, D.F.: siglo ventiuno Editores, s.a. de C.V., 2004.

The Interlinear NASB-NIV Parallel New Testament in Greek and English. Interlinear translation by Alfred Marshall. Grand Rapids, MI: Zondervan, 1993.

The Interlinear NIV Hebrew–English NIV Hebrew–English Old Testament. Interlinear translation by John R. Kohlenberger, III. Grand Rapids, MI: Zondervan, 1987.

Isaiah: Hebrew Text and English Translation with an Introduction and commentary. Introduction and commentary by I. W. Slotki revised by A. J. Rosenberg. London: Soncino Press, 1983.

Isaiah 1–39. A new translation with introduction and commentary by Joseph Blenkinsopp. New York, NY: The Anchor Bible, Doubleday, 2000a.

Isaiah 40–55. A new translation with introduction and commentary by Joseph Blenkinsopp. New York, NY: The Anchor Bible, Doubleday, 2000b.

Isaiah 55–66. A new translation with introduction and commentary by Joseph Blenkinsopp. New York, NY: The Anchor Bible, Doubleday, 2003.

The Book of the Prophet Isaiah 1–39. The Cambridge Bible Commentary on the New English Bible. Commentary by A. S. Herbert. Cambridge: Cambridge University Press, 1973.

The Book of the Prophet Isaiah 40–66. The Cambridge Bible Commentary on the New English Bible. Commentary by A.S. Herbert. Cambridge: Cambridge. University Press, 1975.

Jenkins, Philip. *The Next Christianity: The Coming of Global Christianity.* New York, NY: Oxford University Press, 2007.

Jeremiah: Hebrew Text and English Translation with an Introduction and Commentary. Introduction and commentary by H. Freedman and A. J. Rosenberg. London: Soncino Press, 1985.

Jeremiah. A new translation with introduction and commentary by John Bright. Garden City, NY: The Anchor Bible, Doubleday, 1965.

Jeremiah 1–20. A new translation with introduction and commentary by Jack R. Lundbom. New York, NY: The Anchor Bible, Doubleday, 1999.

Jeremiah 21–36. A new translation with introduction and commentary by Jack R. Lundbom. New York, NY: The Anchor Bible, Doubleday, 2004.

Jeremiah 37–52. A new translation with introduction and commentary by Jack R. Lundbom. New York, NY: The Anchor Bible, Doubleday, 2004.

The Book of the Prophet Jeremiah 1–25. The Cambridge Bible Commentary on the New English Bible. Commentary by Ernest W. Nicholson. Cambridge: Cambridge University Press, 1973.

The Book of the Prophet Jeremiah 26–52: The Cambridge Bible Commentary on the New English Bible. Commentary by Ernest W. Nicholson. Cambridge: Cambridge University Press, 1975.

Jeremiah: Hebrew Text and English Translation with an Introduction and Commentary. Introduction and commentary by H. Freedman and A. J. Rosenberg. London: Soncino Press, 1985.

The Jewish Study Bible. Edited by Adele Berlin and Marc Zvi Brettler. New York, NY: Oxford University Press, 2004.

The Gospel According to John, I–XII. A new translation with introduction and commentary by Raymond E. Brown. New York, NY: The Anchor Bible, Doubleday, 1966.

The Gospel According to John, XIII–XXI. A new translation with introduction and commentary by Raymond E. Brown. New York, NY: The Anchor Bible, Doubleday, 1970.

Josephus: The Complete Works. Translated by William Whiston. Nashville, TN: Thomas Nelson, 1998.

Joshua. A new translation with introduction and commentary by Robert C. Boling and C. Ernest Wright. New York, NY: The Anchor Bible, Doubleday, 1982.

Joshua and Judges: Hebrew Text and English Translation and Commentary. Introduction and Commentary by H. Friedman, A. J. Rosenberg. London: Soncino Press, 1982.

Judges. A new translation with introduction and commentary by Robert G. Boling. Garden City, NY: The Anchor Bible, Doubleday, 1975.

Kass, Leon R. *The Beginning of Wisdom: Reading Genesis.* New York, NY: Free Press, 2003.

Kierkegaard, Søren. "Fear and Trembling: A Dialectical Lyric." In *Fear and Trembling, Repetition.* Edited and translated by Howard V. Hong and Edna H. Hong. Princeton, NJ: Princeton University Press, [1843] 1983.

Kings: Hebrew Text and English Translation with an Introduction and Commentary. Introduction and commentary by I. W. Slotki and E. Oratz. London: Soncino Press, 1990.

I Kings. A new translation with introduction and commentary by Mordechai Cogan. New York, NY: The Anchor Bible, Doubleday, 2000.

II Kings. A new translation with introduction and commentary by Mordechai Cogan and Hayim Tadmor. New York, NY: The Anchor Bible, Doubleday, 1988.

Kershaw, Ian. *Hitler 1936–1945: Nemesis.* New York, NY: Norton, 2000.

Kirsch, Jonathan. *The Harlot by the Side of the Road: Forbidden Tales of the Bible.* New York, NY: Ballantine, 1997.

_____. *King David: The Real Man Who Ruled Israel.* New York, NY: Ballantine, 2000.

Koch, Klaus. *The Prophets: Volume One, The Assyrian Period.* Translated by Margaret Kohl. Philadelphia, PA: Fortress Press, [1978] 1983.

_____. *The Prophets: Volume Two, The Babylonian and Persian Periods.* Translated by Margaret Kohl. Philadelphia, PA: Fortress Press, [1978] 1984.

The Koran, 5th revised edition with minor revisions. Translated with notes by N. J. Dawood. New York, NY: Penguin Books, 2003.

Kristeva, Julia. *Strangers to Ourselves.* Translated by Leon S. Roudiez. New York, NY: Columbia University Press, [1998] 1991.

Kugel, James L. *The Bible as It Was.* Cambridge, MA: Harvard University Press, 1997.

_____. *How to Read the Bible: A Guide to Scripture, Then and Now.* New York, NY: Free Press, 2007.

Lanzmann, Claude. *Shoah: An Oral History of the Holocaust, The Complete Text of the Film.* New York, NY: Pantheon Books, 1985.

Larson, Edward J. *Summer for the Gods: The Scopes Trial and America's Continuing Debate Over Science and Religion.* New York, NY: Basic Books, 1997.

Leviticus, 1–16. A new translation with introduction and commentary by Jacob Milgrom. New York, NY: The Anchor Bible, Doubleday, 1991.

Leviticus, 17–22. A new translation with introduction and commentary by Jacob Milgrom. New York, NY: The Anchor Bible, Doubleday, 2000.

Leviticus, 23–27. A new translation with introduction and commentary by Jacob Milgrom. New York, NY: The Anchor Bible, Doubleday, 2000.

The JPS Torah Commentary, Leviticus: The Traditional Hebrew Text with the New JPS Translation. Commentary by Baruch A. Levine. Philadelphia, PA: The Jewish Publication Society, 1989.

Liebman, Charles S., and Eliezer Don-Yehiya. *Civic Religion in Israel: Traditional Judaism and Political Culture in the Jewish State.* Berkeley, CA: University of California Press, 1983.

Lieu, Judith M. *The Theology of the Johannine Epistles.* Cambridge: Cambridge University Press, 1991.

Lindgren, Torgny. *Bathsheba.* Translated by Tom Geddes. New York, NY: Harper & Row, [1984] 1989.

Locke, John. *Two Treatises on Government and a Letter Concerning Toleration.* Edited by Ian Shapiro with essays by John Dunn, Ruth W. Grant, and Ian Shapiro. New Haven, CT: Yale University Press, [1690] 2003.

Lowance, Mason I. Jr., ed., *A House Divided: The Antebellum Slavery Debate in America, 1776–1865.* Princeton, NJ: Princeton University Press, 2003.

The Gospel According to Luke, I–IX. A new translation with introduction and commentary by Joseph A. Fitzmyer. New York, NY: The Anchor Bible, Doubleday, 1970.

The Gospel According to Luke, X–XXIV. A new translation with introduction and commentary by Joseph A. Fitzmyer. New York, NY: The Anchor Bible, Doubleday, 1985.

MacCulloch, Diarmaid. *Christianity: The First Three Thousand Years.* New York, NY: Viking, 2010.

MacDonogh, Giles. *After the Reich: The Brutal History of the Allied Occupation.* New York, NY: Basic Books, 2007.

Machiavelli, Niccolò. *The Prince.* 2nd ed. Translated by Harvey C. Mansfield. Chicago, IL: University of Chicago Press, [1532] 1998.

Mann, Thomas. *Joseph and His Brothers.* Translated by John E. Woods. New York, NY: Knopf, [1933, 1934, 1936, 1943], 2005.

Mark. A new translation with introduction and commentary by C. S. Mann. New York, NY: The Anchor Bible, Doubleday, 1986.

Mark, 1–8. A new translation with introduction and commentary by Joel Marcus. New York, NY: The Anchor Bible, Doubleday, 2000.

Mark, 8–16. A new translation with introduction and commentary by Joel Marcus. New Haven, CT: The Anchor Yale Bible, Yale University Press, 2009.

Matthew. A new translation with introduction and commentary by W. E. Albright and C. S. Mann. New York, NY: The Anchor Bible, Doubleday, 1971.

Mazower, Mark. *Hitler's Empire: How the Nazis Ruled Europe*. New York, NY: Penguin, 2008.

McGinn, Bernard. "Revelation." In *The Literary Guide to the Bible*, edited by Robert Alter and Frank Kermode, 523–39. *The Literary Guide to the Bible*. Cambridge, MA: Harvard University Press, 1987.

McKenzie, Steven L. *King David: A Biography*. New York, NY: Oxford University Press, 2000.

McPherson, James M. *Tried by War: Abraham Lincoln as Commander in Chief*. New York, NY: Penguin, 2008.

Montesquieu, Charles de. *The Spirit of the Laws*. Translated and edited by Anne M. Cohler, Basia Carolyn Miller, and Harold Samuel Stone. Cambridge: Cambridge University Press, [1748] 1989.

Moorhouse, Roger. *Killing Hitler: The Plots, the Assassins, and the Dictator Who Cheated Death*. New York, NY: Bantam Books, 2006.

The New Bible Dictionary. Organizing editor D. J. Douglas. Grand Rapids, MI: Eerdmans, 1962.

Nicolson, Adam. *God's Secretaries: The Making of the King James Bible*. New York, NY: HarperCollins, 2003.

Norris, Pippa, and Ronald Inglehart. *Sacred and Secular: Religion and Politics Worldwide*. Cambridge, MA: Cambridge University Press, 2004.

Numbers 1–20. A new translation with introduction and commentary by Baruch A. Levine. New York, NY: The Anchor Bible, Doubleday, 1993.

Numbers 21–36. A new translation with introduction and commentary by Baruch A. Levine. New York, NY: The Anchor Bible, Doubleday, 2000.

The JPS Torah Commentary, Numbers: The Traditional Hebrew Text with the New JPS Translation. Commentary by Jacob Milgrom. Philadelphia, PA: The Jewish Publication Society, 1990.

Ozick, Cynthia. "Ruth." In *Reading Ruth: Contemporary Women Reclaim a Sacred Story*, edited by Judith A. Kates and Gail Twersky Reimer, 211–32. New York, NY: Ballantine, 1994.

Paine, Thomas. *Common Sense, Rights of Man, and Other Essential Writings of Thomas Paine*. With an introduction by Sidney Hook and a foreword by Jack Fruchtman Jr. New York, NY: Signet, [1776, 1791] 2003.

Pangle, Thomas L. *Political Philosophy and the God of Abraham*. Baltimore, MD: Johns Hopkins University Press, 2003.

_____. *The Theological Basis of Liberal Modernity in Montesquieu's "Spirit of the Laws."* Chicago, IL: University of Chicago Press, 2010.

Passover Haggadah: A New English Translation and Instructions for the Seder. Revisions by Nathan Goldberg. Hoboken, NJ: Ktav Publishing, 1993.

The Pauline Epistles: Oxford Bible Commentary, updated selection. Edited by John Muddiman and John Barton. Oxford: Oxford University Press, 2010.

Pentateuch and Haftorahs: Hebrew Text, English Translation, and Commentary. 2nd ed. Edited by J. H. Hertz. London: Soncino Press, 1960.

The Letter to Philemon. A new translation with an introduction and commentary by Joseph A. Fitzmyer. New York, NY: The Anchor Bible, Doubleday, 2000.

Philippians. A new translation with introduction and commentary by John Reumann. New Haven, CT: The Anchor Bible, Doubleday, 2008.

Pincus, Steve. *1688: The First Modern Revolution*. New Haven, CT: Yale University Press, 2009.

Pinsky, Robert. *The Life of David*. New York, NY: Schocken, 2005.

Polack, Frank H. "David's Kingship--A Precarious Equilibrium." In *Politics and Theopolitics in the Bible and Postbiblical Literature*, edited by Henning Graf Reventlow, Yair Hoffman, and Benjamin Uffenheimer. Sheffield, England: JSOT Press, 1994.

Polzin, Robert. *David and the Deuteronomist: A Literary Study of the Deuteronomic History, Part 3, 2 Samuel*. Bloomington, IN: Indiana University Press, 1993.

Prewitt, Kenneth. *Politics and Science in Census Taking*. New York, NY: Russell Sage Foundation and Washington, DC: The Population Reference Bureau, 2003.

Proverbs, 1–9. A new translation with introduction and commentary by Michael V. Fox. New York, NY: The Anchor Bible, Doubleday, 2000.

Proverbs, 10–31. A new translation with introduction and commentary by Michael V. Fox. New Haven, CT: The Anchor Yale Bible, Yale University Press, 2009.

Proverbs, Ecclesiastes. A new translation with introduction and commentary by R. B. Y. Scott. New York, NY: The Anchor Bible, Doubleday, 1965.

The Book of Psalms: A Translation and Commentary. By Robert Alter: New York: Norton, 2007.

An English Interpretation of The Holy Qur'an (with Full Arabic Text). 3rd ed. English translation by Abdullah Yusuf Ali. Lahore, Pakistan: Sh. Muhammad Ashraf Publishers, 1938.

Radosh, Allis, and Ronald Radosh. *A Safe Haven: Harry S. Truman and the Founding of Israel*. New York, NY: HarperCollins, 2009.

The Republic of Plato. Translated, with notes, an interpretive essay, and a new introduction by Alan Bloom. New York, NY: Basic Books, 1968.

Revelation. A new translation with introduction and commentary by J. Massyngberde Ford. New York, NY: The Anchor Bible, Doubleday, 1975.

The Revelation of John: The Cambridge Bible Commentary on the New English Bible. Commentary by T. S. Glasson. Cambridge: Cambridge University Press, 1965.

Riker, William H. *Federalism: Origin, Operation, Significance.* Boston, MA: Little, Brown, 1964.

Roberts, Andrew. *Masters and Commanders: How Four Titans Won the War in the West.* New York, NY: HarperCollins, 2009.

Romans. A new translation with introduction and commentary by Joseph A. Fitzmyer. New York, NY: The Anchor Bible, Doubleday, 1993.

Rosenberg, Joel. "1 and 2 Samuel." In *The Literary Guide to the Bible,* edited by Robert Alter and Frank Kermode, 122–43. Cambridge, MA: Harvard University Press, 1987.

Rousseau, Jean-Jacques. *The Social Contract with Geneva Manuscript and Political Economy.* Edited by Roger D. Masters and translated by Judith R. Masters. New York, NY: St. Martins, [1762] 1978.

_____. *The Government of Poland.* Translated and with an introduction and notes by Willmoore Kendall. Indianapolis, IN: Bobbs-Merrill, [1772] 1985.

Ruether, Rosemary. *Faith and Fratricide: The Theological Roots of Anti-Semitism.* Eugene, OR: Wipf and Stock Publishers, 1997.

Ruth. A new translation with introduction and commentary by Edward F. Campbell Jr. Garden City, NY: The Anchor Bible, Doubleday, 1975.

Sabine, George H. *A History of Political Theory,* 3rd ed. New York, NY: Holt, Rinehart and Winston, 1961.

Samuel: Hebrew Text and English Translation and Commentary. Translation with an introduction and commentary by S. Goldman. London: Soncino Press, 1949.

I Samuel. A new translation with introduction and commentary by P. Kyle McCarter Jr. New York, NY: The Anchor Bible, Doubleday, 1980.

II Samuel. A new translation with introduction and commentary by P. Kyle McCarter Jr. Garden City, NY: The Anchor Bible, Doubleday, 1984.

The Septuagint with Apocrypha: Greek and English. Edited by Sir Lancelot C. L. Brenton. London: Samuel Bagster and Sons, Ltd., 1851.

Shamir, Michal, and Asher Arian. "Collective Identity and Electoral Competition in Israel." *American Political Science Review* 93 (June 1999): 265–77.

Sharkansky, Ira. *Ancient and Modern Israel: An Exploration of Political Parallels.* Albany, NY: State University of New York Press, 1991.

_____. *Israel and Its Bible: A Political Analysis.* New York, NY: Garland, 1996.

Shulman, George. *American Prophecy: Race and Redemption in American Political Culture.* Minneapolis, MN: University of Minnesota Press, 2008.

Silver, Allan. "Requesting a King." In *The Jewish Political Tradition: Volume 1: Authority*, edited by Michael Walzer, Menachem Loberbaum, and Noam J. Zohar, 120–26. New Haven, CT: Yale University Press, 2000.

Sloyan, Gerard S. *Jesus on Trial: A Study of the Gospels*. 2nd ed. Minneapolis, MN: Fortress Press, 2006.

Smith, Huston. *The World's Religions*. 50th anniversary edition. New York, NY: HarperCollins, 2009.

Snyder, Timothy. *Bloodlands: Europe Between Hitler and Stalin*. New York, NY: Basic Books, 2010.

The Soncino Chumach: The Five Books of Moses with Haphtoroth. Edited by A. Cohen. London: The Soncino Press, 1983.

Song of Songs. A new translation with introduction and commentary by Marvin H. Pope. New York, NY: The Anchor Bible, Doubleday, 1977.

Stark, Rodney. *The Rise of Christianity: How the Obscure, Marginal Jesus Movement Became the Dominant Force in the Western World within a Few Centuries*. Princeton, NJ: Princeton University Press, 1996.

Steffens, Lincoln. *Moses in Red: The Revolt of Israel as a Typical Revolution*. Philadelphia, PA: Dorrance, 1926.

The Stone Edition Chumach: The Torah, Haftaros, and Five Megillos. 11th ed. General Editor Nosson Scherman. Brooklyn, NY: Mesorah Publications, 2000.

Strauss, Leo. *What is Political Philosophy? And Other Studies*. Chicago, IL: University of Chicago Press and Free Press, 1959.

Suetonius. *The Lives of the Caesars*, vol II. Latin with an English translation by J. V. Rolfe. Cambridge, MA: Harvard University Press, 1997.

JPS Hebrew-English Tanakh: The Traditional Hebrew Text and the New JPS Translation. Philadelphia, PA: The Jewish Publication Society, 1999.

The Koren Tanakh, 2nd Hebrew/English ed. Jerusalem: Koren Publishers, 2010.

Telushkin, Joseph. *Biblical Literacy: The Most Important People, Events, and Ideas of the Hebrew Bible*. New York, NY: HarperCollins, 1997.

The Letters to the Thessalonians. A new translation with introduction and commentary by Abraham J. Malherbe. New York, NY: The Anchor Bible, Doubleday, 2000.

Thieberger, Frederic. *King Solomon*. New York, NY: East and West Library, 1947.

The Landmark Thucydides: A Comprehensive Guide to the Peloponnesian Wars. Translated by Richard Crowley and edited by Robert B. Strausser. New York, NY: Touchstone Books, 1998.

Tolstoy, Leo. *War and Peace*. Translated by Richard Pevear and Larissa Volokhonsky. New York, NY: Knopf, [1869] 2007.

The Torah: A Modern Commentary. Rev. ed. General Editor Gunther W. Plautt. New York, NY: Union for Reform Judaism, 2005, 2006.

The Torah: A Women's Commentary. General Editor Tamara Cohn Eskenazi. New York, NY: UJR Press of Women of Reform Judaism, 2008.

Tuchman, Barbara W. *The March of Folly: From Troy to Vietnam*. New York, NY: Knopf, 1984.

Wald, Kenneth D., and Allison Calhoun-Brown. *Religion and Politics in the United States*. 6th ed. Lanham, MD: Rowman and Littlefield, 2011.

Walzer, Michael. *Exodus and Revolution*. New York, NY: Basic Books, 1985.

Weber, Max. *Ancient Judaism*. Translated by Hans H. Gerth and Don Martindale. New York, NY: Free Press, [1917–1919] 1952.

_____. "Politics as a Vocation." In *From Max Weber: Essays in Sociology*, translated and edited by H. H. Gerth and C. Wright Mills, 77–128. New York, NY: Oxford University Press, [1919] 1946.

_____. *The Theory of Social and Economic Organization*. Translated by A. M. Henderson and Talcott Parsons. New York, NY: Free Press, [1920] 1947.

Weinberg, Gerhard L. *A World at Arms: A Global History of World War II*, new ed. Cambridge: Cambridge University Press, 2005.

Weld, Theodore Dwight. *The Bible Against Slavery: An Inquiry into the Patriarchal Mosaic System, and the Teachings of the Old Testament on the Subject of Human Rights*. New York, NY: American Anti-Slavery Society, 1837.

White, Michael L. *From Jesus to Christianity*. New York, NY: HarperOne, 2004.

Wiesel, Elie. *Messengers of God: Biblical Portraits and Legends*. Translated by Marion Wiesel. New York, NY: Simon and Schuster, 1976.

Wildavsky, Aaron. *The Nursing Father: Moses as a Political Leader*. Tuscaloosa, AL: University of Alabama Press, 1984.

_____. "What is Permissible that This People May Survive? Joseph the Administrator." *PS: Political Science and Politics* 22 (December 1989): 779–88.

_____. *Administration Versus Separation: Joseph the Administrator and the Politics of Religion in Biblical Israel*. New Brunswick, NJ: Transaction Publishers, 1993.

Wills, Lawrence E., ed., "The Marriage and Conversion of Aseneth." In *Ancient Jewish Novels: An Anthology*, translated by Lawrence E. Wills. New York, NY: Oxford University Press, 2002.

Wolin, Sheldon S. *Politics and Vision: Continuity and Innovation in Western Political Thought*. Expanded ed. Princeton, NJ: Princeton University Press, 2004.

Yadin, Yigael. *The Art of Warfare in Biblical Lands in the Light of Archeological Study, Vol. 1.* Translated by M. Pearlman. New York, NY: McGraw-Hill, 1963a.

_____. *The Art of Warfare in Biblical Lands in the Light of Archeological Study, Vol. II.* Translated by M. Pearlman. New York, NY: McGraw-Hill, 1963b.

The Yale Book of Quotations. Edited by Fred R. Shapiro. New Haven, CT: Yale University Press, 2006.

Zornberg, Avivah Gottlieb. *The Murmuring Deep: Reflections on the Biblical Unconscious.* New York, NY: Shochken, 2009.

_____. *Genesis: The Beginning of Desire.* Philadelphia, PA: The Jewish Publication Society, 2010.

Index of Scriptural Passages

Index of Names

Index of Subjects